Florida Landlords' Rights & Strategies

Knowing your Rights, Protecting your Assets and Profiting with Rental Properties

Mark Warda, Attorney at Law

GALT PRESS
a division of
Galt International, Inc.
Post Office Box 186
Lake Wales, FL 33859
Tel: 863.678.0011

First Edition, 2012

ISBN 10:   1-888699-10-8
ISBN 13:   978-1-88699-10-4
LCCN: 2011935846

Manufactured in the United States of America.

This publication is designed to provide accurate and authoritative information in regard to the subject matter covered. It is sold with the understanding that the publisher is not engaged in tendering legal, accounting, or other professional service. If legal advice or other expert assistance is required, the services of a competent professional person should be sought.
—*From a Declaration of Principles Jointly Adopted by a Committee of the American Bar Association and a Committee of Publishers and Associations*

Published by Galt Press, a division of Galt International, Inc., Post Office Box 186, Lake Wales, Florida 33859-0186. This publication is available by mail for $34.95 plus $3.62 postage plus Florida sales tax if applicable. For credit card orders call 863-678-0011 or fax 863-678-0155, or email to mark@warda.net.

Quick Index

Many people who use this book just want a fast answer to an immediate problem. The following index will help you find the answers to the most common problems.

Table of Contents

Introduction

My first book, *Landlords' Rights and Duties in Florida*, published in 1983 and revised in ten editions through 2005, was a simple explanation of Florida's landlord tenant laws. This new book also explains the laws, but adds practical landlording advice and asset protection information that can be even more valuable to landlords.

Besides knowing what the law requires, a landlord should know what the law allows and what the most practical and profitable solutions are to landlord problems. The practical information in this book comes from the author's own landlording experience, that of his clients, and from other landlord friends and acquaintances of the author, most of whom were met at investor club meetings.

Every landlord should belong to a real estate investors club. It puts you in contact with many people who can make your landlording experience easier and more profitable: attorneys, real estate agents, title company employees, and other investors who have had the same problems you have and know the best solutions to them.

When my first book came out one of the main concerns was that landlords had legal duties that they didn't know about that could prove very expensive if a tenant knew about them and went after the landlord.

Today there are so many duties imposed by all branches of government that most landlords know they've got to be extra careful in everything they do. Today the main issue isn't knowing the rules, but employing strategies to survive as a landlord in spite of this new overwhelming regulation.

Gone are the days of freedom of contract where two adults could agree to whatever they wished. Today the state government adds a guaranty to every lease that the premises must be made safe by the landlord, and must warn the tenant about possible though nonexistent hazards. The federal government requires that a landlord must disclose what he knows about lead paint used on the property before 1978. The state government requires that tenants be warned about the possibility of radon gas. Some local government even require that their lackeys inspect every rental unit to be sure the government thinks it is okay for someone to rent.

Government is growing like a cancer at every level with rules and regulations for everything we do. (Did you know there's a new federal law that forbids selling toys and children's books at garage sales?!) And on top of this there are those who are using government to transfer property from those who work for it to those who merely desire it.

Landlords, with very valuable assets that cannot be hidden or moved, are prime and easy targets for these regulators and redistributionists. But while some laws allow people to take your property, other laws allow you to protect it. Only by knowing the laws can you survive and prosper in today's environment.

My Florida land trust seminar was held in Miami a few years back, and shortly thereafter I received a letter from The Florida Bar saying that a lawyer who attended the seminar complained about it to the Bar. She complained that I was teaching people to hide their assets, foreclose mortgages more quickly and take advantage of tenants. Apparently, she was a community organizer who, when she saw "land trust" thought we were going to teach how to set up land trusts to help homeless people!

I answered her complaint by saying that everything we taught was legal and allowed by Florida law and that her complaints were the same kind you would get if a criminal defense attorney stumbled into a prosecutor's seminar or vice versa.

It's a political issue. Some people fight for the rights of one side and some fight for the rights of the other side. I choose to teach people who work for their assets how to keep them from those who want to take them away without working for them.

Our country is going through trying times. Whenever 51% of the population realize that they can do what they want to the other 49%, there is going to be trouble. According to the most recent figures I could find, 47% of the population pays no income tax, and this number is growing!

In some cities, government employees are retiring in their 50s with $100,000 a year or more pensions. Eventually the government is going to run out of money and they are going to have to find new ways to get it from those who have it. Landlords, who cannot move their properties to a different jurisdiction as other business owners can, will be the easiest targets.

Landlording has always been a profitable enterprise. While there are headaches, the pleasure of getting a large check when you unload a property that you have improved and paid down over a number of years can be worth it.

Today there are more headaches than ever, but hopefully the situation will turn around before long. And until then there are ways to beat the system and survive and hopefully prosper. This book was written to help you do just that.

1 Your Landlording Plan and Goal

It is not enough to know that many people have gotten wealthy in real estate and to just start buying some properties. There are several different strategies and you should consider at the beginning which ones you will use. You might change your strategy, if you find out you don't enjoy it or it's not working the way you planned. But to have the most success you will need a plan.

Landlording Strategies

The following are some of the most common landlording strategies.

Buy and hold. Probably the oldest strategy is to buy rental properties that can be managed with at least break-even cash flow until the mortgage is paid off, and then to retire on the rents that formerly went to pay the mortgage. This is a good plan with properties that attract good tenants near good jobs.

Buy, amortize and sell. When properties turn out to be difficult to manage, with tenants who pay late, disappear and damage the properties, a landlord who thought he would buy and hold often prefers to sell the property and take back a mortgage. That way he receives monthly mortgage payments from one owner who is invested in the property, instead of collecting numerous rents from difficult tenants. After a few years of paying down the loan or appreciation in the property value, equity can be built up that can provide cash flow.

Buy, fix and sell. Those who dislike dealing with tenants can profit from buying a property with low rents and improving it in ways that allow higher rents. Rental property values are often based on the cash flow, so if you can double the cash flow (by adding units, charging more for improved units, or lowering expenses) you can theoretically raise the value of the property.

Level of Clientele

Besides different plans for holding properties, there are different levels of clientele (tenants) to rent to.

High end. With high end rentals, you buy expensive units and rent to people whose income is high, which theoretically means you rarely need to worry about missed or late rent. But because high income people can buy a home as easy as renting one, it is harder to find such tenants, and if your expensive unit is empty for very long it can destroy any profit you hope to make.

Before buying an expensive unit to rent you should have some idea how you will find a tenant. Some people with high income rent instead of buy because they change jobs and move regularly (professors, military officers). Others rent because they have no idea how to maintain a house, or don't want to be bothered, or they come from a family that has known nothing other than renting.

Mid level. Many landlords prefer the middle range of properties. Middle income people can be the most steady at staying at their jobs and in the same location close to schools and other amenities.

As this book is being written the real estate market is in a state of flux. (Some would say crisis.) Government programs and bad lender policies allowed many middle and lower-middle class people who never would have been able to buy a home to get mortgages with no money down. Home ownership rates went from about 64% to 69%, but many of those now homeowners, for various reasons ranging from teaser mortgages to inability to save for unexpected repairs, were unable to keep their homes.

The explosion of new homeowners caused a shortage of renters for mid level property landlords, and then cause a crash of mid level values as these properties went into foreclosure.

In the future, if the government can be kept out of helping unqualified people from getting loans, the mid level should again be a good investment area.

Low end. Low end rentals provide some of the best profits in landlording, but they also provide the most headaches. Low end tenants are often late in paying rent, are more likely to damage the property, and end up needing to be evicted more often than others.

But consider the possible numbers. If you bought a $200,000 home you could probably take in $1,500 a month in rent. But if you used the same $200,000 to buy five $40,000 mobile homes, you could probably rent them for $150 a week which would give you $3,225.00 a month. ($150 times 5 units times 4.3 weeks in a month.)

But while the $1,500 check would probably come like clockwork, or be direct-deposited into your account, you would have to personally go to the mobile homes every week, sometimes several times, to collect the rents. Is this worth it? For many people it is.

Now, if we add leverage to the equation, say, using the $200,000 to put 25% down on 20 mobile homes, the cash flow is now $12,900 a month. Once the mortgages are paid off that would be a decent income for just driving around collecting rents. If you start early and buy enough units you could retire very young.

Level of Service

Some landlords try to put nearly all the maintenance responsibilities on the tenants, to save money and aggravation, while others prefer to do everything themselves to be sure their property is repaired correctly.

When you make it the tenant's responsibility to do maintenance, things like water pipe leaks or roof leaks might be ignored by the tenant. These things can cause major damage to the property such as mold, termite infestation or rotten wood that could end up costing many thousands of dollars to remedy. So putting these repairs on the tenant could be risky unless you inspect the property regularly.

But if you can get a conscientious tenant who will take good care of the property, giving a slight reduction in rent in exchange for doing minor maintenance can be worth the avoidance of phone calls at 3 a.m. and on holidays.

One way to get the tenant to take better care of the property and do more repairs is if he has an option to buy the property at the end of the lease. More on this in Chapter 4.

Level of Your Participation

Collecting rents and taking care of the property is something you can do all by yourself, or that you can hire others to do, either as employees or as independent contractors.

Participation in management. To make the most profit from your rental properties you need to manage them yourself. Since they will be producing income and retirement savings for you this can be like a second job (or if you are a masochist, a profitable hobby).

Management companies usually charge about 10% of rents and there are sometimes extra fees for finding and screening tenants, arranging repairs, etc. If you are a high-income professional looking for a passive investment, this may be reasonable to you. If you are an aggressive young investor, this may not be worth it.

Participation in maintenance. The classic landlord rags-to-riches story is the handyman-type guy who has a regular job and buys rental properties as he finds bargains over the years. Being handy, he can fix clogged toilets, patch roof leaks, replace burned-out switches and change leaking faucets.

If you are not able to do things like these, you can either learn or hire someone to do them for you.

If you decide to hire someone to do your repairs, it is much more economical if you can find one handyman who can fix most things than to call an unknown specialist whenever something goes wrong. Going to a landlord club is a good way to find reliable handymen.

If you are mechanically inclined, most repairs are fairly simple and if you cannot figure them out by taking apart the old one, you can get a book with detailed instructions of every type of repair. As a young landlord, the author learned to fix many things by taking them apart and bringing an apparently-broken piece to the hardware store for a replacement.

Since hiring someone to do a repair can cost many times the cost of a part ($80 labor and travel to install a $20 faucet), you can greatly increase your real estate profits by doing your own repairs. Of course, if you make $100 or $200 an hour for your own time, and value your free time, you may prefer to pay a specialist.

Choosing You Help

If you decide to hire someone to help with maintenance or management or both, the first question you will need to consider is whether they will be your employee or whether you will hire them as an outside business or "independent contractor."

If you have a lot of properties you may want an employee who can be available as needed to do everything that comes up. And for a large enough number of properties, it may be the best plan.

But today hiring an employee carries a much higher cost and much greater risks than it did years ago. (No wonder unemployment is so high.) Besides the risk of being liable for an employee's acts such as sexual harassment, discrimination or injury to a tenant, there are new taxes and mandates such as worker compensation, unemployment taxes, and much more. Once you hire your first employee you will need to start filing state and federal forms every quarter, and summaries every year. This is explained in the author's book, *How to Start a Business in Florida.*

If you pay someone who works for another company or has their own company you can avoid collecting and paying employment taxes and can avoid some kinds of liability.

Some people game the system by having a helper who acts like an employee but is listed as an independent contractor. The IRS is cracking down on this and assessing tax penalties on those who mis-classified employees. This is explained in detail in Chapter 10.

2   Protect Your Assets Before You Start

The most frustrating consultation a lawyer can have with a client is when the client comes in with a judgment filed against him, and all of his life's assets at risk of being lost. Once a judgment has been filed it is too late to do most of the important things that can protect your assets, but even the mere filing of a lawsuit limits some of the things you can do.

Imagine working for decades managing properties, building up your net worth, and then just when you are ready to retire, losing it all, not because you did something terrible, but because your tenant did something stupid. Some real cases:

➲ A tenant was running a day care center in her rental unit and she owned a pit bull. The dog killed one of the children in her care. Who was liable? The landlord, for several million dollars, because the lease said that no dogs were allowed and the landlord failed to force her to get rid of the dog.

➲ A water heater broke and the grandmother living in the unit boiled pots of water on the stove to make hot baths for the children. While carrying the water to the bathroom she spilled it on one of the children burning him severely. Liability? Landlord had to pay $775,000 because he had not gotten the heater fixed within 3 days.

➲ A man paid a $25 deposit to start moving his things into a mobile home. The gas was turned on outside the unit and he smelled gas inside the house. What did he do? Light a match, causing himself serious injuries. Who was liable? You guessed it. The Florida Supreme Court used this case to change the centuries-old tradition that the person in physical control of a house is liable for its condition. From this case forward, tenants are given an invisible "warranty of habitability" whenever they rent a dwelling unit.

➲ A woman was raped by someone who broke into the management office and stole the keys to the rental units and won a $17 million judgment against the landlord because the landlord refused to give her a better lock when she requested one. (Not a Florida case, but this shows where this type of thing is going.)

No landlord but the largest has insurance enough to cover a $17 million judgment. But the same legal system that allows such judgments also allows opportunities to protect yourself against them. But for most kinds of protections **you must set them up before something happens**.

My book, *Complete Guide to Asset Protection Strategies*, explains each possible strategy in detail, but this chapter will provide an overview of the ones most useful to landlords in Florida.

Three Approaches to Asset Protection

The three ways to achieve asset protection are first, to keep claims from reaching you personally, second, to protect the assets you own from any claims that do reach you, and third, to have property not in your name so it is not subject to claims that do reach you.

One way to keep claims from reaching you is to form a limited liability company (LLC) in which to operate your business.

Unlike some states, Florida makes it relatively easy and inexpensive to form and maintain an LLC.

A corporation can be used just like an LLC, and years ago most people used corporations, but LLCs are entities invented about twenty years ago that today are better than corporations for these reasons:

1. LLCs require less paperwork. Corporations are supposed to have regular meetings of their shareholders and board of directors, and keep written copies of minutes of the meetings, and elect officers. If you forget to do the paperwork, you can lose the asset protection. The purpose of the LLC was to give people limited liability with less formality and less paperwork.

2. LLCs offer double asset protection. Both LLCs and corporations protect their owners from liability for things they do, but only LLCs offer protection to LLC assets from claims against owners unrelated to the LLC.

> **Example:** If you own stock in General Motors, stock in an S corporation and a membership interest in an LLC, then if General Motors or the S corporation of the LLC are bankrupted by some great liability, you as the stockholder or member have no liability. But, if you are liable for something unrelated, such as you kill someone in a car crash, a court can take your GM stock away, it can take your S corporation stock away, but it cannot take your LLC membership away (if you have another, innocent member). This is the double asset protection that LLCs offer over corporations.

3. LLCs can choose whatever tax reporting they wish. They can file like a sole proprietor, a partnership or like a C corporation or an S corporation.

Besides LLCs, another way to keep claims on real property from reaching you is to use land trusts. Years ago it was said that land trusts only offer privacy of ownership, but not liability protection. But a few years ago the law was changed to say that a beneficiary of a land trust is not liable for claims against the property. [F.S. §689.071(8)(a)].

> **Example:** An attorney from one of those billboard accident chasing law firms called the trustee of a land trust to say that a child was seriously injured by a dog bite on a rental property in trust, and to ask for the name of the insurance company. The trustee told him that the property had no insurance, but that the injured child was welcome to have the property (subject to a large mortgage). The attorney never called back.

Second, if claims do reach you, the next type of asset protection is to protect the property you own from being seized. Two ways to do this are having adequate insurance for any claims, and having assets that cannot be taken from you, called *exempt assets*.

Insurance. Typical insurance policies with liability limits of $300,000 or $500,000 are not adequate to cover a major accident such as discussed previous. But "umbrella" policies are available to landlords which extend that coverage to a million dollars, $2 million, or more. These are usually not expensive, just a couple hundred dollars with additional properties added for a few dollars each.

Exempt assets. When a person files bankruptcy because they have more debts than they can ever hope to pay, the bankruptcy trustee takes all their property away, except their exempt assets, and uses it to pay their debts at 50¢ or 10¢ on the dollar, or however much there is.

So asset protection planning involves making sure, in case you ever need to file bankruptcy, that you as much of your wealth in exempt assets and as little as possible in non-exempt assets. As explained in my asset protection book, you are allowed in some cases, even if you have claims against you, to convert non-exempt assets to exempt assets. But that right is limited, so long term planning involves getting as many exempt assets and as few non-exempt assets as possible.

All of the details would not fit into this chapter, but briefly, the most useful exempt asset categories are:

• *Homestead.* Remember a certain football player who sliced up his ex-wife and a friend and moved to Florida and bought a $15 million home which could not be seized by the friend's estate? The homestead is one of the most strongly protected assets in Florida. Since then the law has been changed to require four years residency to avoid abuse, but it can still offer unlimited protection with the right planning.

• *Retirement accounts.* When I was young I didn't want to tie up my money in retirement accounts, I preferred to invest it in real estate, but now I put as much as legally possible into my IRA because they are exempt and can never be taken away. As explained in Chapter 10, you can now use a self-directed IRS to invest in single family homes.

• *Annuities.* Every year a couple financial magazines publish articles about how annuities are not a good deal because you get a small percentage less return due to the annuity aspect of the investment. However, these articles rarely discuss the fact that annuities are exempt from creditor claims. How much lower return on your investment would you be willing to take, knowing that this would be safe from any lawsuits that might be filed against you?

For extra protection annuities can be purchased easily from companies based in Switzerland which offer protection from both creditors and from a possible collapse in the value of the dollar.

• *Wages.* A certain amount of your wages cannot be seized. If you set up a separate bank account just to deposit your wages into, this money can be safe from creditors. You could use rent money to live on and build up your wage account into a nest egg that could not be touched.

Tenancy by the entireties. One of the strongest asset protection devices in Florida, especially the homestead is limited for the first four years, is tenant by the entireties.

In all states property can be owned either by "tenants in common" or by "joint tenants" but in 26 states including Florida property can be owned a third way, tenancy by the entireties. This is based upon the ancient concept that a husband and wife are united as a single entity, and that a claim against only one of them is not a claim against property owned by both of them.

In making your asset protection plan using this method, you should seek to title your properties (including personal things like furniture, gold and collectibles) in your names as tenants by the entireties, and most important, to avoid whenever possible signing debts in both names.

Lenders always want both spouses to sign, even hospitals try to get spouses to co-sign admission papers, but you should avoid this whenever you can.

The third approach to asset protection is to have assets that are not in your name so that if the claims did reach you and if they are not exempt, they would still be unavailable to your creditor.

The big issue with this is that while you want the assets to be out of your name so that they are not your assets that can be seized, most people don't want to just give them away, they still want to maintain control. And maintaining control is what often lets a creditor get to it.

Some of the ways to have property under your control but not owned by you are LLCs, trusts, limited partnerships, nonprofit corporations and gifts to other family members.

Detailing most of these is beyond the scope of this book, but when your assets become considerable you should look into these possibilities. Using family members can work well but only as long as the family gets along. Many a man has put all his assets in his wife's name only to have her leave him. And putting property into young children's names means that when they turn 18 they get to do whatever they want with it

Five Most Important Rules of Asset Protection

I have been specializing in asset protection for over 15 years and the five things I have learned to be most important in asset protection planning are:

1. Set up your plan as soon as possible. After you have a claim against you it is too late to do some things, and even if you have no claims, some things must be done four years before they can give you protection. Procrastination is the easiest thing to do, but considering that your entire fortune and retirement plans are at stake, you should put asset protection planning at the top of your list of things to do.

2. Know and use all your exemptions. The above explanation includes the most important ones, but there are several others, such as insurance, tools, and alimony. Be sure to make the highest use of all that are available to you.

3. Don't put all your eggs in one basket. Whatever plan you use to protect your assets there is always the possibility that a judge will find a flaw in it. By using several techniques you give yourself a better chance that at least some of your assets will not be lost even in the worst of circumstances.

4. Review your plan regularly. Laws change, exemptions change, new court cases throw out old rules, and your mix of assets changes. After you set up your plan, be sure, every few years to do research or talk to a lawyer who can advise you if anything has changed.

5. Don't look like the "bad guy." In every area of law the rules are mostly gray, not black and white, and a judge has a lot of leeway in deciding who will win. You can have the most iron clad asset protection arrangement, with your assets all in an untouchable trust in the Cook islands, and if the judge thinks you are a crook, we will order you to sit in jail until you figure out a way to get your assets out of the trust. (This has actually happened!)

If you get in an accident and maim a person for life and you deed your properties to your children's college fund, a judge will probably take them back and give them to the injured person. But if you set up a college fund when your kids were infants (early planning) and you had those properties in those funds, a judge will probably not touch them.

3 Getting the Right Property

Getting the first rental property must be one of the scariest possible events for some people, as there are many potential investors who go to seminars and buy books on investing and look at properties for years without making an offer much less a purchase.

Then there are investors so seasoned that they make offers without even going inside a property (much less having it inspected) or buy it without even driving by!

The four main variables to consider when buying a rental property are where to buy, what to buy, who to buy from, and how to buy. You should consider your goal and your plan in order to decide how to answer these questions.

Where to Buy

The oldest rule in real estate investing is that there are three things to consider when buying a property, location, location, and location. But it is easy to forget when you think you have found a bargain. New investors often jump at a property that seems to be a great bargain at a fraction of the price of similar homes, without realizing that the difference is because it is on a busy road or behind a noisy factory.

While some people do too much research before buying a property, the most important thing to do is to thoroughly check out the neighborhood you are buying in.

Besides current factors, try to find out if there are any changes coming. Are established residents moving away because crime is rising? Are road expansions planned? Are factories or schools moving away?

Because this kind of local information is important in the value of property it is best to buy property in the area where you live. After a few years of living in an area you will know a lot about its trends. Buying a property in another city or state makes it a lot harder to make good decisions.

Pension crisis. It has come to light that many municipalities throughout the country have promised unreasonable pensions to their employees. In some areas they are allowed to retire after 20 years with pensions of over $100,000 a year. Doing the math on these, in many cities it will be impossible to make the payments without raising taxes to ridiculous levels. Some cities will likely go bankrupt, as a couple already have. But others may prefer to keep raising taxes for as long as they can.

When buying a property for long term investment, you should investigate whether the municipality has unfunded pension requirements. The higher taxes could make your property too expensive to rent out and impossible to sell.

What to Buy

The two decisions on what to buy are what type of property and what condition of property.

Types of property. Like many things in life, people often just fall into one type of investment or another. A neighbor needs to sell and move away so they buy the house and eventually buy a few more on the block. Or they somehow come across an RV storage lot for sale, and find it so profitable they start buying any others they can find for sale.

Good profits can be made on every kind of real estate from vacant land and mobile home lots to apartment buildings and shopping centers

Condition of property. Another classic rule of investing is to buy the worst property on the best street. Much profit can be made in improving a dilapidated property. If you are ambitious and talented with tools this is the best kind of property to buy. But it also offers risk. An old property that looks like it would just need a new coat of paint could have structural problems from settling or hidden termite damage.

When the author started investing it wasn't common to have a property professionally inspected, and of course most properties don't have hidden problems. You could look through a property and only if you notice something unusual ask a contractor for an opinion if it might be a big problem.

Today there is a whole industry of home inspectors who carefully check every system in a property, and with so many of them (due to unemployment in the construction industry) the prices are often reasonable.

So getting a professional inspection is a good idea. Just be sure that your contract says that the purchase is contingent on a satisfactory inspection by whomever you use.

One important thing about using an inspector. If an inspector is paid a few hundred dollars and says he didn't find anything wrong with a property it will look like he didn't do much checking. So inspectors will almost always find a bunch of things, mostly all minor. Don't let this scare you away from the property unless they might really lead to costly repairs.

One advantage of an inspector is that even after you have negotiated the best possible price for the property, a list of defects discovered by your inspector could get the seller to lower the price even more to save the deal.

Who to Buy From

The most common sources of real estate investments are real estate agents and for sale by owner properties (FSBOs), but today a lot of good deals can be gotten from bank holdings from foreclosures (REOs), people in foreclosure, and foreclosure sales at the courthouse. Other possibilities are tax deed sales, wholesalers at real estate clubs who find good deals and are willing to flip them to you for a small profit, and writing or calling the owners of properties you notice that look empty and neglected.

Contrary to what some investment gurus suggest, calling all the probate lawyers and funeral directors in town isn't one of the best plans.

How to Buy

How to buy refers to the financing used on the deal. Few investors use all cash to buy. Even if they have enough cash, it is better to only put a small percentage down in order to have leverage and use "other people's money" or OPM.

If you buy a property with $100,000 cash and it goes up 3% a year in value you make 3% profit. If you are able to put $10,000 down on ten $100,000 properties that go up 3% a year, you made 30% profit.

As this is written the real estate market is still in crisis mode so financing possibilities are in flux. When money is available for investment properties it usually requires much more of a down payment than in the recent past. Traditionally, 20% down was required for getting a loan on an investment property and it may be headed back there if not higher.

Two alternatives to bank financing are seller financing and buying properties with existing loans.

Seller financing. When a seller does not need to get all their cash out of a property in a sale, he or she might consider doing the financing for you. This can be done by a mortgage to the seller or by an agreement for deed, or contract for deed. A long time ago a contract for deed was good for the seller and bad for the buyer because the seller could take back the property faster. But the laws have changed and such an agreement has to be foreclosed just like a mortgage. Sellers sometimes ask the buyer to sign a deed back to them at the same time as the contract for deed or mortgage is signed so they can record it and take back the property immediately when there is a missed payment, but such deeds are void and a title company will not insure a future sale of the property until the buyer's interest is foreclosed in court

Subject to. If a seller has a mortgage on a property you may be able to pay the seller the difference between the current balance and the ales price and then just take over payments on his mortgage.

Most mortgages today are "due on sale" meaning that the lender can call the entire loan due if the property is sold, and foreclose if not paid. In the current climate, it is unimaginable that a bank would foreclose a loan that is current with record numbers of loans delinquent. So it is probably safe to take over a loan. But in the future things could change and if interest rates rise the loan could be called due.

One way to avoid getting caught is to have the seller put the property into a land trust with the seller as the beneficiary of the trust, and then assign the trust to you. The federal Garn-St. Germain Act says that a lender can't call a loan due on sale if a person put it into his own trust. So if the lender complains that the title was changed, you could show them the trust showing the seller as beneficiary (without showing the assignment of the trust to you).

One issue is insurance because the new buyer needs to be on the insurance. Some investors buy duplicate insurance if the cost is low enough compared to the amount saved. Others just replace the insurance and hope the lender's insurance department does not notice and tell the other departments. And others add themselves as an additional insured to the policy.

There has been a debate among some attorneys and investors as to whether violation of a due-on-sale clause is illegal or immoral or otherwise not the right thing to do. Those supporting lenders say it is fraudulent and those supporting investors say that it is a remedy in the mortgage that can be invoked at any time (any time the lender finds out).

In a United States Supreme Court case regarding a due-on-sale clause in a mortgage there is an interesting footnote. The party to the case was guilty of fraud in a bankruptcy because he quietly transferred the property after asking permission of the lender and not paying the $10,000 that the lender required. The footnote speculated that if the party had just transferred the property without asking or telling the lender anything, he would not be guilty. As one commentator says, "There is no due on sale jail."

How to Know What to Pay

One thing a new investor needs to do to get started in real estate is to drive around looking at properties and comparing prices. This is the best way to learn what are good deals.

Whenever you see a property that is priced below what you have seen others priced at, investigate further to find out the reason. If it just came on the market, perhaps it is just underpriced because the seller didn't know the market or wants to sell quickly. If it has been on the market for a long time, there must be a reason no one else grabbed it up. Some possible factors could be a loud train line or factory nearby, pending road widening, occasional flooding, poor construction, or other nearby nuisance.

If you will be using bank financing you will need to get an appraisal and that should note any negative factors affecting the property. But if you pay cash or use a private lender who doesn't require an appraiser, you will need to take more time to determine the value.

Beware of Condos and Associations

Did you know that a condominium association can vote to forbid all rentals? If you owned a unit in such a building your only option would be to sell, and if other landlords own units in the same building, the value might be reduced.

Some condominiums forbid short-term rentals, or have other rules regulating how units can be rented. Before buying a condo unit, you should read the documents carefully, or get your attorney's opinion on them.

Homeowners' Associations also sometimes have rules regarding rentals, but these are less common. Be sure to make your purchase offer contingent on review of and satisfaction with condominium and homeowner and association documents.

4 Getting the Right Tenants

The second most common mistake of a new landlord (after picking the wrong property) is accepting the wrong tenant. With a mortgage payment due and an inclination not to be disagreeable, a new landlord will often accept the first person who asks to rent a vacant unit. This can be a mistake.

Realize that you are turning over to a stranger one of the most valuable assets you own. He can let water run for days, punch holes in all the walls, live rent-free for months and years as you pay the mortgage and maybe even his electric bill. You need to screen people carefully before you entrust them with your property.

While you cannot legally discriminate for reasons of race, religion, children, etc., you can discriminate based on ability to pay, credit worthiness, past rental history, and other factors which affect the chances that the rent will be paid.

Finding Tenants

The best method for finding tenants depends on the type of tenants you want for your property and the location of your property. While a sign in the window usually works for all types of rentals, other methods, such as ads, bulletin boards, and web sites.

If your property is near a school, hospital, military base or similar source of well-paid tenants, you should see if you can put a vacancy notice on one of their bulletin boards, or in their newsletter if they have one.

Here are some methods and the pros or cons:

Friends of tenants. If you have high class tenants they are good for referrals as they wouldn't want to be embarrassed by their friends. But if you have low class tenants they might get together and start a rent strike or call the building inspector in unison.

Sign in the yard. Good because it is cheap and focuses on local people. Note, some cities and associations don't allow signs. Rather than ask if it is allowed, you might use the "easier to get forgiveness than permission" tactic. Also, some courts have ruled that such prohibitions are illegal.

Sign down the street. These are illegal in most areas but are usually not penalized except that you lose the sign. Some landlords feel a few lost signs are worth the cost to find a tenant.

Newspaper classifieds. They are usually the most expensive, but in some areas work very well and quickly. You should carefully review the rates and look for discounts that are often hidden. Some papers allow the ad to be cancelled and not billed for the rest of the term.

Online. Besides Craigslist, check for local rental bulletin boards. Ask other landlords which work best in your area.

Bulletin boards. These are good ways to focus your search on people who work for a good employer.

Rental guides. These are good for large properties with frequent vacancies. For one unit the lead time for publication is usually too long.

One thing to beware of when advertising for tenants, don't be too cheap! One rental property I had rented very quickly with a tiny ad in the major newspaper. It was ridiculously high priced, something like $150 for 3 tiny lines for 10 days (25 years ago), but I usually got a couple calls the first day and could cancel the ad, just paying for the one day. When I sold the building the new landlord was too cheap to use that newspaper, so he put free ads in the local shopper paper and had the unit vacant for months.

Screening Prospective Tenants

The first step in avoiding legal problems with tenants is to carefully choose who will be your tenant. As long as you do not discriminate based on categories such as race, sex, and age (see pages 58-63), you can be selective as to whom you rent your property. A tenant who has had the same apartment and job for the last five years will be a better tenant than one who has been evicted several times.

You should get a written application from all prospective tenants (Form 1). Besides allowing you to check their past record as a tenant, the information can be helpful in tracking them down if they disappear owing you rent or damages. Be sure that the form you use does not ask illegal questions such as those concerning an applicant's nationality.

Some landlords use a tenant application packet which includes a credit check permission form (Form 2), tenant rules and regulations, such as number of people allowed in the unit, and a notice that their backgrounds will be checked and that prior landlords will be asked about late rent and noise problems. Besides helping you screen the tenants, such a system can deter people with a bad rental history from even applying and wasting your time.

Since 9/11 you should ask every prospective tenant for a government-issued photo identification.

You should check the *defendant index* of the court records (not just the *official records* which lists deeds, mortgages and final judgments) of your county or the last county the applicants lived in to see if they have ever been evicted or sued. It would also be wise to check the *plaintiff index* to see if they have ever sued a landlord or anyone else for that matter. In some counties these indexes are combined.

You should check with a prior landlord to see if he or she would rent to them again. Do not bother checking with their present landlord. He or she may lie just to get rid of them. Be sure the people you talk to are really landlords. Some tenants use friends who lie for them.

There are some companies that, for a fee, will investigate tenants, including employment, previous landlords, court cases, and their own files of *bad tenants.* Some landlords require a nonrefundable application fee to cover such an investigation. CBI/Equifax offers a Tenant Apartment Protection Service which you can reach at 800-685-1111. Another company is Tenant Chek at 800-927-2214. You can also check your phone book under Credit Reporting Agencies, or ask at your local landlord club who they use.

If you decline to rent to someone because of information you found on their credit report federal law requires that you disclose this to them (15 USC 1681 *et seq.*)

Negotiation with an Applicant

While in some areas where rentals are scarce you may have an advantage, today there is a glut of empty units in many areas with many landlords desperate for tenants offering discounts and other incentives. In such an area you may be at a disadvantage in negotiations with a prospective tenant.

One negotiating trick is to "turn the tables" on a well qualified applicant. Such people are looking for the right place for themselves, knowing that they qualify for any place and they expect to do the picking. But if you hint that they might not qualify, or that someone else has applied first, you might be able to get them to feel that getting accepted by you is an important goal.

5 Using the Right Lease

It cannot be stressed too strongly how important it is to have a good lease or rental agreement. This defines your relationship with the tenant and can save you time, money and stress when it protects your interests.

Lease and Rental Agreement Forms

The Florida Supreme Court has approved some lease forms which were put together by a committee of the Florida Bar. And they look like they were put together by a committee!

The original versions from 1992 were ten pages long and included whole sections of the statutes explaining the parties' duties and obligations. (If they are already included in the law, why do they have to be repeated in the lease?)

The newest versions, which came out in April, 2010 added more material, including the already required federal lead form, and then calls for attaching a copy of the entire Florida Landlord Tenant Act for a total of about 20 pages.

How many contracts or agreements do you sign that include the entire statute related to the transaction? Apparently, someone feels tenants are not quite up to finding their own statutes so they should be spoon-fed.

Well, fortunately these leases are not required, unless a non-lawyer is providing legal services to a client. As a landlord you are free to use whatever lease meets your needs. In the author's experience a 20 page lease would be intimidating to a tenant who would much prefer a two or three page lease.

The leases in this book were prepared by the author for his own use and the use of his clients. They were put together over many years after various experiences with tenants. For example, the parking clause was added when a client had a tenant who parked in the middle of the front lawn and tried to argue that nothing in the lease said he couldn't.

These simple forms are meant to be used with the other required notices such as the Lead Paint Notice and Holding Security Deposit Notice.

If you really want them, the Supreme Court approved leases and other approved forms are available here:

http:////www.floridasupremecourt.org/decisions/2010/sc09-250.pdf

But be forewarned!

If you have a situation that you feel requires a longer, more detailed lease than those included in this book, the author wrote The *Complete Guide to Real Estate Leases* which includes a CD and explains how to put a lease together clause by clause.

However, that is a book meant for a national audience and you should be sure to read the rest of this chapter for the specific requirements of Florida law.

Lease or Rental Agreement

There are different opinions as to whether or not a landlord should use a lease with a set term, such as one year, or a rental agreement which is an open-ended agreement. Some argue that they would rather not have a lease so they can get rid of a tenant at any time. Others would rather have a lease where they know the tenant is locked in for a certain time and they won't have to look for a new tenant for at least a year.

Those who like rental agreements say that tenants usually break the lease anyway if they want to leave and it is not easily enforceable. The others say that better tenants don't usually break the lease and they would be much less likely to stay if they knew there was some risk for breaching a signed lease.

Your decision of what to use should be based on your goals (do you want to lock tenants in or be able to get rid of them easily?) and your clientele (those who don't care if they breach a lease or those who want to keep their credit good?)

Whichever you use you should be sure it covers all the possible problems that could come up during the tenancy. There are certain clauses that must be in a lease to make it valid and there are other clauses that are to your benefit to have in a lease.

Required Clauses. The minimum elements that a lease must contain to be valid are:

🖎 name of lessor (landlord) or agent;

🖎 name of lessee (tenant);

🖎 description of the premises;

🖎 rental rate;

🖎 starting date; and,

🖎 granting clause ("Lessor hereby leases to Lessee...").

(There have been cases in which a lease has been valid when one or more of these terms has been omitted if there was an objective means to determine the missing term. Such exceptions are beyond the scope of this book, and it is best that all the required terms are present.)

Management Disclosure. At or before the beginning of a residential rental, the landlord must disclose to the tenant either his or her name and address or the name and address of his or her agent. The agent, if any, retains authority until the tenant is given written notice of a change of agent. (Fla. Stat., Sec. 83.50(1).) In most cases the landlord's name and address in the lease or rental agreement is sufficient and no other notice need be given. If an agent collects rent after he or she is discharged and absconds with the money, it is the landlord's loss if the landlord did not inform the tenants in writing that the agent no longer had authority to collect rents.

Termination Clause. Section 83.575, added to the Landlord-Tenant Act in 2003, allows a landlord to require a tenant to give notice to a landlord before vacating the premises at the end of a lease term. The notice cannot be required more than sixty days in advance. The lease can require the tenant to pay liquidated damages if the tenant fails to give such notice.

Radon Clause Whenever a building is leased or sold in Florida, at least one document which is part of the transaction must contain the following clause. (Fla. Stat., Sec. 404.056(5).)

> RADON GAS: Radon is a naturally occurring radioactive gas that, when it has accumulated in a building in sufficient quantities, may present health risks to persons who are exposed to it over time. Levels of radon that exceed federal and state guidelines have been found in buildings in Florida. Additional information regarding radon and radon testing may be obtained from your county public health unit.

Placing this clause in a lease can help protect the landlord against suits from tenants who may claim injury from radon gas. Landlords who omit this clause risk liability.

Lead Paint Disclosure. Notice must be given to tenants of rental housing built before 1978 that there may be lead-based paint present and that it could pose a health hazard to children. This applies to all housing except housing for the elderly or zero-bedroom units (efficiencies, studio apartments, etc). It also requires that a pamphlet about lead-based paint titled *Protect Your Family From Lead in Your Home* be given to prospective tenants. The recommended **DISCLOSURE OF INFORMATION ON LEAD-BASED PAINT AND/OR LEAD-BASED PAINT HAZARDS** form is included in this book as Form 14.

More information and copies of the pamphlet can be obtained from the National Lead Information Center at 800-424-5323. The information can also be obtained at: **www.nsc.org/issues/lead.** You are also required to make disclosures to the tenants when you do any work on the property that disturbs more than six square feet of paint.

Suggested Clauses. The following clauses are not required by any law, but are suggested by the author to avoid potential problems during the tenancy:

  security and/or damage deposit;

  last month's rent;

  use clause (limiting use of the property);

  maintenance clause (spelling out who is responsible for which maintenance);

  limitation on landlord's liability;

  limitation on assignment of the lease by tenant;

  clause granting attorney's fees for enforcement of the lease;

  clause putting duty on tenant for own insurance;

  late fee and fee for bounced checks;

  limitation on number of persons living in the unit;

  in a condominium, a clause stating that the tenant must comply with all rules and regulations of the condominium;

  requirement that if locks are changed, the **landlord** is given a key (forbidding tenants from change locks may subject the landlord to liability for a break-in);

  limitation on pets;

🍃 limitation on where cars may be parked (not on the lawn, etc.);

🍃 limitation on storage of boats, etc., on the property;

🍃 in a single-family home or duplex, a landlord should put most of the duties for repair under Florida Statutes, Section 83.51 on the tenant;

🍃 in commercial leases there should be clauses regarding the fixtures, insurance, signs, renewal, eminent domain, and other factors related to the business use of the premises; and,

🍃 to protect the landlord if it is necessary to dispose of property left behind by a tenant, a clause cited in Florida Statutes, Section 83.67(3) should be in the lease. (See "Property Abandoned by Tenant" in Chapter 9.)

Oral Leases A lease of property for *less than one year* does not have to be in writing to be valid. Oral leases have been held up in court. However, written leases are recommended even for tenancies less than one year, since oral leases are hard to prove and risk having the other party get away with lying.

📄 *Proof.* To prove an oral lease of one year, the evidence must be "clear, full and free from suspicion." Eli *Einbinder, Inc. v. Miami Crystal Ice Co.,* 317 So.2d 126 (Fla. 3 DCA 1975).

📄 *Part Performance.* When a landlord gave a tenant the key to the premises and the tenant paid rent, improved the property, and stopped looking for other locations, partial performance of the contract made it unnecessary for it to be in writing. *Poinciana Properties Ltd. v. Englander Triangle, Inc.,* 437 So.2d 214 (Fla. 4 DCA 1983).

Problem Clauses

If a judge feels that a rental agreement is grossly unfair, he or she may rule that it is *unconscionable* and unenforceable. (Fla. Stat., Sec. 83.45.) In such a case, the judge may ignore the entire lease or may enforce only parts of it. Therefore, making your lease too strong may defeat your purpose. There is not much guidance as to what may or may not be unconscionable, so what the judge believes reasonable will prevail.

A cost of living adjustment in the rent was found not to be unconscionable. *Bennett v. Behring Corp.,* 466 F. Supp. 689 (1979).

Waivers of Liability or Rights. If either of the following kinds of clauses are included in a lease, it is void and unenforceable, and a party suffering damages because of the clause may recover money from the landlord for any losses so caused. (Fla. Stat., Sec. 83.47.)

➢ A clause waiving the rights, remedies, or requirements of the Florida Landlord/Tenant Law.

➢ A clause limiting the liability of the landlord to the tenant or of the tenant to the landlord, arising under law.

Hidden Clauses. Because of examples, of landlords trying to slip a bad clause into a long lease, if a lease contains a clause which falls outside standard lease terms, it should not be buried in the lease. It should be pointed out, and initialed by the tenant. Otherwise, its enforceability could be questioned in court, and it could be found *unconscionable.*

Water Beds. If a flotation bedding system (water bed) does not violate the building codes, a landlord cannot prohibit it in the rental unit. (Fla. Stat., Sec. 83.535.) A lease clause prohibiting it would be unenforceable. However, Florida law requires a tenant to carry insurance on the water bed to cover personal injury and property damage, which names the landlord as the loss payee. Such a requirement should also be in the lease to avoid misunderstandings later.

Waivers in Commercial Leases. In a commercial lease, a tenant may waive rights that may not be waived in a residential lease. A commercial lease spells out nearly all of the rights and obligations of the parties. The statutes concerning landlord/tenant law are very limited in scope, so it is important to spell everything out carefully in the lease.

Notice. The right to a three-day notice may be waived in a commercial lease. However, even if a three-day notice is waived, some type of notice of termination should be used. *Moskos v. Hand*, 247 So.2d 795 (4DCA 1971). If a lease provides for notice on default longer than three days, then that would be controlling and the landlord would have to give whatever notice is required by the lease. Cricket Club Management *Corp. v. Cricket Club Condominium, Inc.*, 510 So.2d 1162 (Fla. 3 DCA 1987)

Default. The three options that a landlord has when a tenant defaults (see "Remedies for Breach" in Chapter 8) may be waived in a lease if the lease specifies the rights of the landlord. *Linens of Paris, Inc. v. Cymet*, 510 So.2d 1021 (Fla. 3 DCA 1987)

Limiting Similar Businesses. Provisions in a lease that limit the landlord's right to lease to similar businesses should be strictly construed. A lease providing that a tenant would be the only appliance store in a shopping center will not prevent a landlord from leasing to a department store that also sells appliances.

Options

Both residential and nonresidential leases may contain clauses that grant the tenant an option to extend the lease for another term or several terms. Often these options provide for an increase in rent during the renewal periods. Some general rules regarding renewal options to keep in mind include the following.

▤ An option to renew a lease is valid and enforceable, even if not all of the terms are spelled out. *State Road Dept. v. Tampa Bay Theatres, Inc.*, 208 So.2d 485 (Fla. 2 DCA 1968)

▤ Some terms may be left open for future negotiation or arbitration, but when no terms are stated, the court can assume that the terms will be at the same terms as the original lease. *Grossman v. Fontainebleau Hotel Corp.*, 273 F.2d 720 (1960)

▤ Leases that can be renewed indefinitely are not favored by the courts and when doubt exists as to the terms, they may be limited to one renewal term. *Sheradsky v. Basadre*, 452 So.2d 599 (Fla. 3 DCA 1984)

⤫ If a lease contains a notification clause for vacating, a renewal option may go into effect if a tenant vacates without the required notification.

Options to Purchase. An option to purchase is one of the best ways to get a tenant to take good care of the property, but it can be one of the most costly clauses to use and can give a tenant years of free use of the property.

The law says that the landlord tenant eviction procedures do not apply to situations where the tenant is buying the property or has an option to buy it.

This means that you can't get the tenant out quickly if he stops paying, you need to file another type of case such as an ejectment or possibly a foreclosure. These cases can take years to get through the courts. So unless a tenant either puts a large deposit down (tens of thousands of dollars) or has sterling credit and other wealth, never grant a tenant an option.

The author and another investor have devised a system of dividing a lease with an option arrangement to a lease and then a separate "agreement for option" on a land trust beneficial interest (like an agreement for deed, you don't get the option until you make all the payments for the option). This is explained in the book *Secrets of Lease Option Profits*.

▤ If a lease contains an option to purchase, it will usually be enforceable exactly according to its terms. When a tenant continued renting the property as a tenant-at-will after his lease expired, the court ruled that his option to purchase the property expired at the end of the lease. *Gross v. Bartlett*, 547 So.2d 661 (Fla. 2 DCA 1989).

Signatures

If you do not have the proper signatures on the lease, you could have problems enforcing it or evicting the tenants. If the property is owned by more than one person, it is best to have all owners sign the lease.

In most cases, it is best to have all adult occupants sign the lease so that more people will be liable for the rent. But in inexpensive rentals in which evictions are frequent, having just one person sign will save a few dollars in fees for service of process.

Initials. Some landlords have places on leases for tenants to place their initials. This is usually done next to clauses that are unusual or very strongly pro-landlord. This might be helpful because in one case a judge refused to enforce a clause that was "buried" on page two of the lease, even though the judge admitted it was highlighted. *Chancellor v. Garrett*, 2 FLW Supp. 125 (Escambia Co. 1993). Even initials might not help if a judge really does not like a clause.

Witnesses. No witnesses are required for a lease of one year or less. A lease of over one year is not valid without two witnesses to the Landlord's signature. (Fla. Stat., Sec. 689.01.) If a party accepts the benefits of a lease, even if it is not properly witnessed, that party may be estopped from contesting the lease's validity. *Bodden v. Carbonell*, 354 So.2d 927 (Fla. 2 DCA 1978). *Arvanetes v. Gilbert*, 143 So.2d 825 (Fla. 3 DCA 1962).

Notary. A lease does not need to be notarized to be valid.

Warning: A landlord should not allow his or her signature on a lease to be notarized because the lease could then be recorded in the public records. This could cloud his or her title to the property and cause a problem when the property is sold.

Co-signers

When renting to someone with poor credit or no credit history, some landlords require a co-signer to guaranty the payment of the rent, usually by a parent. Of course if the parents are as destitute as the tenant, this may not be worth anything financially. But it could put extra pressure on the tenant not to break the lease.

Oral Leases

A lease of property for less than one year does not have to be in writing to be valid. Oral leases have been held up in court. However, written leases are recommended even for tenancies less than one year.

▤ Proof To prove an oral lease of one year, the evidence must be "clear, full and free from suspicion." *Eli Einbinder, Inc. v. Miami Crystal Ice Co.*, 317 So.2d 126 (Fla. 3 DCA 1975).

▤ Part Performance. When a landlord gave a tenant the key to the premises and the tenant paid rent, improved the property, and stopped looking for other locations, partial performance of the contract made it unnecessary for it to be in writing. *Poinciana Properties Ltd. v. Englander Triangle, Inc.*, 437 So.2d 214 (Fla. 4 DCA 1983).

Agreements to Lease

What are your rights if a tenant agrees to rent your unit but then backs out? An agreement to enter into a lease may be a valid and binding contract even if a lease has not yet been signed. *Clark & Lewis v. Gardner,* 109 So 192 (Fla. 1926).

As a practical matter, it will probably not be worth the time and expense to sue someone for breaching an oral agreement to lease. Whether or not a landlord could keep a deposit after a prospective tenant changed his or her mind would depend upon the facts of the case and the understanding between parties. Writing "nonrefundable" on the deposit receipt would work in the landlord's favor.

Backing Out of a Lease

There are circumstances in which a party can back out of a lease. However, these circumstances are limited and subject to misconceptions.

Rescission. Contrary to the beliefs of some tenants, there is no law allowing a rescission period for a lease. Once a lease has been signed by both parties, it is legally binding on them.

Fraud. If one party fraudulently misrepresents a material fact concerning the lease, the lease may be unenforceable. *Oceanic Villas v. Godson*, 4 So.2d 689 (Fla. 1942).

Impossible Purpose. If the lease states that the premises are rented for a certain purpose and it is impossible to use the premises for that purpose, then the lease may not be enforceable.

▤ When property was rented for a moving and storage business and the zoning laws made it illegal to operate the business on the premises, the landlord could not sue the tenant for failing to pay the rent. *La Rosa v. G.S.W.*, 483 So.2d 472 (Fla. 3 DCA 1986).

▤ When the tenant could not operate his business because of difficulty in getting insurance, this was found to be not enough to make it impossible to use the property, and the tenant had to pay the rent. *Home Design Center -Joint Venture v. County Appliances of Naples, Inc.*, 563 So. 2d 767 (Fla. 2 DCA 1990).

Illegal Purpose. If a lease is entered into for an illegal purpose, then it is void and unenforceable by either party. An example of void leases includes situations in which the property, which is the subject of the lease, is not owned by the landlord. *Escambia Land & Mfg. Co. v. Ferry Pass Inspectors' & Shippers' Asso.*, 52 So. 715 (Fla. 1910). *Daytona Village Apartments v. Neal*, 3 FLW Supp. (Volusia Co. 1995).

6 Landlording Laws & Rules

This chapter covers the laws that govern rental property:

To successfully accomplish anything you need to know what the rules and limitations are. Landlording has become one of those things with more rules than you could imagine and harsh penalties if you break them. For hundreds of years people were free to enter into whatever agreements they wished to regarding real property, but in this modern age, some have decided that some people in society need to be protected from others, and from themselves, so that the agreements that can be made are severely limited today.

Probably half the rules explained in this book didn't exist thirty years ago. And more are being proposed all the time. Just recently a lawyer wrote an article in a Florida Bar magazine proposing a law that tenants should all have an option to renew whether the landlord wants them or needs the unit himself, or not!

Luckily the bureaucrats who work in government are usually not especially ambitious or clever, so violations of the rules by a landlord might not be noticed. But the penalties can be so harsh, that every landlord should know the rules to avoid getting trapped by them.

This chapter contains a summary of the state and federal laws. There is more detail on some important elements in other chapters. And some municipalities and counties have their own rules, some of which are much worse than the state laws.

At this point I want to make a plug for participating in the political process and trying to keep people out of government who want to increase the laws that restrict our freedoms. Some people don't vote because they don't want to be called for jury duty (but jurors are now chosen from driver license lists) or don't want to take the time. But when you see what kind of inane laws we get when the wrong people get elected, you should realize how important it is to help choose the people who write the laws.

Good Faith Obligation

Every residential rental agreement and duty under the landlord/tenant law requires good faith, which is defined as "honesty in fact." Any sort of dishonesty or trickery could cause a loss of valuable rights. (Fla. Stat., Sec. 83.44). While this requirement is not in the nonresidential act, any lack of good faith in a nonresidential tenancy would likely have just as bad consequences for the perpetrator.

In fact, this is one of the basic rules of asset protection planning, and every other area of law. If you appear to a judge or jury to have tried to take advantage of people or use trickery or bad faith, you will likely lose your case no matter what your paperwork says in black and white.

Florida Landlord Tenant Statutes

Florida's original landlord tenant laws were passed in 1828, before Florida was even a state, and most of the original ones are still on the books, applying today mostly to non-residential rentals. These laws are pretty strongly pro-landlord.

The laws that apply to residential rentals were first passed in 1973 and are more protective of tenants' rights, but compared to many states, they give the landlord a lot of protections, *if* the landlord knows the rules and follows them carefully.

Applicability of the Residential Act

The residential portion of the Landlord-Tenant Act applies to most residential tenancies but does not apply to hotels; motels; rooming houses; religious, educational, geriatric, or medical facilities; transient rentals; condominium owners; or, proprietary leases in cooperatives. It also does not apply to contracts to purchase property.

Purchase Contracts. In a contract for sale of property that provided the Landlord-Tenant Act would apply in the event of default, the court held this invalid and said that rules for foreclosing a mortgage would apply. *Purcell v. Williams*, 511 So.2d 1080 (Fla. 1 DCA 1980).

De Facto Purchase Agreements. Where an agreement was titled "Real Estate Lease" but was in fact a twelve-year purchase agreement, a court held that the Landlord-Tenant Act did not apply and a foreclosure was necessary to remove the buyer. *Buyer's Advantage Finance Co. Inc. v. Morse*, 4 Florida Law Weekly Supplement (FLWSupp.) 475 (Co.Ct. Santa Rosa 1997).

One possible way to use landlord/tenant law in a purchase or option situation would be with a land trust. If the purchaser signs a lease with the trustee for possession of the property and a separate purchase or option agreement with the beneficiary of the trust for purchase of the beneficial interest, the arrangement may allow use of landlord/tenant law for an eviction. No case is known to have ruled on this issue, but one case allowed a similar situation. *Ferraro v. Parker*, 229 So.2d 621 (Fla. 2 DCA 1969).

Mobile Home. When a mobile home and lot are rented, Florida Statutes, section 723.002 states that the Landlord-Tenant Act applies. When a lot is rented to the owner of a mobile home, then Chapter 723 applies. *Saoud v. Skorski*, 3 FLW Supp. 35 (Manatee Co. 1994). If the unit rented is a "recreational vehicle" in a recreational vehicle park (as defined in Florida Statutes, section 513.01), then the tenant is a transient guest and can be removed like a nonpaying hotel guest. *Dehnel v. Paradise R. V. Resort*, 588 So.2d 668 (1991).

Vacant Land. One Florida court has held that this chapter does not apply to vacant land onto which a tenant moves a mobile home to use as a residence. *Russo v. Manfred*, 35 Fla. Supp. 2d 23 (Cir.Ct. Citrus Co. 1989).

Boat. At least one case has allowed a landlord to evict a boat from a marina using the residential landlord/tenant procedure, because the boat was being used as a residence. However, the landlord did not follow the exact notice requirement, so he lost the case. *TCY Ltd., Inc. v. Johnson*, 3 FLW Supp. 72 (Dade Co. 1995).

Applicability of the Nonresidential Act

The nonresidential landlord/tenant laws apply to nonresidential tenancies, to residential tenancies that do not fall into the definition of the residential act, and to any other tenancies that are not covered by the mobile home park or self-storage laws.

Commercial. The nonresidential act applies to nearly all rentals of commercial property, but at least one case has held that it does not apply to stalls in markets such as flea markets. *Jarrouj v. LJS Realty, Inc.*, 31 Fla. Supp.2d 10 (Cir.Ct. Dade Co. 1988).

Residential in Fact. The nonresidential act could apply to tenancies that are, in fact, residential but which do not fall under the definition of the residential or mobile home chapters. Florida Statutes, Section 83.001, states that it applies to nonresidential tenancies "and all tenancies not governed by part II of this chapter." This would indicate that it could cover unusual residential tenancy arrangements if they did not fit into the definition of residential tenancies in part II.

▤ It has been held that the residential tenancy rules do not apply to land rented to a person who placed a mobile home on it. *Russo v. Manfredo*, 35 Fla.Supp.2d 23 (Cir.Ct. Citrus Co. 1989).

▤ The residential tenancy laws do not apply to occupancy under a contract of sale. Therefore, if a party was renting a property under a contract of sale, this section of landlord/tenant law might apply. However, one appeals court has ruled otherwise. *Casavan v. Land O'Lakes Realty, Inc.*, 542 So.2d 371 (Fla. 5 DCA 1989).

Rules of the Division of Hotels and Motels

Under Florida Statutes, Chapter 509, the Division of Hotels and Motels of the Department of Business Regulation has the power to regulate the rental of apartment buildings of five units or more. The division says that any five units or homes on a contiguous piece of property comes under their jurisdiction, but the statute excludes buildings that have less than five units. (Fla. Stat., Sec. 509.013(4) (b)4.)

Owners of buildings that come under the jurisdiction of the Division of Hotels and Motels are required to be registered with them and are subject to their rules, which are contained in the Florida Administrative Code, Chapters 61C-1 and 61C-3. These can be photocopied at a law library or obtained from the Department of Business and Professional Regulation. Their number is 850-487-1395.

Rules of the Florida Department of Legal Affairs

The Florida Department of Legal Affairs at one point issued rules purporting to cover residential tenancies. They were repealed. Future attempts to regulate landlord/tenant relations should be considered questionable because two courts have ruled that the Florida statutes covering deceptive trade practices, under which the rules are promulgated, do not apply to mobile home or real estate transactions. *State v. DeAnza Corporation*, 416 So.2d 1173 (Fla. 5 DCA 1982). *Kingswharf, Ltd. v. Kranz*, 545 So.2d 276 (Fla. 3 DCA 1989).

Nursing Homes and Related Facilities

Nursing homes and related facilities are not covered by the landlord/tenant statute. Florida has special statutes regulating "Nursing Homes, Assisted Living Facilities, Home Health Care Facilities, Adult Day Care Centers, Hospices, and Adult Foster Homes," These are found in Florida Statutes, Chapter 400.

Licensing

Four or less units. Buildings with four or less rental units do not need to be licensed with the state but some cities and counties are starting to require that all rental units be licensed and inspected.

Licensing is a way for cities to collect more fees, and to have an excuse to inspect every rental unit and force them to be brought up to the latest codes. Check with your city clerk or with other landlords at your local landlord club. Be grateful if you still live in an area without these laws.

Five or more units. Apartment buildings of five or more units are regulated by Florida Statutes Chapter 509, and must be licensed by the Division of Hotels and Motels of the Department of Business Regulation. If the units are in separate buildings on the same property the Division says they must be licensed. Breaking a property into separate ownership, such as separate trusts might avoid this requirement.

Owners of such units are subject to the rules the Department published in the Florida Administrative Code, Chapters 61C-1 and 61C-3. You can read them at most libraries or here:

http://www.flrules.org

Using a Fictitious Name

Anyone doing business in Florida under a name other than his or her own personal or corporate name must register the name with the Secretary of State. (Fla. Stat., Sec. 865.09.) This applies to landlords who use management company names or apartment building names. The law is contained in the criminal section of the statutes and it is a misdemeanor to fail to register.

A corporation that does business under its own name does not have to register. The procedure is to advertise the name once in a local newspaper and then to file a form with the Secretary of State with the filing fee (currently $50).

Registration lasts for five years and expires on December 31st of the fifth year. It may be renewed for $50. If a business is sold, the old registration may be assigned and the name reregistered for $50.

Sales and Use Tax

Since Florida doesn't have an income tax like most states, it needs to find other ways to cover its revenue needs. One of the favorite ways for states to collect taxes is to get it from people who don't even live in the state, like tourists, and people who come down for short periods and can't vote.

Florida's sales and use tax exempts most permanent residents, so it only applies to tourists, part-time residents and commercial rentals. The rules are explained in detail in Chapter 10 Taxes.

Discrimination

Since Congress passed the *Civil Rights Act of 1968,* it has been a federal crime for a landlord to discriminate in the rental or sale of property on the basis of race, religion, sex, or national origin. In addition, Florida passed its own antidiscrimination statute in 1983, which makes such acts a state crime and adds the additional category of handicapped persons. In 1988, the United States Congress passed an amendment to the Civil Rights Act that bans discrimination against both the handicapped and families with children. Except for apartment complexes that fall into the special exceptions, such as those designated senior living facilities, all rentals must now allow children in all units.

Civil Rights Act of 1968. Under the Civil Rights Act of 1968, any policy that has a discriminatory effect is illegal. (United States Code (U.S.C.), Title 42, Section 3631.) This means that even if you do not intend to discriminate, if your policy (such as requiring a certain income level) has the effect of discriminating, you can be liable. Failure to attend a hearing or to produce records can subject you to up to a year in prison or a $1000 fine.

Penalty. A victim of discrimination under this section can file a civil suit, a HUD complaint, or request the U.S. Attorney General to prosecute. Damages can include actual losses and punitive damages of up to $1000.

Limitation. The complaint must be brought within 180 days.

Exemptions. This law does not apply to single-family homes if:

➲ the owner owns three or less;

➲ there is no more than one sale within twenty-four months;

➲ the person does not own any interest in more than three at one time; and,

➲ no real estate agent or discriminatory advertisement is used.

It also does not apply to a property that the owner lives in if it has four or less units.

Coercion or Intimidation. If coercion or intimidation is used to effectuate discrimination, there is no limit to when the action can be brought or the amount of damages that can be received. For example, firing a real estate agent who rented to African-Americans was found intimidating enough to warrant unlimited damages. *Wilkey v. Pyramid Construction Co.*, 619 F. Supp. 1453 (D. Conn. 1983).

Civil Rights Act, Section 1982. The Civil Rights Act, *Section 1982* is similar to the previously discussed statute but whereas Section 3631 applies to any policy that has a discriminatory effect, this law applies only when it can be proved that the person had an intent to discriminate. (U.S.C., Title 42, Section 1982.)

Penalty. Actual damages plus unlimited punitive damages. In 1992, a jury in Washington, D.C. awarded civil rights groups $850,000 in damages against a developer who only used Caucasian models in rental advertising.

The *Washington Post* now requires that 25% of the models in the ads it accepts be African-American to reflect the percentage of African-Americans in the Washington area.

Limitation. None.

Exemptions. None.

Civil Rights Act 1988 Amendment. The 1988 Amendment to the Civil Rights Act, also known as the *Fair Housing Act,* bans discrimination against the handicapped and families with children. (U.S.C., Title 42, Sec. 3601.) Unless a property falls into one of the exemptions, it is illegal under this law to refuse to rent to persons because of age or to people with children. While landlords may be justified in feeling that children cause damage to their property, Congress has ruled that the right of families to find housing is more important than the rights of landlords to safeguard the condition of their property, and ensure the peace and quiet of other tenants.

Regarding the disabled, the law allows them to remodel the unit to suit their needs as long as they return it to the original condition upon leaving. It also requires new buildings of four units or more to have electrical facilities and common areas accessible to the disabled.

Penalty. $10,000 for first offense; $25,000 for second violation within five years; and up to $50,000 for three or more violations within seven years. Unlimited punitive damages in private actions.

A federal appeals court ruled that if a party who is discriminated against because of his her race does not have any actual monetary damages, he or she is not entitled to punitive damages. Punitive damages can be awarded without monetary damages when a person is denied constitutional rights, but not under the Fair Housing Act. *Louisiana Acorn Fair Housing v. LeBlanc,* 211 F.3d 298 (5th Cir. 2000).

Limitation. Complaint must be brought within two years for private actions.

Exemptions. This law does not apply to single-family homes if the owner owns three or less; if there is no more than one sale within twenty-four months; if the person does not own any interest in more than three at one time; and if no real estate agent or discriminatory advertisement is used. (A condominium unit is not a single-family home, so it is not exempt.) The law also does not apply to a property that the owner lives in if it has four or less units. There are also exemptions for dwellings in state and federal programs for the elderly, for complexes that are solely used by persons 62 or older, and for complexes where at least 8% of the units are rented to persons 55 or older.

Testers. You should be aware that there are people hired by the government to pretend to apply for rental units to see if landlords are discriminating. If someone with a foreign accent or African American dialect calls you and asks if you have a rental available and you say no, and then shortly thereafter someone with a more white dialect calls and you say you do have a vacancy, you can be fined.

Americans with Disabilities Act. The ADA requires that *reasonable accommodations* be made to provide the disabled with access to commercial premises and forbids discrimination against them. This means that the disabled must be able to get to, enter, and use the facilities in commercial premises. It requires that if access is *readily achievable* without *undue burden* or *undue hardship,* changes must be made to the property to make it accessible.

The law does not clearly define important terms like "reasonable accommodations," "readily achievable," "undue burden," or "undue hardship," and does not even explain exactly who will qualify as handicapped or disabled. The law includes people with emotional illnesses, AIDS, dyslexia, and past alcohol or drug addictions, as well as hearing, sight, and mobility impairments.

Under the ADA, if any commercial premises are remodeled, then the remodeling must include modifications that make the premises accessible. All new construction must also be made accessible.

What is reasonable will usually depend upon the size of the business. Small businesses will not have to make major alterations to their premises if the expense would be an undue hardship. Even large businesses would not need shelving low enough for people in wheelchairs to reach so long as there is an employee to assist the person.

However, there are tax credits for businesses of less than thirty employees and less than one million dollars in sales that make modifications to comply with the ADA. For more information on these credits, obtain IRS forms 8826 and 3800 and their instructions. Get them online at www.irs.gov.

Some of the changes that must be made to property to make it more accessible to the disabled are:

➲ installing ramps;

➲ widening doorways;

➲ making curb cuts in sidewalks;

➲ repositioning shelves;

➲ repositioning telephones;

➲ removing high pile, low-density carpeting; and,

➲ installing a full-length bathroom mirror.

Both the landlord and the tenant, for example a store lessee, can be liable if the changes are not made to the premises. Most likely, the landlord would be liable for common areas and the tenant for the area under his or her control.

Penalty. Injunctions and fines of $50,000 for the first offense or $100,000 for subsequent offenses.

Exemptions. Private clubs and religious organizations are exempt from this law, and the ADA does not apply to residential property.

Florida Discrimination Law. The Florida Discrimination Law is very similar to the federal statutes. (Fla. Stat., Sec. 760.20-.37.) The reason for a duplicate state statute is to give victims of discrimination a state remedy that may be easier to pursue than a federal one. This statute does not, however, require apartment owners to make all areas accessible to the handicapped.

Military Personnel. Section 83.67 of the landlord Tenant Law was amended in 2003 to forbid discrimination against military personnel. This was part of a bill allowing military personnel out of their lease agreements, (see Chapter 8.)

Florida HIV Law. Under Florida Statutes, Section 760.50, it is illegal to discriminate against persons with HIV. One tenant who was evicted by his landlord was awarded $5,000 plus attorney's fees against a landlord who was found to have discriminated against him because he had AIDS. *Meli Investment Corp., etc., v. O.R, et al*, 18 FLW D1557 (Fla. 3 DCA 1993) Under Florida Statutes, Section 689.25, HIV or AIDS status does not have to be disclosed in a real estate transaction.

Local Laws. Landlords should check their city and county ordinances before adopting a discriminatory policy such as an adult-only complex. A Dade County ordinance prohibits even federally subsidized housing for the elderly because it is discriminatory.

Lead Paint and Radon Gas Warnings

Federal and state laws require warning be given to tenants about the hazards of lead paint and radon gas. While these may be slightly burdensome, they could help protect the landlord from liability for any injuries caused by these conditions.

Lead paint. The federal Environmental Protection Agency has decided that tenants must be given a warning whenever they move into a dwelling unit built before 1978, and that only certified trained professionals can perform repairs that disturb more than six square feet of paint in a house built before 1978.

The are official forms that must be used to give these warnings that are explained in the sections on leasing and maintenance and are included in the Appendix.

Radon Gas. A Florida statute [404.056(5)] requires a written warning be given to a tenant about the risk from radon gas escaping out of the ground and into a dwelling unit. Failure to include the clause could subject the landlord to claims for damages from any injuries caused to the tenant by the gas. The clause is included in the leases in this book.

Security Deposits

Florida's Landlord Tenant law has strict requirements regarding handling of tenant security deposits and failure to follow them could mean loss of the deposit even if the tenant damaged the premises and paying the tenant's attorney thousands of dollars in fees.

Amount. Unlike some states, Florida does not have a law limiting the amount of security deposit a landlord may require. What to charge should be made based on the practical consideration of what is the most you can get without scaring away possible tenants.

Bank account. All types of damage, rent, pet, and other tenant advance deposits, must be kept in a separate account "for the benefit of the tenant" unless a surety bond is posted. (Fla. Stat., Sec. 83.49(1).) The separate account may be interest bearing or noninterest bearing, and the landlord cannot pledge the money, use it in any way, or mix it with his or her own money.

🖹 When a tenant sued a landlord over a security deposit and asked for punitive damages because he had not kept it in a separate account, a county court held that the tenant was not entitled to punitive damages. *Williams v. Scrima,* 18 Fla. Supp. 2d 72 (Co.Ct. Palm Beach Co. 1986).

If the landlord posts a surety bond for the amount of the deposit, or $50,000, whichever is less, the funds may be commingled with his or her own, but tenants must be paid 5% interest on their deposits. If a landlord (or his or her agent) rents properties in five or more counties, a bond may be posted with the Secretary of State. (Fla. Stat., Sec. 83.49(1)(c).)

These provisions will probably be a surprise to most landlords. Very few landlords or tenants are aware of these rules and even fewer understand them. Because of the expenses of a surety bond, the small landlord is stuck with the separate account alternative. However, tenants come and go, and with deposits of only several hundred dollars, banks are not pleased with the opening and closing of accounts with each new tenant. The landlord technically cannot commingle even $ 10 of his or her own in the account to keep it open.

As a practical matter, a $5 or $10 deposit of a landlord's own money to keep an account open during periods when there were no security deposits on hand would probably not be considered an actionable violation of the statute. In fact, it appears that most small Florida landlords do not keep the funds separate, and this is seldom brought up by tenants.

Notice. Under Florida Statutes, Section 83.49(2), landlords must give notice to tenants within thirty days of receiving a deposit of how the deposit is held, as follows:

➲ Within thirty days of receipt of a deposit, written notice must be given in person or by mail to the tenant, which includes the following (a **NOTICE OF HOLDING SECURITY DEPOSIT** can be used for this purpose see Form 18):

➲ name and address of the depository;

➲ whether it is in a separate account or commingled with the landlord's funds;

➲ if it is commingled, whether it is in a Florida interest-bearing account; and,

➲ a copy of Florida Statutes, Section 83.49(3).

If any of the above information changes, a new notice must be given within thirty days. The interest, if any, must be paid or credited to the tenant at least once a year. All of the information required in the notice can also be included in the lease the tenant signs when starting the tenancy.

Interest. The deposits do not have to be placed in an interest-bearing account, but if they are, the tenant must be given either 75% of the interest paid or 5% interest (at the landlord's option). Considering the current low interest rates, it won't be worth the bookkeeping for most landlords to use an interest bearing account. But for landlords with hundreds of properties or if rates rise, it might be profitable.

In those cases in which interest must be paid to a tenant, it must be either paid or credited against the rent at least once a year. No interest need be paid to a tenant who wrongfully terminates his or her tenancy prior to the end of the term. (Fla. Stat., Sec. 83.49(9).)

Most tenants do not even know they are entitled to interest on their deposit, but occasionally a vacating tenant will demand interest. A landlord who has not followed the separate account rule is better off paying it and avoiding a suit that could cost attorney's fees.

Keeping the Deposit. Unless the landlord follows the notice requirements, he or she cannot keep the security deposit no matter how much damage the tenant has done. (Fla. Stat., Sec. 83.49(3).) The landlord must return the tenant's security deposit together with interest, if any, within fifteen days of the day the tenant vacated the premises.

Notice of Intention to Impose a Claim on Security Deposit If the landlord wishes to keep any part of the security deposit, he or she must send the following notice by certified mail to the tenant's last known address within thirty days of the date that the tenant vacated the unit, (see Form 29.)

THIS IS NOTICE OF MY INTENTION TO IMPOSE A CLAIM FOR DAMAGES IN THE AMOUNT OF $ UPON YOUR SECURITY DEPOSIT, DUE TO [state any reasons]. IT IS SENT TO YOU AS REQUIRED BY §83.49(3), FLORIDA STATUTES. YOU ARE HEREBY NOTIFIED THAT YOU MUST OBJECT IN WRITING TO THIS DEDUCTION FROM YOUR SECURITY DEPOSIT WITHIN FIFTEEN (15) DAYS FROM THE TIME YOU RECEIVE THIS NOTICE OR I WILL BE AUTHORIZED TO DEDUCT MY CLAIM FROM YOUR DEPOSIT. YOUR OBJECTION MUST BE SENT TO [landlords address].

If, as happens in many cases, the damages exceed the deposit, then you should show this in the notice. You can sue the tenant in small claims court for the balance, but this is rarely worth the expense.

If you try to send the tenant the balance of a deposit but cannot find the tenant, then the money is considered abandoned and is supposed to be turned over to the State of Florida.

If this notice is not sent as required, the deposit must be returned to the tenant, even if the tenant caused damage to the premises. If the tenant must sue for return of his or her deposit, the landlord will have to return the deposit and pay the tenant's attorney's fees.

⬚ If the tenant sues the landlord for the deposit and the landlord sues the tenant for damages, the court could order the landlord to return the deposit and pay the tenant's attorney's fees immediately and then hold a trial for the damages later, at which time the tenant can spend the money and be judgment proof. *(Durene v. Alcime,* 448 So.2d 1208 (Fla. 3 DCA 1984).)

⬚ When the tenant won his security deposit back and the landlord won recovery for damages, the landlord had to pay both his and the tenant's attorneys fees. *Malagon v. Solari,* 566 So.2d 352 (Fla. 4 DCA 1990).

⬚ When the parties bitterly fought over a security deposit for over a year, and the file grew to nine volumes of depositions, motions, notices, and documents, the tenant ended up settling for a return of $1,525.00, and the tenant's attorney was awarded $20,000.00 in attorney's fees. On appeal, this amount was reduced to "only" $5,000.00 (plus $1,100.00 in costs). *Missilian v. Zimmerman and Permulter,* 22 Fla. Supp. 2d 185 (llthCir.App. Div. 1987).

Early Termination by Tenant. If the tenant vacates the premises prior to the end of the term of the lease, he or she must give at least seven-days' notice of leaving early or the landlord does not have to send the notice. The tenant's notice can be sent by certified mail or personally delivered, and it must include an address at which the tenant can be reached. Failure to give the notice is not a waiver on any rights the tenant may have to the security deposit. A landlord is well-advised to send the **NOTICE OF INTENTION TO IMPOSE CLAIM ON SECURITY DEPOSIT** (see Form 29) even if the tenant fails to send his or her notice to avoid any problems in case the tenant lies about giving notice.

📃 A Miami court ignored the statute and said that even when the tenant did not give the seven-days' notice, the landlord still had to give the fifteen days' notice. *Rollo v. Armesto,* 6 FLW Supp. 398 (11th Cir. App. Div. 1999).

Forwarding Address. If the tenant has not left a forwarding address, the notice must be sent to the property address even though you know the tenant is gone. (The tenant might have given a forwarding address to the post office.) If you would like to know the tenant's new address, you can write "ADDRESS CORRECTION REQUESTED" on the front of the envelope and the post office will send you the address for a small fee.

📃 Where a landlord did not know the tenant's new address but did know the tenants attorney, the landlord was still correct in mailing the certified notice to the vacated property. *Newman v. Gray,* 4 FLW Supp. 271 (CC 11th Cir. Dade 1996).

Objection to Deductions. If the tenant does not object to the amount claimed in the notice within fifteen days of receipt of the notice, then the landlord may deduct the amount claimed and must then remit the balance to the tenant within thirty days of the date the notice was first sent. If the tenant objects, he or she would have to file a suit against the landlord. It appears that a tenant may have up to five years to file the suit.

To make it more tempting to the tenant, the landlord should include a check for the balance of the deposit, if any, with the notice. The landlord might want to write on the back of the check, "Accepted in full payment of claims against security deposit." However, this might make a tenant want to sue immediately.

A check without this language might be cashed by the tenant who plans to sue later but never gets around to it.

Wear and Tear. The landlord may deduct *damages* from a security deposit, but may not deduct normal *wear and tear.* What is normal is subjective and only a judge or jury can decide. A hole in a wall is clearly not normal. An apartment needing painting after a tenant lived there ten years is normal. You have to use your best judgment of what is regular wear and tear or what is excessive. If you have any doubts, you should get a second opinion from a disinterested person or an attorney.

A landlord making a claim on a deposit should always take pictures of the damage.

If a security deposit claim goes to court, it is also good to have receipts for the repairs that were done. However, a court will probably allow a landlord to do the work him- or herself and charge a reasonable value of the work. Getting a written estimate before doing the work yourself may be helpful for larger repairs.

📄 A Florida court allowed a landlord to charge a former tenant for the cost of a real estate agents fee for finding a new tenant for a rental unit. *McLennan v. Rozniak,* 15 Fla. Supp. 2d 42 (Palm Beach 1985).

Some leases have clauses that allow a landlord to keep the entire deposit or a certain portion of it if the tenant leaves before the lease is up. When the clause has been considered a *liquidated damages* clause, it has usually been upheld.

However, when it has been considered a penalty, it has been thrown out. It is not possible to say for certain whether a clause will be considered one or the other because judges have a wide leeway in their rulings. Usually the decision depends upon who the judge considers the good guy and the bad guy in the case.

Special Rules. In addition to all of the rules previously discussed in this chapter regarding security deposits, there are some special rules of which you should be aware.

Real Estate Brokers. If there is a conflict with the rules of Chapter 475 regarding what real estate brokerage licensees must do with deposits, Florida Statutes, Section 83.49(3)(d) prevails and licensees must follow these rules.

Hotels and motels. These security deposit rules do not apply to transient rentals by hotels and motels. (Fla. Stat., Sec. 83.49(4).) Any person who is licensed under Section 509.241 (public lodging and food service establishments) who does not comply with this law (if it applies) may lose his or her license or be fined. (Fla. Stat., Sec. 83.49(8).) Since the law does not apply to transient rentals, this would only apply to hotels or motels that rented to permanent residents or to those without another place of residence.

Public housing. These security deposit rules do not apply to instances (other than for rent stabilization) in which the amount of rent or deposit, or both, is regulated by laws or rules of a public body. This includes public housing authorities and federal housing programs including Section 202, Sections 221(d)(3) and (4), Section 236 or Section 8 of the *National Housing Act.* (Fla. Stat., Sec. 83.49 (4).)

Except for the requirement of a Notice of Claim on Security, these rules do not apply to public housing under Florida Statutes, Chapter 421. (Fla. Stat., Sec. 83.49(4).)

Municipal housing authorities. According to an opinion of the Florida Attorney General, municipal housing authorities do not have authority to require security deposits. (Op. Atty. Gen. 078-104.)

Renewals. If a rental agreement is renewed, the security deposit is considered a new deposit. This means that when a lease is renewed, a new notice as explained on pages 28 and 29 must be sent. (Fla. Stat., Sec. 83.49(6).)

Sale Of the Property. Upon sale of the property or change of the rental agent, all deposits and interest must be transferred to the buyer or agent together with an accurate accounting. (Fla. Stat., Sec. 83.49(7).)

Bank Seizure. When a bank seizes an account containing security deposits belonging to tenants for debts owed by landlord, either the landlord or the tenant can take court action against the bank for return of the deposits. *Nardi v. Continental Nat. Bank*, 559 So.2d 307 (Fla. 3 DCA 1990).

Warranty of Habitability

Did you know that every tenant who rents from you gets a Warranty of Habitability? You don't have to give it to them, the Florida Supreme Court did.

In recent years, the centuries-old theories of landlord/tenant law have been replaced with new obligations on landlords to protect their tenants. One of these new obligations is the *implied warranty of habitability,* which has been accepted in over forty states. Under this doctrine, any time a dwelling unit is turned over to a tenant, the tenant is automatically given a warranty by the landlord that the premises are in safe and habitable condition and will remain so during the term of the lease.

🗐 The case of *Mansur v. Eubanks* officially made the doctrine of habitability the law in Florida. In this case, the tenants gave a $25 deposit and started moving things into the premises. They turned on the gas outside the dwelling and when they went inside, they smelled gas. A resulting explosion seriously injured one of the tenants. The court ruled that the landlord was liable for the tenant's injuries. *Mansur v. Eubanks,* 401 So.2d 1328 (Fla. 1981).

🗐 In another case, a landlord did not repair a broken hot water heater for three days and was liable for $775,000.00 in damages when a woman carrying boiling water to the bathtub spilled it on her grandson. *Bennett M. Lifter, Inc. v. Varnado,* 480 So.2d

1336 (Fla. 3 DCA 1985). This case showed that the duty of the landlord is not just to turn over a safe dwelling unit, but to *keep* it safe.

In a single-family home or duplex, a landlord can attempt to protect him- or herself by stating in the lease that the tenant is responsible for maintaining the premises. This cannot be done in larger buildings.

➲ If a lease states that a tenant is responsible for maintenance, then the landlord should not voluntarily do repairs. Otherwise, the landlord can be held responsible for the safety of the premises. If something comes up that the tenant cannot handle and the landlord would rather do it, he or she should have the tenant sign an agreement that the landlord will repair this one item one time, but that the landlord assumes no other responsibilities.

➲ Although Florida Statutes, Section 83.51 allows the landlord and tenant to agree that the tenant shall have the duty of maintenance, Section 83.47 states that a lease cannot limit a landlord's liability. Where the line will be drawn between these two statutes is not yet known.

Maintenance Requirements

Responsibility for maintenance depends on whether the unit is an apartment versus a home or duplex, and on what the terms of the lease are. With an apartment the law requires the landlord to do much more of the maintenance than if the rental is a single-family home or duplex.

Residential Apartments. The landlords' duties of maintenance are included in Florida Statutes, Section 83.51(1). Under this law, the landlord must comply with health, housing, and building codes. If there are no codes, the landlord must "maintain the roofs, windows, screens, doors, floors, steps, porches, exterior walls, foundations, and all other structural components in good repair and capable of resisting normal forces and loads and the plumbing in reasonable working condition."

Under Florida Statutes, Section 83.51(2), unless the landlord and tenant agree that these shall be the tenant's responsibility, the landlord must make *reasonable provision* for:

➲ exterminations of rats, mice, roaches, ants, wood-destroying organisms, and bedbugs;

NOTE: *When the premises must be vacated for extermination, the tenant must vacate for up to four days upon being given seven days' written notice. The landlord is not liable for damages but must prorate the rent and not charge for the days that tenant is unable to stay in the premises. The landlord does not have to pay for the tenant to stay at a hotel.*

➲ locks and keys;

➲ clean and safe condition of common areas;

➲ garbage removal and outside receptacles; and,

➲ functioning facilities for heat during winter, running water, and hot water.

Some specific areas of additional consideration under the statute include the following.

➲ These rules do not apply to mobile homes owned by tenants. (Fla. Stat., Sec. 83.5 l(2)(d).)

➲ The landlord may require the tenant to pay for garbage removal, water, fuel, or utilities. (Fla. Stat., Sec. 83.51(2)(e).)

➲ The landlord is not responsible for conditions that are caused by the tenant, the tenant's family, or guests. (Fla. Stat., Sec. 83.51(4).)

Single Family Homes & Duplexes. Florida law offers special exceptions for single-family homes and duplexes. The only requirements specifically in the law are that the landlord comply with building, housing, and health codes (Fla. Stat., Sec. 83.51(1)) and supply working smoke detectors. (Fla. Stat., Sec. 83.51(2)(b).) However, these duties can be put on the tenant if it is so agreed in the lease.

Nonresidential rentals. Florida statutes do not specify who is responsible for maintenance in nonresidential rentals. All of the responsibilities should be spelled out in the lease. If the lease puts the responsibility for maintenance on the landlord and the premises are "wholly untenantable," Florida Statutes, Section 83.201 allows the tenant to withhold rent and gives the landlord twenty days to complete the repairs.

When a unit was uninhabitable at the beginning of the lease, the tenant was allowed to recover the fair rental value from the landlord for the time up to when the repairs were completed. *Zais v. CF West Florida, Inc.,* 505 So.2d 577 (Fla. 4 DCA 1987).

Tenants' Responsibilities. Under Florida Statutes, Section 83.52, at all times the tenant must:

⊃ comply with all building, housing, and health codes;

⊃ keep his or her part of the premises clean and sanitary;

⊃ remove his or her garbage in a clean and sanitary manner;

⊃ keep all plumbing fixtures in the unit (or used by him or her) clean and sanitary and in repair;

NOTE: *Although the law clearly puts this obligation on tenants, the Division of Hotels and Motels has required landlords to clean up bathrooms that tenants have soiled by allowing the toilet to back up. The rationale of the Division is that, while the law allows the landlord to evict a tenant for sanitary problems, the ultimate responsibility is on the landlord.*

⊃ use and operate in a reasonable manner all electrical, plumbing, sanitary, heating, ventilating, air conditioning, and other facilities and appliances, including elevators;

⊃ not destroy, deface, damage, impair, or remove any part of the premises or property therein belonging to the landlord nor permit any person to do so; and,

⊃ conduct him- or herself and require other persons on the premises to conduct themselves in a manner that does not unreasonably disturb his or her neighbors or constitute a breach of the peace.

The constitutional conflict. There is a problem with Florida Statutes, Section 83.51 of which landlords should be aware. In stating that landlords must comply with "building, housing, and health codes," it has been argued that the legislature has included "any law, ordinance, or governmental regulation concerning health, safety, sanitation, or fitness for habitation, or the construction, maintenance, operation, occupancy, use, or appearance of any dwelling unit."

This language is so broad and vague that it includes any minor regulation by a municipality, and Section 83.56(1) allows a tenant to withhold rent for a violation.

➲ In Coral Gables, the colors of the buildings must be approved by the Board of Architects. If the color of a building was not approved, a tenant could argue that this gives him the right to withhold rent.

➲ The Division of Hotels and Restaurants has applied its rules to apartment houses and required a landlord to clean a tenant's bathroom when the tenant kept using the toilet after it malfunctioned.

➲ Even though Section 83.51(4) states that a landlord is not responsible for conditions caused by the tenant's own negligence, the Division of Hotels and Restaurants has ignored this and made its own rules under Section 83.51(1).

➲ Section 26-26 of the Code of the City of Miami requires landlords of furnished rentals to provide "housecleaning equipment," and many tenants demand vacuum cleaners.

➲ In Dade County, a vegetable garden has been cited as a sanitary nuisance. In all of these cases, the tenant could withhold rent because there was a violation. It has been pointed out by John J. Boyle, an attorney in the Miami area, that Section 83.51 may be unconstitutional. Anyone faced with problems in this area should have his or her attorney obtain a copy of Boyle's book, *Landlords Remedies in Florida,* published by D&S Publishing, or Boyle's CLE materials for good arguments and case law in this area.

Code violations. Landlords should be aware that governmental bodies can levy fines of hundreds of dollars a day for minor violations. Ignoring notices of violation can be expensive. Whenever you receive a governmental notice, you should read it very carefully and follow it to the letter. One landlord who sold his property and thought the problem was solved was fined $11,000 ($500 a day for the last twenty-two days he owned the property) for a violation. After you correct a violation, be sure that the governmental body that sent the notice gives you written confirmation that you are in compliance.

Lead paint notice. Under rules of the Environmental Protection Agency, if any repairs are done to the property during a tenancy and more than six square feet of interior or twenty square feet of exterior lead paint is disturbed, notice must be given to the tenants and the landlord must obtain a receipt from the tenant for the notice. (The notice and receipt are included as form 15 in this book.) The following rules also apply:

➲ any work by plumbers, painters, electricians, and others is included;

➲ the tenants must be given the pamphlet *Protect Your Family From Lead in Your Home;*

➲ if the work is done on common areas of the building, all tenants must be notified; and,

➲ emergency renovations and repairs are excluded.

Retaliatory Conduct

In 1983, the Florida legislature passed a law prohibiting landlords from "retaliating against a tenant." (Fla. Stat., Sec. 83.64.) It can be argued that the law is too vague but it would be expensive to take the argument to court. The best strategy is to read the following rules carefully and avoid any conduct that might look like a violation.

Under Florida Statutes, Section 83.61(1), a landlord must not discriminatively do any of the following acts in retaliation against a tenant:

➲ raise rent;

➲ reduce services; or,

➲ threaten court action.

The key is the word *discriminatively.* It is okay to raise all rents but you cannot raise one tenant's rent to retaliate against that tenant.

▤ When a tenant sued a landlord for damage to his personal property from water leaks, and the landlord chose not to renew the tenant's lease, the court held that the landlord did not violate either the landlord/tenant retaliatory eviction law or the anti-discrimination law (Chapter 760) *Chancellor v. Garrett, 2* FLW Supp. 125 (Escambia Co. 1993).

The conduct of a tenant that a landlord may not retaliate against, under Florida Statutes, Section 83.64(1), is unlimited but specifically includes:

➲ tenant complaints to governmental agencies about code violations;

➲ tenant participation in tenant's organizations; and,

➲ tenant complaints to landlord about maintenance.

To defend an eviction, a tenant may say that the landlord is retaliating. However, the law states that it is not a defense if the landlord brings a good faith action for nonpayment of rent, violation of the rental agreement, or violation by the tenant of the landlord/tenant laws.

▤ When a tenant admitted to breaching his or her lease by having unauthorized pets, moving a rug to the garage, and other violations, he or she was not allowed to use the retaliatory eviction defense. *Salmonte v. Eilertson,* 526 So.2d 179 (Fla. 1 DCA 1988).

Interrupting Utilities

Under Florida Statutes, Section 83.67, a landlord who terminates or interrupts utilities such as water, heat, light, electricity, gas, elevator, garbage collection, or refrigeration can be held liable for three month's rent for each violation, plus the tenant's court costs and attorney s fees. This can be frustrating to a landlord whose tenant is intentionally wasting utilities to hurt the landlord. The correct response in such a situation would be to get an emergency restraining order under Florida Statutes, Section 83.681.

A court ruled that although the statute seems to say that any interruption of utilities entitles a tenant to three months' rent, it could not possibly mean that, since that would be absurd and unreasonable. Therefore, a landlord was not liable for damages when he shut off water and elevator services during conversion of an apartment building to condominiums. *Badaraco v. Suncoast Towers V Assoc.,* 676 So.2d 502 (Fla. 3 DCA 1996).

When landlords pay for utilities and tenants stop paying rent and utilities it can be extremely frustrating to pay utilities for a tenant, especially if it drags on for months and especially if the tenant is clearly wasting the utilities.

Thus a landlord should whenever possible avoid setting up a tenancy where the utilities are in his name. If there is no other alternative, one possibility for protection might be to put a clause in the lease that if utilities become x number of days or weeks late, then they shall be converted to the name of the tenant.

In such a case a landlord might get away with telling the utility to take his name off. If the tenant fails to put his name on, they it might not be considered interrupting utilities. However, a pro-tenant judge probably would fine the landlord anyway. If you have already filed an eviction you might be able to get some information on how the judge in your case would react to this.

Abandoned Property

The abandoned property law is another one that, while a little burdensome at times, can protect the landlord from liability. What it does is give you procedures to follow that will protect you from claims by a former tenant. A landlord was once liable for thousands of dollars for throwing out junk furniture when the tenant claimed they were valuable antiques and the landlord couldn't prove otherwise.

The abandoned property laws are explained in Chapter 9, After the Tenancy.

Towing Vehicles

Of course there is a special law providing rules on how and when you can tow a vehicle from your rental property.

The law, section 715.07 of the Florida Statues is contained in the appendix and mostly controls how towing companies can operate, but the following riles are of concern to landlords.

➲ In most cases, in order to tow vehicles from your property, you must have signs with the proper wording and correct-sized letters.

➲ The sign rules do not apply to single-family homes or when you personally informed the vehicles owner.

➲ If you do not follow the rules, you can be liable to the vehicles owner for damages and attorney's fees.

➲ Municipalities can have stricter laws than the state statute, so check with your police department.

Know Your Legal Rights

Do not assume that every law is constitutional or that every government employee is right. You may have to bring your case to a higher court to get all of the rights you are entitled to. In one case, some tenants who were being evicted filed a complaint with a state civil rights commission. The commission held a hearing at which it both represented the tenants and ordered the landlords to pay the tenants $40,000 in damages and not to evict the tenants. The daughter of one of the landlords filed a suit against the commission, and the court held that the landlords had been denied several constitutional rights. The commission agreed to pay the landlords $100,000.

Doing Further Research

This book contains a summary of most of the court cases and statutes that affect landlord/tenant law in Florida. However, you may want to research your predicament further by reading the entire statute section or court case. To do this, you should use the statute section number or case citation. Florida Statute citations appear in this book as "Fla. Stat., Sec. 00.00" All of Florida's landlord/tenant statutes are included in Appendix A.

As described in the "Using Self-Help Law Books" section, court cases are noted by the following research symbol 📑. Where you see the 📑, a point of law being made is supported by a court decision. You can find the citation for that decision in the Table of Authorities found in Appendix A. Other cases are summarized throughout the text, with their citations being given with the summary and in the Table of Authorities. Case citations include the name of the case, the volume and page of the reporter, the court, and the year. For example, *Clark & Lewis v. Gardner,* 109 So. 192 (Fla. 1926) means that the case is found in volume 109 of the Southern Reporter on page 192, and that it is a 1926 case from the Florida Supreme Court. The notation "(Fla. 3 DCA 1964)" means the case was decided in Florida's third district court of appeals. The notation "(11 th Cir. App. Div. 1987)" means it was in a circuit court acting as an appeals court from county court in the 11th circuit, and "(Co.Ct. Broward 1996) means it is from a county court in Broward County.

7   Issues During the Tenancy

It's nice to have a rental property where you just get a check in the mail the first of the month like clockwork. But there aren't too many like this. Usually at least some issues come up. Depending on how you screened your clients and your luck, you could have calls monthly or more often! This chapter explains how to deal with some of the more common issues.

Landlord's Access to the Premises

Under the historic principles of landlord/tenant law, which still apply to nonresidential tenancies, the landlord has no right to enter the premises unless the right is given to the landlord in the lease. Under Florida's residential landlord/tenant law, the landlord does have a right to access, even if it is not in the lease, and the tenant cannot unreasonably withhold consent for the landlord to enter the dwelling unit. (Fla. Stat., Sec. 83.53.) The landlord may enter the premises to make repairs between 7:30 a.m. and 8:00 p.m. if at least twelve hours' notice is given. The landlord may also enter to:

⊃ inspect the premises;

⊃ make necessary or agreed repairs, decorations, or improvements;

⊃ supply agreed services; or,

⊃ exhibit the dwelling to prospective or actual purchasers, mortgagees, tenants, workmen, or contractors.

However, the landlord may enter for the reasons in the previous paragraph only under the following circumstances:

⊃ with the consent of the tenant;

⊃ in case of emergency;

⊃ when the tenant unreasonably withholds consent; or,

⊃ if the tenant is absent from the premises for one-half of the rental period without notice.

The landlord may enter the premises at any time if it is necessary to protect the premises. The landlord must not abuse the right of access or use it to harass the tenant.

Violations of privacy. The tenant's exclusive use of the premises includes the right not to be observed by the landlord, especially surreptitiously. One court found a landlord and his wife both liable for $1,286,582 in damages because the landlord made a peephole in a closet through which he could look into the tenants' apartment.

Lease Violations by the Tenant

Since the main duty for the landlord is to accept the rent, the most common problems during the tenancy are ones caused by tenants not following the obligation in the lease.

Rent Due Date. In a residential tenancy, unless otherwise stated in a lease, rent is due at the beginning of each rent payment period (Fla. Stat., Sec. 83.46(1)), and in a nonresidential tenancy the rule is the opposite; meaning, unless a lease or rental agreement states that rent must be paid in advance, it does not have to be paid until the end of the term. (This is because hundreds of years ago feudal tenants paid a share of their crops at the end of the season as rent.) *De Vore v. Lee*, 158 Fla. 608, 30 So.2d 924 (1947).

Mailing of Rent. If a lease says that rent is due on a certain date, it is not good enough if the tenant mailed it on that date. In some situations (such as paying income tax) the mailing date is important, but not when the lease clearly states when the rent is due. *Green v. Redfield*, 6 FLW Supp. 413 (19th Cir. App. Div. 1998).

Bad Checks. The procedure for collecting on bad checks is contained in Florida Statutes, Section 68.065. It provides for a service charge based on the amount the check was written for, ranging from $25 to $40 or 5% of the amount of the check (whichever is greater), and for triple damages (or a minimum of $50).

The procedure is to send a notice by certified mail and then file suit on the check. (See Form 62.) However, if a tenant cannot immediately pay the check, the landlord would be better advised to immediately start the eviction rather than sue on the bad check.

There is also a criminal law against writing a bad check found in Section 832.07. You may get your sheriff to prosecute the tenant. However, you must comply with certain requirements, such as checking the identification of the maker of the check and not accepting a post-dated check.

Damage to the Premises. If the tenant does intentional damage to the premises, the landlord can terminate the tenancy (see Chapter 8) and can also get an *injunction* against the tenant. (Fla. Stat., Sec. 83.681.) This can be done by filing a complaint with the county or circuit court. For an injunction to be issued, the damage must be over twice the amount of the security deposit or $300, whichever is greater.

Lease Terms Violations. Before taking action for a lease violation, the landlord must decide whether the breach is *curable* or *incurable*. If it is curable, then the tenant must be given seven days to fix the problem. If it is incurable, then the landlord may immediately terminate the tenancy. However, in deciding that a breach is incurable, the landlord takes a risk that if the tenant fights it, the court will say it was curable and the landlord will have to pay the tenant's attorney's fees.

➲ Examples of noncompliance that are incurable are destruction, damage, or misuse of the landlord's or other tenant's property by intentional act or continued unreasonable disturbance. (Fla. Stat., Sec. 83.56(2)(a).)

Examples of noncompliance that the tenant should be allowed to cure are unauthorized pets, guests, or vehicles; parking in an unauthorized manner; or failing to keep the premises clean and sanitary. (Fla. Stat., Sec. 83.56(2)(b).) In one case, a tenant's son's harassment and hitting of another tenant's son was held to be curable. *Hobbs v. Lyons*, 2 FLW Supp. 128 (Escambia Co. 1993).

If the violation is curable, the landlord must give the following notice to the tenant, (See form 32.):

YOU ARE NOTIFIED THAT YOU HAVE VIOLATED YOUR RENTAL AGREEMENT AS FOLLOWS:_____

_____

DEMAND IS HEREBY MADE THAT YOU REMEDY THIS NONCOMPLIANCE WITHIN SEVEN DAYS OF RECEIPT OF THIS NOTICE OR YOUR LEASE SHALL BE DEEMED TERMINATED AND YOU SHALL VACATE THE PREMISES UPON TERMINATION. IF THIS SAME CONDUCT OR CONDUCT OF A SIMILAR NATURE IS REPEATED WITHIN TWELVE MONTHS, YOUR TENANCY IS SUBJECT TO TERMINATION WITHOUT YOUR BEING GIVEN AN OPPORTUNITY TO CURE THE NONCOMPLIANCE.

If the violation is not curable or if the tenant repeats a noncompliance after receiving the notice, then the landlord may terminate the tenancy. See Chapter 8.

Tenant Vacating Early. If the tenant breaches the lease by vacating the property before the expiration of the lease, the landlord has the choice of doing one of four things:

1. terminate the lease and take possession of the property for his or her own account (relieving the tenant of further liability);

2. take possession of the premises for the account of the tenant and hold the tenant liable for the difference in rent due under the lease and the rent eventually received; or,

3. let the unit sit vacant and sue the tenant for the full rent as it comes due. (Fla. Stat., Sec. 83.595.) *CB Institutional Fund VIII v. Gemballa U.S.A., Inc.*, 566 So.2d 896 (1990).

4. The fourth remedy was just added by the legislature in 2008, the landlord can charge a liquidated damages or early termination fee, if it is no more than two months rent and this has been agreed to in writing, either in the lease or in a separate agreement signed at the time of the lease. (F.S. §83.595(4)) (See Form 9.)

The law in this area is very complicated. The Florida Supreme Courts decisions have caused confusion in the appellate courts, and many landlords have lost in their attempts to collect damages from tenants. Before taking action regarding large sums of money, a landlord should consult an attorney and request that the attorney review the latest cases in this area as well as the latest publications on landlord/tenant law.

Suing for Rent. The problem in most of the cases in which landlords have lost their suits against tenants is that they have tried to terminate the lease and sue for the rent, combining option (1) with option (2). When this is done, the courts have usually found that the landlord accepted a surrender of the premises and lost all rights to sue for damages.

If a landlord wishes to terminate the lease, then instead of suing for accelerated rent, the landlord should sue for breach of contract. *Hudson Pest Control Inc. v. Wesford Asset Management, Inc.*, 622 So.2d 546 (Fla. 5 DCA 1993).

If the landlord wishes to sue the tenant for rent for the period up to the point when a new tenant is found, or for future rent, he or she should not terminate the tenancy, but use option (2) and take possession for the account of the tenant.

> When a landlord evicts a tenant, some courts have held that this terminates the rental agreement (option (1)) and precludes a suit for future rent. However, a recent decision has made it clear that even when a tenant is evicted, the landlord can choose option (2) and sue the tenant for future rent. *Colonial Promenade v. Jubus,* 541 So.2d 1313 (Fla. 5 DCA 1989).

The usual problem in the court cases is a misinterpretation of the landlord's intent. To avoid this, the landlord should analyze the options and make his or her intent clear either in the form of a certified letter to the tenant or in the allegations of the landlord's complaint.

Some other points that a landlord should know about include the following.

➲ Where the landlord has many vacant units, he or she can elect option (3) and just sue the tenant for the rent due without trying to rent the unit.

➲ If the landlord expects to rent the unit out at a lower rate, then it should be made clear that he or she is taking possession for the account of the tenant and will hold the tenant liable for the difference.

> When a tenant broke the lease and the landlord sued for the rent for the period before it was re-rented, the court held that the landlord was renting the property for the account of the tenant and that the tenant could get credit for the higher rent the landlord was receiving from the new tenant. *Gould v. Vitiello,* 526 So.2d 1018 (Fla. 2 DCA 1988).

> Unless the lease provides that the balance owed under a lease can be accelerated upon default, the landlord

cannot sue for the rent until it comes due. *National Advertising Co. v. Main Street Shopping Center,* 539 So.2d 594 (Fla. 2 DCA 1989).

When a lease stated that the landlords remedy, in the event of tenant's breach, was to terminate the lease and to relet the premises on account for the tenant, the landlord lost the right to use other remedies usually available and could not sue for rent as it came due. *Linens of Paris, Inc. v. Cymet,* 510 So.2d 1021 (Fla. 3 DCA 1987).

Code Violations

Violations of city, county and state building and health codes can result in fines against a property for $1,000 a day or more. So of course you need to quickly take care of any violations for which you receive notice. Usually these fines are not imposed until you have received a certified letter and been given a time to fix the situation.

The most common reason to get a notice of violation is a complain by a tenant. If your property is in poor condition it is best not to get in a battle with a tenant. As explained in the previous chapter you are not allowed to evict a tenant for complaining about a violation, but you are not required to renew his lease. A good reason not to renew the lease is to renovate the unit.

Injuries on the Premises

The landlord has a duty to inspect and repair *common areas* in a rental building with more than one unit. *Hester v. Guarino,* 251 So.2d 563 (Fla. DCA 1971). This does not apply to a single-family home. In a duplex, a landlord may state in the lease that the tenants assume the duty to take care of the common areas.

The general rule is that a landlord is not liable for injuries on parts of the premises that are *not under his or her control* except in the following circumstances:

◒ when there is a danger known to the landlord;

◒ when there is a violation of law in the condition of the premises;

◒ when there is a preexisting defect in construction;

◒ when the landlord undertakes repairing the premises or is required by the lease to do the repairs;

◒ when the landlord did a negligent act; or,

◒ when the premises were a nuisance at the time of the making of the lease or would become one upon tenant's expected use of the premises. *Bowen v. Holloway,* 255 So.2d 696 (Fla. 4 DCA 1971)

Cases Holding a Landlord Not Liable

The following are cases that held that a landlord would not be liable for injuries. It must be kept in mind that the holdings in some of the earlier cases may have been modified by the rulings in later cases.

▤ When no one knew about a hole under a concrete slab that broke when a tenant stepped on it, the landlord was not liable since the tenant was in a position to know about the danger. (*Zubowicz v. Warnock,* 149 So.2d 890 (Fla. 2 DCA 1963).)

▤ When a landlord rented a single-family home to a tenant and a salesman slipped on a painted concrete step wet with rainwater, there was no liability since there was no concealment—even though it was the landlord who originally painted the step. (*Wingard v. McDonald,* 348 So.2d 573 (Fla. 1 DCA 1977).)

▤ When a tenant was responsible for doing maintenance at his own cost, the landlord was not liable for the tenant's fall on the carpet. *Stolzenberg v. Forte Towers South, Inc.,* 430 So.2d 558 (Fla. 3 DCA 1983).

📑 A landlord was not liable for the death of a patron at a bar when the landlord's only interest in the premises was to receive the rent and to receive a reversion of the premises and the liquor license at the end of the lease. *Santiago v. Allen,* 449 So.2d 388 (Fla. 3 DCA 1984).

📑 When a tenant saw that a chair was being used to hold a door open but tripped over it when she was momentarily distracted, the landlord was not liable because it was not a dangerous condition, and there was sufficient light and space beside it to get by. *Schoenbach v. VMS Realty, Inc.,* 503 So.2d 382 (Fla. 3 DCA 1987).

📑 When a child was injured by falling from a tree onto broken glass at an apartment complex, the landlord was not liable because there was no evidence to show that the landlord knew the glass was there or how long the glass had been there. *Haynes v. Lloyd,* 533 So.2d 944 (Fla. 5 DCA 1988).

📑 When employees of a tenant were injured by a gas explosion in a commercial rental unit, the landlord was not liable because he had turned possession of the premises over to the tenant. *Veterans Gas Co. v. Gibbs,* 538 So.2d 1325 (Fla. 1 DCA 1989).

📑 When the daughter of a tenant's guest ran through a sliding glass door, the landlord was not liable since he was not in possession of the premises, had no duty to ascertain that the glass was not safety glass, and had no duty to put decals on the glass. *Fitzgerald v. Cestari,* 569 So.2d 1258 (1990).

📑 When a woman went into an office building to look for a telephone and slipped on an overripe mango that had fallen from a tree near the entrance, the landlord was not liable because she was not an *invitee,* but only an *uninvited licensee.* In English, this means that since the building owner had no interest in her coming into the building, he was not liable. If she were coming in to visit one of the businesses, the landlord could have been liable. *Iber v. R.P.A. International Corp.,* 585 So.2d 367 (Fla 3 DCA 1991).

Cases Holding a Landlord Liable

The following cases are examples of when a landlord was held liable for injuries to a tenant or a guest.

▤ When a landlord continues to do repairs on the premises after turning them over to the tenant, he or she may be liable for injuries on the premises. *McDonald v. Wingard,* 309 So.2d 192 (Fla. DCA 1975).

▤ The fact that the landlord used to have carpet in the elevator was evidence that it was negligent not to have carpet when an elderly tenant slipped on the linoleum floor. *Firth v. Marhoeffer,* 406 So.2d 521 (Fla. 4 DCA 1981).

▤ When a child being cared for by the tenant was bitten by the tenant's pit bull, the landlord was liable because he should have known about the dog and could have terminated the tenancy. *Vasquez v. Lopez,* 509 So.2d 1241 (Fla. 4 DCA 1987).

▤ When a tenant's son was bitten by a neighbor's pit bull, a court held that the landlord could be held liable even if its management company only found out a day or two earlier about the dog. *Giaculli v. Bright,* 584 So.2d 187 (Fla. 5 DCA 1991).

Protection from Liability for Injuries

The basis for liability in these cases is that the landlord breached a duty to keep the premises safe. If a landlord puts the duty to keep the premises safe on the tenant, there will be less likelihood that the landlord can be held liable. Florida Statutes, Section 83.51 allows a landlord to put certain duties of maintenance on the tenant in a single-family dwelling or duplex. A nonresidential lease can probably do the same. But in a multifamily building, the landlord cannot get out of the burden of making sure the premises are safe at all times.

▤ A landlord cannot immunize him- or herself against liability for his or her own negligent actions. *Johns Pass Seafood Co. v. Weber,* 369 So.2d 616 (Fla. 2 DCA 1969).

The result of all this is that the landlord is the insurer of the safety of tenants and must therefore carry adequate insurance to cover any liability. Many landlords raise their rents to compensate for this additional insurance expense.

Crimes on the Premises

Crimes against Tenants

Another area where liability of landlords has been greatly expanded is in the area of crimes against tenants. The former theory of law was that a person cannot be held liable for deliberate acts of third parties. This had been the theory for hundreds of years but has recently been abandoned in favor of a theory that a landlord must protect tenants from crimes.

Basis for Liability. The theory has been stated to be that when the landlord can foresee the possibility of criminal attack, the landlord must take precautions to prevent it. But some have said that this means any time an attack is possible, the landlord must protect the tenant. This would include nearly every tenancy, especially in urban areas.

New Jersey has gone so far as to hold landlords strictly liable for every crime committed on their property whether or not they knew there was a risk or took any precautions. This liability for crime, unlike the warranty of habitability, applies to both residential and commercial tenancies. However, it has not been extended to single-family homes, yet.

🗐 When owners of an apartment complex knew about the "sexually aberrant and bizarre behavior" of a tenant's child, they were liable when that child committed a sexual assault upon another child. *Lambert v. Doe,* 453 So.2d 844 (Fla. I DCA 1984).

🗐 When a landlord failed to provide adequate locks pursuant to Florida Statutes, Section 83.51(2)(a), the landlord was liable when tenant was raped by an intruder. *Paterson v. Deeb, All* So.2d 1210 (Fla. 1 DCA 1985).

▤ When a landlord temporarily provided an armed guard on premises, this was used as evidence that the landlord knew of a dangerous condition and could be liable for the rape and murder of a tenant. *Holley v. Mt. Zion Terrace Apartments, Inc.,* 382 So.2d 98 (Fla. 3 DCA 1980).

▤ When an apartment manager shot tenants during a dispute over an eviction, the landlord was liable for damages. *Gonpere Corp. v. Rebull,* 440 So.2d 1307 (Fla. 3 DCA 1983); compare however, a similar case in which an apartment manager knifed a tenant who was asking for hot water—the landlord was not liable because the event was not foreseeable or in furtherance of the landlord's interests. *Perez v. Zazo,* 498 So.2d 463 (Fla. 3 DCA 1986).

▤ When a tenant in an office building was mugged by an intruder, the landlord was held liable based in part on the fact that the landlord "should have known" of the dangers in the building and taken measures to protect commercial tenants. *Green Cos. v. DiVincenzo,* 432 So.2d 86 (Fla. 3 DCA 1983).

Protection from Liability for Crimes. The law is not clear in Florida as to just how far courts will go in holding landlords liable for crimes against tenants. A clause in a lease that makes a tenant responsible for locks and security may provide some protection to landlords in some situations, especially in single-family homes and duplexes.

In apartment complexes where crime is common, landlords may be required to provide armed guards or face liability. Again, insurance is a must and this additional cost will have to be covered by rent increases.

Crimes by Tenants against Nontenants

Courts in Florida have not yet held landlords liable for crimes by tenants against nontenants. It is, however, happening elsewhere in the country, so landlords should be careful not to get in a situation where tenants are using the property for illegal activities.

Subletting and Assignment

In most leases a tenant is not allowed to sublet or assign the unit. (Sublet means that the tenant is still your tenant but he rents all or part of the unit to a sub-tenant; assignment means the tenant assigns his interest in the lease to someone else and leaves, with the assignee paying the rent to you in his place.)

From your point of view it should not be allowed without your permission because you want to be as careful in screening the persons living in the unit as you were when you rented to the tenant in the first place.

Before allowing a sublease or assignment you should require the same application package as you did in the beginning of the tenancy. You should not accept rent from someone who is not a tenant without making it clear that they are not accepted as a tenant and that any payment is being applied on the original tenant's account.

Validity. If a lease is for over a year, an assignment of that lease would not be valid unless it had two witnesses. (Fla. Stat., Sec. 689.01.)

Liability. If a lease contains a covenant to pay rent and the landlord does not release the tenant upon the assignment, then the landlord may sue the original tenant if the new tenant defaults. *Kornblum v. Henry E. Mangels Co.*, 167 So.2d 16 (Fla. 3 DCA 1964).

Waiver. If a landlord knowingly accepts rent from an assignee or a sublessee of a lease, then the landlord waives his or her right to object to the assignment. But if the landlord was unaware of the assignment it does not constitute a waiver. *El Prado Restaurant, Inc. v. Weaver*, 268 So.2d 382 (Fla. 3 DCA 1972).

Approval. Some leases provide that a lease may only be assigned with the approval of the landlord. However, these clauses are not always enforced.

Where a lease required written consent to subleases, a court allowed subleases without written consent since the landlord acquiesced in the subleases and did not contest them until the parties got into litigation. *Holman v. Halford*, 518 So.2d 442 (Fla. 1 DCA 1988).

Where a lease said that a landlord could not unreasonably withhold consent to an assignment but that the landlord could terminate the lease upon notice of the assignment, the court found the clauses repugnant to each other and struck the second one, denying the landlord's right to terminate the lease. *Petrou v. Wilder*, 557 So.2d 617 (Fla. 4 DCA 1990).

Sale or Loss of Property by Landlord

A landlord has the right to sell property covered by a lease, but the new owner takes the property subject to the terms of the existing leases. In most cases, a landlord is relieved of his or her obligations under a lease upon sale of the property. *Gray v. Callahan*, 197 So.2d396 (1940).

The new owner cannot cancel the old leases or raise the rent while the leases are still in effect (unless the leases have provisions allowing the landlord to do so).

The new owner must do any repairs to the property that the old owner would have had to do under the terms of the lease. *City of St. Petersburg v. Competition Sails*, A49 So.2d 852 (Fla. 2 DCA 1984).

When the purchaser of a property sent a tenant a notice that his month-to-month tenancy was terminated and that he would be evicted, the tenant moved out and sued the landlord for wrongful eviction. The landlord said that he did not know that the tenant had a written lease, but the jury awarded the tenant $7,000.00 in damages. *Ruotal v. Ottati*, 391 So.2d 308 (Fla. 4 DCA 1980).

When selling property, a landlord must specify in the sales contract that the sale is subject to existing leases. Otherwise, the buyer may sue for failure to deliver the premises free and clear of other claims. At closing, the leases should be assigned to the buyer.

Foreclosures. When property is purchased at a foreclosure sale, the leases of the tenants are terminated if they were signed after the date of the mortgage and if the tenants were joined as parties to the suit. *Redding v. Stockton, Whatley, Davin & Co.,* 488 So.2d 548.

Raising the Rent

If a tenancy is for a set term (such as a one-year lease) at a specified rent, then the landlord cannot raise the rent until the term ends unless the lease allows for this.

If the tenancy is month-to-month, then the landlord would be able to raise the rent if he or she gives notice at least fifteen days prior to the end of the month. This is based upon the law that the landlord can cancel the tenancy by giving fifteen days' notice. To raise the rent in a month-to-month tenancy, you can use the NOTICE OF CHANGE OF TERMS, (see Form 23.)

In such a case, the tenant would probably not have to give fifteen days' notice if he or she decided not to stay at the end of the month. This is because by raising the rent the landlord would be terminating the previous tenancy and making the tenant an offer to enter into a new tenancy at a different rental rate.

Modifying the Terms of the Lease

If you agree to modify the terms of your lease with a tenant, you should put it in writing. If you do not and you allow a tenant to do things forbidden in the lease, you may be found to have waived your rights. A simple AMENDMENT TO LEASE/ RENTAL AGREEMENT modification form is included in this book, (see Form 19).

Destruction of the Premises

If the premises are damaged by fire, hurricane, or other casualty, such event does not automatically terminate the lease.

Nonresidential. In nonresidential tenancies, the rights of the parties are usually spelled out in the lease. If they are not, Florida Statutes, Section 83.201 allows nonresidential tenants to withhold rent if the premises are *wholly untenantable,* if under the lease it is the landlord's duty to maintain the premises. The landlord must first be given notice and twenty days to complete the repairs. If the repairs are not complete, then the tenant may vacate the premises and keep the withheld rent.

Residential. Florida Statutes, Section 83.63 states that if the enjoyment of the premises is substantially impaired, then the tenant may terminate the tenancy and immediately vacate the premises. The tenant also has the option of vacating the part of the premises that is unusable and paying partial rent. The landlord does not have the right to terminate the tenancy unless such a right is spelled out in the lease.

> In a case in Miami-Dade County after Hurricane Andrew, a landlord attempted to terminate the lease to do repairs. Because of the shortage of housing after the hurricane, the court was quite upset that the landlord was trying to evict the tenants and their three children. It awarded attorney's fees to the tenant and severely criticized the landlord's attorney for bringing the case. *Baldo v. Georgoulakis,* 1 FLW Supp. 432 (11 Cir. 1993).)

8 Terminating a Tenancy

The tenancy may be terminated in several ways. Unless the tenancy is terminated properly, the tenant may not be evicted. If you file an eviction without properly terminating the tenancy, then the tenant may win the case and you may be ordered to pay damages to the tenant as well as the tenant's attorney's fees.

Tenancies with No Specific Term

Even when there is no written lease between the parties, the law is strict about how the tenancy may be terminated. Any variation from these procedures can delay the eviction for months. If done right, however, a tenant can be removed quickly.

Residential. Under Florida Statutes, Section 83.57, if a unit is rented without a specific term, either party may terminate the rental by giving written notice as follows:

➲ when the rent is paid yearly, the notice must be given at least sixty days prior to the end of the rental year;

➲ when the rent is paid quarterly, the notice must be given at least thirty days prior to the end of the quarter;

⊃ when the rent is paid monthly, the notice must be given at least fifteen days prior to the end of the month; and,

⊃ when the rent is paid weekly, the notice must be given at least seven days prior to the end of the week.

This means that if a tenant paying rent monthly, for example, does not give notice fifteen days prior to the end of the month that he or she plans to terminate, the tenant is liable for the rent for an additional month. Likewise, if a landlord wants to terminate a monthly rental, then he or she must give the tenant notice fifteen days prior to the end of the month or the tenant may stay another month.

A tenancy may not be terminated in the middle of a term. For example, if a landlord or tenant on a monthly basis gives notice on August 12th that they wish to terminate the tenancy, then they may terminate effective August 31st (not August 27th). If they give notice on August 17th then they may terminate it effective September 30th and not sooner. (Unless both parties agree.)

Unwritten tenancies are considered *tenancies at will*. This means they can be terminated at any time by giving the proper notice. If the length of the tenancy of an unwritten lease is not agreed upon, then the term is determined by the frequency rent is paid. If the rent is paid monthly, it is a month-to-month tenancy.

If the rent is paid yearly, it is a yearly tenancy, if paid monthly, a monthly tenancy, etc. (Fla. Stat., Sec. 83.01.) When the length of a written lease is not specified, it is considered a tenancy at will and can be terminated the same as an unwritten lease, as explained in the previous paragraph. (Fla. Stat., Sec. 83.02.)

This law also applies to tenancies in which the tenant stays after a lease expires. If the tenant fails to give the notice required by Section 83.57, the tenant is liable for one month additional rent after leaving. (Fla. Stat., Sec. 83.575.)

Nonresidential. Under Florida Statutes, Section 83.03, if a unit is rented without a specific term, either party may terminate the rental by giving written notice as follows:

➲ when the rent is paid yearly, the notice must be given at least three months prior to the end of the year;

➲ when the rent is paid quarterly, the notice must be given at least forty-five days prior to the end of the quarter;

➲ when the rent is paid monthly, the notice must be given at least fifteen days prior to the end of the month; and,

➲ when the rent is paid weekly, the notice must be given at least seven days prior to the end of the week.

Local Laws. The City of Miami Beach asked the attorney general if it could require a longer period of notice to terminate a tenancy and was told it could. Therefore, you should find out if the city in which your unit is located has rules different from the above. (AGO 94-41, May 5, 1994.)

Expiration of Rental Term

In some states, a lease is presumed to automatically renew unless a tenant gives the landlord notice that he or she is leaving. In Florida, however, the law is that a lease ends at its term unless the parties agree to renew it.

A lease can require that a tenant give up to sixty days' notice that he or she will leave at the end of the lease and that it can require the tenant to pay liquidated damages if he or she does not. (Fla. Stat., Sec. 83.575(1) and (2).)

However, it does not say that the lease automatically renews. It will take a few court cases to see how this statute will be interpreted. If you want a tenant to leave at the end of a lease, and do not expect that he or she will, you can use the **NOTICE OF NON-RENEWAL** (see form 34.)

If a tenant continues to rent the premises with your permission after a lease expires, the tenant is required to give notice before leaving just as if there were no lease. If the tenant fails to give such notice, he or she must pay one month rent as damages. (Fla. Stat., Sec. 83.575(3).)

Early Termination by Tenant

If the tenant leaves the premises before the end of the lease agreement, he or she may be liable for damages unless the tenant is able to legally terminate the tenancy under Florida Statutes, Section 83.56(1) or 83.63.

Destruction of the Premises. If the premises are damaged or destroyed other than by wrongful or negligent acts of the tenant, and if the premises are *substantially impaired,* the tenant may immediately vacate the premises and terminate the rental. (For more information see "Destruction of the Premises" on page 96.)

Landlord's Noncompliance. If the landlord materially fails to comply with the maintenance obligations or with the terms of the lease and does not comply seven days after written notice is given by the tenant, the tenant may terminate the rental and vacate the premises. (Fla. Stat., Sec. 83.56(1).) If the tenant fails to give proper notice, then he or she is not entitled to damages. *Linker v. Rosse and Zager*, 49 Fla. Supp. 22 (17th Cir. Broward 1991).

Efforts to Cure. If the landlord makes every reasonable effort to comply with his or her maintenance obligations and the noncompliance is beyond the control of the landlord, then the parties may terminate or amend the rental agreement as follows:

➲ if the premises are not livable, the tenant may vacate and not be liable for rent as long as it remains unlivable and

➲ if the premises are livable, the tenant may pay reduced rent based on the lost value of the premises.

Remedies for Breach. If the tenant breaches the lease by vacating early, the landlord has four options (Fla. Stat., Sec. 83.595.):

1. the landlord may retake the premises for his or her own account, thereby terminating all further liability of the tenant;

2. the landlord may retake the premises for the account of the tenant, relet the premises, and hold the tenant liable for any difference in the rent received;

3. the landlord may do nothing and sue the tenant for the lost rent as it comes due; or

4. as of 2008 the landlord has a fourth remedy, he can charge a liquidated damages or early termination fee, if it is no more than two months rent and this has been agreed to in writing, either in the lease or in a separate agreement signed at the time of the lease. (F.S. §83.595(4)) (See Form 9.)

If the landlord opts to find a new tenant, he or she must make a good faith effort and use the same efforts used previously or for other units. If the landlord has other vacant units, then he or she does not have to rent out the tenant's unit first.

Early Termination of Residential

Tenancy by Landlord

A landlord may terminate a tenancy before the end of the term for three reasons:

1. nonpayment of rent; or

2. breach of the lease other than nonpayment of rent; or

3. violation of Florida statutes.

Strict Requirements. The laws are very strict about terminating a tenancy and if they are not followed, the landlord may lose in court and be required to pay the tenant damages and attorney's fees. Be sure to read all of these instructions carefully and follow them exactly.

Wording of the Notice. The notice should use the exact wording shown. The law states that the notice is invalid if it does not substantially comply with the wording. *Hunt v. Hiland*, 366 So.2d 41 (1979).

▤ When a landlord added the words "in cash" to the three-day notice, it was eventually held to be valid since all obligations are due in cash. However, it took three different courts and eighteen months for the landlord to prevail. *Moskowitz v. Aslam*, 575 So.2d 1367 (Fla. 3 DCA 1991).

▤ One Florida case has held that a notice that did not state when the three-day period began or ended and did not include the landlord's address was adequate. *Multach v. Snipes*, 15 Fla. Supp. 2d 52 (Palm Beach Co. 1986).) However, this was a local court decision and is not binding on other courts and may not be followed.

▤ In a case in which extra wording was added to the three-day notice, a court said that it was confusing to the low-income tenant and ruled the notice to be void. *Housing Authority of Ft. Lauderdale v. Butts,* 1 FLW Supp. 529 (Broward Co. 1993).

Delivery of the Notice. These notices may be mailed, hand-delivered, or posted on the tenant's door. (Fla. Stat., Sec. 83.56(4).) If they are mailed, then the tenant will probably be entitled to five extra days for mailing time. *Le v. Green*, 11 FLW Supp. 358a (1777th Cir. 2004), *Investment & Income Realty, Inc. v. Bentley*, 480 So.2d 219 (Fla. 5DCA 1985). The notice should only be posted if the tenant is absent from the premises.

Waiver. If either the landlord accepts rent or the tenant pays rent after a known violation, that person has waived the right to terminate the rental for the period, but they may terminate it the next time rent comes due if the violation continues. (Fla. Stat., Sec. 83.56(5).)

If the tenant fails to pay the rent, the landlord may send the following three-day notice, NOTICE FROM LANDLORD TO TENANT–TERMINATION FOR FAILURE TO PAY RENT (See Form 31.)

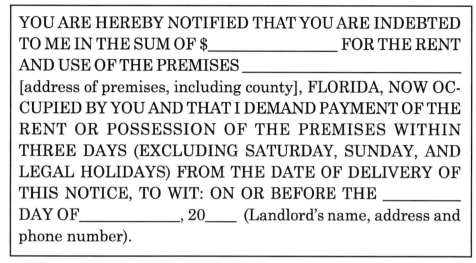

YOU ARE HEREBY NOTIFIED THAT YOU ARE INDEBTED TO ME IN THE SUM OF $_____ FOR THE RENT AND USE OF THE PREMISES _____ [address of premises, including county], FLORIDA, NOW OCCUPIED BY YOU AND THAT I DEMAND PAYMENT OF THE RENT OR POSSESSION OF THE PREMISES WITHIN THREE DAYS (EXCLUDING SATURDAY, SUNDAY, AND LEGAL HOLIDAYS) FROM THE DATE OF DELIVERY OF THIS NOTICE, TO WIT: ON OR BEFORE THE _____ DAY OF_____, 20____ (Landlord's name, address and phone number).

Calculating Three Days. The most common reason for a landlord to lose an eviction is because he or she wrongly executed the three-day notice. The most common mistake is getting the three-day period wrong. If you make such a mistake, you can lose the case and be forced to pay the tenant's attorney's fees.

One big problem with this in the past has been that landlords did not know about Florida's obscure legal holidays such as Confederate Memorial Day (April 26) and Jefferson Davis' Birthday (June 3). Now the law states, "Legal holidays for the purpose of this section shall be court-observed holidays only." This will eliminate some surprises, but it should still be noted that when a holiday falls on Sunday, Monday is considered a holiday, and some counties have their own legal holidays such as Parade Day and Gasparilla Day in Hillsborough County, and DeSoto Day in Manatee County. Also, judges may declare Rosh Hashanah, Yom Kippur, and Good Friday as court holidays. A full list of Florida legal holidays is included on the last page of this chapter.

NOTE: *Call your court clerk to see what days are "court observed holidays" in your area before preparing your three-day notice.*

Amount Due. The second most common mistake landlords make is in the amount of rent due. The notice should only include amounts due for rent, not late charges or utility bills. If the lease clearly states that late charges are part of the *rent,* then you may get away with including them. *Hoche v. Berry*, 5 Fla. Supp. 2d 110 (Co.Ct. Orange 1983), *Housing Authority of Daytona Beach v. Smith*, 27 Fla. Supp. 2d 30, (Co.Ct. Volusia 1988).

▤ One court has held that even if they are included in the rent, they may not be included in the notice. If the three-day notice does include other charges, then you may lose your case and be required to pay the tenant's attorney's fees. *Metropolitan Dade County v. Dansey*, 39 Fla. Supp. 2d 216 (1990).

▤ One case held that an eviction suit does not have to be dismissed because of a defective three-day notice, but that the landlord can be given an opportunity to deliver a proper notice to the tenant. This well-reasoned opinion should be pointed out to any judge who is considering dismissing a suit for a defective notice. *Levenshon Emerald Park Partners, Ltd. v. Walantus*, 3 FLW Supp. 556 (Broward Co. 1995).

▤ In another good case for landlords, a court ruled that if a case is dismissed for some procedural error rather than on the merits of the case, then there is no prevailing party who can be awarded attorney's fees. *Paramount v. P.R.D. Holding*, 4 FLW Supp. 683 (Cir.Ct. Dade 1997).

▤ When a tenant was discovered to owe back rent due to a miscalculation, a court held that the back rent could not be included in a three-day notice. *Flagship Property Management, Inc., v. Mannings*, 46 FLW Supp.2d 136 (Co.Ct. Palm Beach, 1990).

▤ When a landlord sued for eviction for failure to pay for repairs, eviction was denied because the landlord had not yet done the repairs. *Gunby v. Caldwell*, 4 FLW Supp. 609 (Co.Ct. Putnam 1997).

Address. The landlord's address on the three-day notice should not be a post office box. Otherwise, the tenant must be given an additional five days for the rent to arrive by mail. *Wint v. McCarty*, 10 FLW Supp. 66 (Broward Co. 2002)

Attempts to Pay. If a tenant attempts to pay the rent before the three-day notice is up, then the landlord must accept it. *Curley v. McMillan*, 4 FLW Supp. 475 (Co.Ct. Escambia 1996). If the landlord wants to evict the tenant anyway, the only way to do it is if the tenant violates another clause in the lease. If the tenant attempts to pay the rent after the tenancy has been terminated (after the three days are up), then the landlord does not have to accept it. *Helga Skin Therapy Inc. v. Dead River Properties Inc.*, 478 So.2d 95, (Fla. 2 DCA 1985).

Acceptance of Rent. If the landlord accepts rent with the knowledge that the tenant is not complying with some aspect of the lease, then the landlord waives the right to evict for that noncompliance. (Fla. Stat., Sec. 83-56(5).)

Early Notice. In a case in which a landlord routinely delivered a notice of nonpayment of rent to tenants before it was due, the notice was held to be invalid. *Housing Authority of St. Petersburg v. Bullard*, 45 Fla. Supp. 2d 130, (Co.Ct. Pinellas, 1990)

Undated Notice. The notice should explain in detail when, how, and what violation occurred. When landlords merely cite which clause is violated, the notice has been held by some courts to be defective. *Dragoslavic v. Rountree*, 10 FLW Supp. 2d 1 (Broward Co. 2002).

If the tenant violates the terms of the lease or the maintenance obligations under Florida Statutes, Section 83.52, and if the violation is material, then the landlord can terminate the rental agreement by using the notices provided in the statutes.

Attorneys. If an attorney sends a three-day notice for a tenant, some courts have held that the federal *Fair Debt Collection Act* applies, and the attorney can be liable for thousands of dollars in damages for failure to comply with the act.

Breach of Lease. As explained in Chapter 7, the landlord must decide whether the breach of the lease is curable or incurable. If it is curable, then the landlord must use the notice in Chapter 7 to give the tenant seven days to cure the breach. To be safe, a landlord should always assume a breach is curable unless it is really bad, such as intentional damage of property or continued unreasonable disturbance.

If the violation is not curable or if the tenant repeats a violation after receiving the above notice, then the landlord may terminate the tenancy by sending the following notice to the tenant. (See Form 33.)

YOU ARE ADVISED THAT YOUR LEASE IS TERMINATED EFFECTIVE IMMEDIATELY. YOU SHALL HAVE SEVEN (7) DAYS FROM THE DELIVERY OF THIS LETTER TO VACATE THE PREMISES. THIS ACTION IS TAKEN BECAUSE_____

_____.

The notice should explain in detail when, how, and what violation occurred. When landlords merely cited which clause was violated, the notice has been held by some courts to be defective. *Dade County v. Malloy*, 27 Fla.Supp. 2d 1 (Dade Co. 1988)

Public and Subsidized Housing

For nonpayment of rent, the landlord must give the tenant fourteen days' notice rather than a three-day notice, and it **must** be mailed or hand-delivered, not posted. (C.F.R., Title 24, Sec. 866.4(1)(2).) The notice must inform the tenant of his or her right to a grievance procedure.

It is suggested that the landlord only use a fourteen-day notice. If both a fourteen day and three-day notice are given, deliver the three-day notice so that the deadline is the same as for the fourteen-day notice. *Broward Co. Housing Authority v. Simmons*, 4 FLW Supp. 494, (Co.Ct. Broward 1996)

For breach of the terms of the lease other than payment of rent, a thirty-day notice must be given, except in emergencies, and it must inform the tenant of the reasons for termination, the right to reply, and the right to a grievance procedure. (C.F.R., Title 24, Sec. 366(4)(1).) If the tenant requests a grievance hearing, a second notice must be given, even if the tenant loses in the hearing.

Section 236 Apartments. For nonpayment of rent, tenants must be given the three-day notice and be advised that if there is a judicial proceeding, they can present a valid defense, if any. Service must be by first-class mail and hand-delivered or placed under the door. (C.F.R, Title 24, Sec. 450.4(a).)

For breach of the terms of the lease other than payment of rent, the tenant must first have been given notice that in the future such conduct would be grounds for terminating the lease. The notice of termination must state when the tenancy will be terminated, specifically why it is being terminated, and it must advise the tenant of the right to present a defense in the eviction suit. (C.F.R., Title 24, Sec. 450.)

Section 8 Apartments. The section of the law that states acceptance or payment of rent is a waiver of any past noncompliance does not apply to the portion of the rent that is subsidized. (Fla. Stat., Sec. 83.56 (5).) However, waiver will occur if legal action is not taken within forty-five days.

Under the Code of Federal Regulations, Section 882.215(c)(4), the landlord must notify the housing authority in writing at the commencement of the eviction proceedings. Also, the previous paragraph applies to Section 8 housing as well.

Early Termination of Nonresidential Tenancy

by Landlord

The rules for terminating a nonresidential tenancy are much more lenient than for residential tenancies. In most cases, the procedure can be spelled out in the lease itself, since the statutes do not give detailed rules. The rules that are in the statute are as follows.

➲ A three-day notice must be given to the tenant as with residential tenancies. (Fla. Stat., Sec. 83.20 (2).)

➲ In nonresidential tenancies, the wording of the notice does not have to match the statute, and nothing states that the three days excludes Saturdays, Sundays, and legal holidays. A waiver of the right to a three day notice in the lease may also be legal. To avoid letting the tenant make an issue out of it, it would be prudent to use the residential three day notice form, (see Form 31).

➲ The notice must be given to the tenant, or if the tenant is absent from the rented premises, it may be left at the rented premises.

Acceptance of Rent. If the landlord accepts the full amount of past due rent, then the landlord waives his or her right to proceed with eviction. (Fla. Stat., Sec. 83.202.)

Early Termination by Armed Forces Member

Any member of the armed forces may cancel a rental agreement by giving at least thirty days' notice if:

➲ he or she is permanently stationed thirty-five miles or more from the rental unit; or

➲ he or she is prematurely or involuntarily discharged or released from active duty; and,

➲ the written notice to cancel is accompanied by a copy of the orders or written verification signed by the commanding officer. (Section 83.682.)

If a member dies during active duty, a family member may terminate the tenancy under the same terms.

The tenant must pay prorated rent to the termination date. If the rental agreement is terminated fourteen or more days before occupancy of a unit, no rent is due. In the past, law required the tenant to pay liquidated damages.

NOTE: *These rules may not be waived or modified by either landlord or tenant.*

Employment Rentals

Where a dwelling unit is furnished without rent as part of employment, the rental period is determined by how often the employee's salary is paid. If no salary is paid, it is considered a month-to-month tenancy. If the employee ceases

employment, the employer is entitled to rent for the unit from the day after the employment is terminated until the day the former employee vacates the premises at a rate equivalent to similar units in the area. This does not apply to resident apartment managers when there is a written contract to the contrary. (Fla. Stat., Sec. 83.46.)

Death of a Tenant

If a lease contains a clause binding the "heirs, successors, and assigns" of the lessee, then the lease continues after the death of the tenant unless cancelled by the lessor and the heirs, *Kensington Associates v. Moss*, 416 So.2d 1076 (Fla. 4 DCA 1983). Otherwise, it is a personal contract that expires at death, *Goodman v. Jardine*, 353 So.2d 896 (Fla. 3 DCA 1977)

What the landlord's options are upon a tenant's death were not clear until 2007 when the legislature amended §83.59, adding a subsection (d). This says that if a tenant dies (and there are no other co-tenants), personal property is left on the premises, rent is unpaid, sixty days have elapsed since the death and the landlord has not been notified of a probate, then the landlord can take over possession of the unit. Abandoned property should be treated as required by the abandoned property laws explained in the next chapter.

Options to Cancel Lease

Generally, when a lease allows one party to cancel it at will, the lease is not considered binding and the courts will allow either party to cancel it at will. A lease will probably be held to be valid if the option to cancel is contingent upon some event.

If a lease may be cancelled by the landlord upon sale of the property, the lease is valid and the option may be exercised by the new owner. *Manzo v. Patch Publishing Co., Inc.,* 403 So.2d 469 (Fla. 5 DCA 1981).

When a lease provided for termination only if the landlord decided to alter or demolish at least part of the premises and also returned the security deposit and gave the tenant sixty-days' notice, it was enforceable. *In re Alchar Hardware Co., Inc.,* 759 F.2d 867 (11th Cir. Fla. 1985).

A lease that did not specify whether an option to cancel upon sale of the property was to be exercised by the buyer or seller, the buyer was allowed to exercise it. *Manzo v. Patch Publishing Co., Inc.,* 403 So.2d 469 (Fla. 5 DCA 1981).

Legal Holidays in Florida
(Florida Statutes Chapter 683)

These are days that are not counted when figuring a three-day notice for unpaid rent or for the five days that a tenant has to answer an eviction complaint.

Note that you only need to count as holidays those observed by the court in the county where the property is located. Call the court clerk to be sure.

Every Sunday	
New Year's Day	Jan. 1
Martin Luther King, Jr.'s Birthday	Jan. 15
Robert E. Lee's Birthday	Jan. 19
Abraham Lincoln's Birthday	Feb. 12
Susan B. Anthony's Birthday	Feb. 15
George Washington's Birthday	Third Mon. in Feb.
Good Friday	(varies)
Pascua Florida Day	April 2
Confederate Memorial Day	April 26
Memorial Day	Last Mon. in May
Jefferson Davis' Birthday	June 3
Flag Day	June 14
Independence Day	July 4
Labor Day	First Mon. in Sept.
Columbus Day and Farmers' Day	Second Mon. in Oct.
Veterans' Day	Nov. 11
General Election Day	(varies)
Thanksgiving Day	Fourth Thurs. in Nov.
Christmas Day	Dec. 25

Shrove Tuesday (in counties where carnival associations are organized to celebrate Mardi Gras)

Parade Day (in Hillsborough County)

Gasparilla Day (in Hillsborough County)

DeSoto Day (in Manatee County)

The chief judge of any circuit may designate Rosh Hashanah, Yom Kippur, and Good Friday as legal holidays for the courts within the circuit.

NOTE: *When a legal holiday falls on a Sunday, the next day is considered a legal holiday.*

9 After the Tenancy

Just because the lease is about to end, doesn't mean the problems are over, some may be just beginning.

Tenant Holding Over

When the tenant *holds over* at the end of a lease, the landlord has three options. The landlord can:

1. demand double rent and possession of the property;

2. demand a specific amount of continuing rent; or,

3. sue for possession of the property plus damages including special damages for loss of the property's use.

In a nonresidential tenancy, the landlord has to demand double rent. This is not the case in a residential tenancy because of the wording of the statutes. The statutes allowing double rent are Florida Statutes, Section 83.06 (nonresidential) and Section 83.58 (residential).

A landlord can collect double rent and remove the tenant in an eviction proceeding or may bring an action for the double rent after the tenant moves. If a landlord accepts regular rent after the lease expires, the landlord loses his or her right to double rent, and can only terminate the tenancy under the rules for tenancies with "no specific term."

No notice is required at the end of a lease, but a letter to the tenant expressing an intention to terminate or to renew is a good idea. When trouble is expected, a **LETTER TO VACATING TENANT** can be used, (see form 24.) In Public Housing, Section 8 housing, and Section 236 housing, a landlord cannot refuse to renew a lease without good cause.

Damage to the Premises

If the landlord finds damage at the end of a tenancy, then he or she may deduct the amount of the damage from the security deposit. In a residential tenancy, the landlord forfeits that right if he or she does not send the correct notice within fifteen days of when the tenant vacates the premises, (see Chapter 6.)

If the damages exceed the amount of the security deposit, the landlord may sue the tenant. If they are under $5,000, the landlord can file the case in small claims court.

Abandoned Property

Landlords have two options for disposing of property abandoned by the tenant. If they have a written agreement with the tenant, they are free to dispose of it as they wish. If not, they can follow the procedures in Chapter 715 of Florida Statutes.

For residential tenancies, landlords are allowed to have an agreement with the tenants that they are not responsible for storage or disposition of property left behind when a tenant leaves. Under Florida Statutes, Section 83.67(3), the agreement can be included in the lease or as a separate agreement. A separate **AGREEMENT REGARDING ABANDONED PROPERTY** is included in this book, (see Form 8). The clause that must be in the lease is:

BY SIGNING THIS RENTAL AGREEMENT THE TENANT AGREES THAT UPON SURRENDER OR ABANDONMENT,

AS DEFINED BY CHAPTER 83, FLORIDA STATUTES, THE LANDLORD SHALL NOT BE LIABLE OR RESPONSIBLE FOR STORAGE OR DISPOSITION OF THE TENANT'S PERSONAL PROPERTY.

NOTE: *The statute has the clause capitalized, so it should be in the lease.*

Under Florida Statutes, Sections 715.10-715.111, the landlord may protect him or herself from liability for disposing of personal property left behind by a tenant, or by someone else who left property in the rental unit, by following certain procedures.

Applicability. The law applies to both residential and non-residential tenancies. It is an optional procedure that a landlord can use to protect him- or herself.

Procedure. In order to take advantage of the law, the landlord must follow the procedures laid out in the statute.

Notice. A notice must be sent to the tenant (or to any person the landlord believes owns the property, such as a cable TV company or telephone company) carefully describing the property.

Form. The form of the notice is printed in the statute, (see Forms 63, 64, 65, and 66.)

Delivery. It should be personally delivered to the "last known address" of the tenant or the person believed to be the owner. It may be sent to the premises that had been rented, but if the landlord knows that the mail is not being forwarded, then it should be sent to any address known to the landlord at which the tenant may receive it.

Storage Costs. A reasonable storage charge may be required before release of the property. The property may be stored on the premises or in a place of safekeeping. Tenants may be required to pay all costs of storage, but owners other than tenants need only pay storage costs for their own items. No more than one person may be charged for the same costs. If the property is stored on the premises, only the fair value of the space used may be charged.

Date. A date by which the property may be claimed must be given. It must be at least ten days after notice is personally given or fifteen days after notice is mailed.

Liability. The landlord must exercise reasonable care in storing the property, but he or she is not liable for any loss unless caused by his or her deliberate act.

Release. The landlord must release the property to the tenant or person reasonably believed to be the owner upon payment of the storage charges and advertising. It must be released if claimed at any time before a landlord takes possession or holds the sale as described as follows:

Property Valued under $500. If the value of all abandoned property is reasonably believed to be under $500, it may be kept, sold, or destroyed by the landlord after the date given in the notice. If a landlord is not sure of the value, it is always safer to assume it is worth over $500.

Property Valued over $500. If the value of the abandoned property is over $500, it must be sold at a public sale. A landlord or tenant may bid at the sale. The sale must be held in the nearest suitable place to where the property is stored. Notice of the time and place of the sale must be advertised in a newspaper of general circulation once a week for two weeks. The sale must not be sooner than ten days from the first ad and five days from the second ad.

If there is no newspaper of general circulation, then a notice must be posted in six conspicuous places in the neighborhood of the sale. The notice must adequately describe the property except that contents of a locked or fastened container need not be listed.

If there is a surplus of funds after storage, advertising, and sale costs are deducted, they must be turned over to the treasury of the county within thirty days. Any person claiming an interest in the funds may apply to the county treasurer for them within one year.

Municipal Liens

Florida Statutes, Section 180.135 states that no municipality may refuse utilities, water, or sewer services or assert a lien against a property for nonpayment by a former occupant. The municipality also may not force the landlord to guarantee the tenant's bills.

Not all municipalities in Florida comply with this law. Many require landlords to put the bills in their name, which in effect makes the landlord guarantee the bill for the tenant. Unfortunately, if a city refuses to follow the law, your only recourse is to file suit, which is more expensive than the utility bills would be.

Money Damages and Back Rent

Trying to collect on a judgment against a former tenant is usually not worth the time and expense. Most landlords are just glad to regain possession of the property. Tenants who do not pay rent usually do not own property that can be seized, and it is very difficult to garnish wages in Florida. However, occasionally former tenants come into money, and some landlords have been surprised many years later when called by a title insurance company wanting to pay off their judgment. Therefore, it is usually worthwhile to put a claim for back rent into an eviction complaint.

Making a Residential Claim. To make a claim against a tenant for back rent, you can include a *Count II* in your **COMPLAINT FOR EVICTION AND DAMAGES** (see Form 36) asking for the rent owed. However, if you do so, the complaint must be filed by the owner or an attorney, not a non-attorney agent. In a residential eviction, if you have not included a demand for rent, the court should still award rent in the case but only if the tenant was personally served or properly served with certified or registered mail. This is because Florida Statutes, Section 83.625 states that the court "shall direct... the entry of a money judgment."

At least one county court has ruled that if a Count II for rent is not included in the complaint, it must at least make a demand for rent or the court cannot grant it. *Pollard v. Alpert,* 48 Fla. Supp. 2d 127 (Palm Beach Co. 1991). However, this is not what the statute says, and other courts are not following this case.

If you forgot to ask for rent, did not get personal service, or if the tenant moved out without the need for an eviction preceding, you can file a separate suit for the rent owed. If the amount is less than $5,000, then the suit can be filed in small claims court.

Making a Nonresidential Claim. In a nonresidential tenancy, a demand must be made for rent in the eviction complaint or it cannot be awarded. However, you can sue for it separately in small claims court.

Amount. In county court, the limit on claims is $15,000. When the tenant has breached the lease, the landlord is entitled to several types of monetary damages. However, the landlord should review his or her options on default before deciding which type of claim to make against the tenant.

Pro-rated Rent. Under Florida Statutes, Section 83.46(1), rent is uniformly pro-rated over the month. Therefore, if a landlord took possession of the dwelling unit for his or her own benefit, then the tenant would be liable for rent only until he or she vacates the premises.

Future Rent. Under Florida Statutes, Section 83.595(l)(c), the landlord can sue the tenant for future rent if he or she takes possession for the benefit of the tenant.

Interest. A landlord is entitled to interest on the rent from the day it is due until the date of the judgment.

Double Rent. Under Florida Statutes, Section 83.58, if the tenant holds over at the end of the rental period, the landlord is entitled to double rent for the period during which the tenant refuses to surrender the dwelling unit.

▤ The landlord is not entitled to double rent when the tenant is evicted, only when he or she holds over at the expiration of the lease. *Wagner v. Rice*, 97 So.2d 267 (Fla. 1957).

▤ There can be double rent when a tenant holds over after a periodic tenancy even if there was no lease. *Eli Einbinder, Inc. v. Miami Crystal Ice. Co.*, 317 So.2d 126 (Fla. 3 DCA 19975).

Damage to the Premises. The landlord may sue the tenant for damage to the premises, but this does not include *normal wear and tear.*

Other Losses. A landlord may make a claim against the tenant for other losses related to the damage or breach.

▤ When a landlord lost rent while he was repairing the premises, he was allowed to claim this amount against the tenant. *Waters v. Visage,* 20 Fla. Supp. 2d 93 (Co.Ct. Orange Co. 1986).

Hearings. When asking for a money judgment in an eviction action, it is usually necessary to have two hearings. This is because the judgment for possession can be granted after five days, but a money judgment may not be granted until twenty days after the complaint was served.

Usually after the first hearing, the landlord is granted a FINAL JUDGMENT—EVICTION (Form 49), and after the second hearing the landlord is granted a FINAL JUDGMENT—DAMAGES (Form 50).

If the tenants move out prior to holding the first hearing, then it can be skipped. But, if it was already scheduled, be sure to check with the judge's office to see if it can be rescheduled after the twenty-day period has ended. Also, if the first hearing is cancelled because the tenants move out, the FINAL JUDG-

MENT—EVICTION should also state that the landlord is entitled to possession to be sure the tenant does not make trouble later.

Defenses. Although the law states that failure to deposit rent into the registry of the court shall be an absolute waiver of all defenses, that only applies to the eviction portion of the case. The tenant is still able to assert any defenses he or she has to the money damages portion of the case, *Premici v. United Growth Properties, L.P.*, 648 So.2d 1241 (Fla 5DCA 1995).

Liens

There are three types of landlord liens that can apply to tenants property—statutory liens, judgments, and nonresidential statutory liens.

Statutory Liens. Under Florida Statutes, Section 713.691, a landlord is given a lien on the property of the tenant that has been brought onto the premises.

➲ The statute states that a head of household can claim $1,000 in exempt property; however, the Florida constitution gives that right to every natural person and not just heads of households. In any event, a landlord does not want to risk getting into an extended court case with a tenant who has unlimited free legal aid would be advised to avoid using the lien, *Roberts v. Jackson*, 4 FLWSupp. 549 (CoC Marion 1997).

➲ One way the landlord's lien might be useful would be when following the procedures for abandoned property. The landlord's lien could be asserted against any surplus proceeds.

Judgments. If a court issues a money judgment against the tenant, it can be a lien against property of the tenant. First, by filing a certified copy of the judgment in the official records of any county you can make the judgment a lien on any real estate owned by the tenant. This lien is good for seven years but can be re-filed twice for a total of up to twenty years. (You can obtain a certified copy of the judgment from the recording office where you file the judgment.)

Second, by filing a judgment lien certificate with the secretary of state you can make it a lien on personal property owned by the tenant anywhere in the state of Florida. This lien is good for five years and can be renewed for a second five years. Information on how to do this is available on the secretary of state's website:

www.sunbiz.org/corpweb/inquiry/jlien_info.html

Nonresidential Statutory Liens. A landlord has a lien for rent against property of the tenant. (Fla. Stat., Sec. 83.08-83-10.) The only property of the tenant which is exempt is clothing apparel, bedclothes, and beds. Since this law only applies to nonresidential tenancies, this may not seem to make sense, but the reason is that when the law was written, it applied to all tenancies. When the new residential law was passed, it was changed to apply to nonresidential tenancies, but this exemption was not removed.

Some other things about nonresidential statutory liens you should know include the following.

▤ The lien can also be for loans made to the tenant.

▤ The landlord's lien is superior to all other liens on agricultural products raised on the land.

▤ The lien on property brought to the premise is superior to liens given after the date the property is placed on the land.

▤ The lien does not start on the tenant's other property until the county sheriff has made a *levy* on the property. This means that the sheriff either seizes the property or posts a notice on it that they are under the sheriff's control.

▤ A liquor license is not considered tangible property on which a landlord can have a lien, *Flanigan's Enterprises, Inc. v. Barnett Bank of Naples*, 639 So.2d 617 (Fla. 1994).

▤ The landlord's lien is superior to other "unperfected" liens. For example, if a store takes goods on consignment and the owners of the consigned goods do not perfect their liens on the goods by filing a UCC financing statement, then the landlord's lien is ahead of the rights of the owners of the goods. *Lynch Austin Realty, Inc. v. Engler*, 647 So.2d 988 (Fla. 2DCA 1994).

NOTE: *Before attempting to enforce a landlord's lien, be sure to consult an attorney. The law is complicated. For a horror story in which a court said a landlord could be liable for civil theft, see Seymore v. Adams,* 638 So.2d 1044 (Fla. 1 DCA 1994).

Distress for Rent and Replevin

In nonresidential tenancies there is a procedure for posting a bond and having the sheriff levy upon the tenant's property and forbid him or her to move it from the premises. (Fla. Stat., Sec. 83.12- .13.) It is called *distress for rent.* It is complicated and should be handled by an attorney. (Forms for this procedure are published by the Florida Bar in their continuing education legal forms workbook.)

In nonresidential tenancies, there is also a procedure called *replevin,* by which the property of the tenant may be sold to pay the rent owed to the landlord. (Fla. Stat., Sec. 83.13- .19.) The sale must be advertised and the landlord has the right to bid for the tenant's property. A replevin action is also complicated and should be handled by an attorney.

10 Taxes

This chapter is intended to give you an overview on how rental property is taxed and to point out some important provisions that you might have overlooked that could save you considerable money.

The author is not a tax specialist and as this is written the tax laws expected to be subject to many changes. So just use this as a checklist of things to be aware of when doing your taxes.

Sales and Use Tax

Florida sales and use tax applies to certain types of rentals. Technically, all rentals are subject to the tax, unless they are exempt. Some of the exemptions include the following.

➲ Transient rentals of over six months. (Fla. Stat., Sec. 212.03(1).) To qualify, a landlord should get written leases of longer than six months from each tenant.

➲ Permanent places of residence. (Fla. Stat., Sec. 212.03(7)(c).) To qualify, at least half the rental units must rent for over three months.

 Rentals to full-time students. (Fla. Stat., Sec. 212.03(7)(a).)

Agricultural, recreational, condominium recreational, airport, port facilities, qualified production facilities, movie theatre concessionaires, and those exempt under F.A.C. 12A-1.070(19) (c). (Fla. Stat., Sec. 212.031 (l)(a).) See the statute for more details.

 Property already subject to parking, dock, or storage space tax. (Fla. Stat., Sec. 212.031(1)(a).)

This means that generally all commercial rentals and transient rentals of six months or less are taxed, while all permanent residential rentals are exempt

An issue sometimes comes up between a landlord and the Florida Department of Revenue when the landlord rents only to permanent residents, but uses a month-to-month rental agreement or oral rental agreement.

In one case the DOR argued that tax was always due unless the landlord used a lease of longer than six months and won in trial court but the landlord appealed and the appeals court said that was only one of many factors to consider to determine if the rentals are permanent or transient. *Fla. Dept. of Revenue v. Hale*, 808 So.2d 237 (Fla. 1st DCA 2002). While the Hales won, they spent 10 years in court and because of procedural errors the state didn't have to pay their attorney fees.

Many rental complexes require seven month minimum leases to avoid this problem. Theoretically a six-months-and-a-day lease would work. Possibly a clause in a rental agreement stating that the rental was for a permanent residence would work.

If you rent someone a condominium unit or apartment with a separate parking space, garage, or storage unit you would need to collect tax on the separate unit only if it is rented under a separate lease agreement (which some management companies do). To keep it tax-free, put it on the residential lease.

Who pays. The tax is paid by the tenant to the landlord in addition to the rent. This should be spelled out clearly in the lease. (If the landlord didn't collect the tax and later is required to pay it to the state, it would come out of the landlord's pocket.)

➲ Since 1989, when a commercial lease does not state who pays the tax, the tenant must pay the tax in addition to the rent. *Schnurmacher Holding, Inc. v. Noriega*, 542 So.2d 1327 (Fla. 1989). A precious case held that the landlord had to pay the tax out of the rent but the Florida Supreme Court overruled that.

➲ If a tenant pays rent by performing services or trading some piece of property, the tax is still due.

Registration to collect tax. Each property manager or owner who collects the tax must first obtain a tax number from the Florida Department of Revenue and then make payments to the state of the taxes collected. These payments are made monthly, quarterly, or semi-annually, depending on the amount collected. Property managers of facilities that are exempt from the tax must still register with the state and file a declaration each year that the property is exempt.

You must register to collect and pay the tax. If you register online it is free or you can submit a written application with a $5 fee. You can get the application by calling 800-352-3671 or you can download it online. The web site for registering or getting the form is:

http://dor.myflorida.com

As compensation of your time in collecting the tax for the state of Florida, you are allowed to keep 2.5% of the tax collected (if you file on time) but you are asked if you want to donate it to education. If you forget to file your tax return on time there is a $50 penalty but they will waive it if you have a good record.

Property Taxes

Since, unlike about 45 other states, Florida does not have an income tax, a bulk of the state's revenue comes from real estate taxes. This puts a strain on the income of retirees and those with limited income. To remedy this the homestead exemption was devised to make the first $25,000 of value tax-free. As values rose this was raised to $50,000, but to be sure that people whose property was worth less than $50,000 paid at least some taxes, the second $25,000 exemption is on the $50,000 to $75,000 of value.

Also, to protect homeowners who have lived in their properties for decades and intend to stay in them, a 3% cap on the increase in assessed value was passed. This means that two identical properties next door to each other can have different tax bills, with one possible double or triple the other one. It also meant that a person who moved from one house to another could have taxes which were double even if the houses were the same. However this last problem was fixed by making the cap portable.

A cap in the amount that the assessed value of non-homestead property can be raised each year was recently passed. So if the value goes up, say 25%, the assessment can only be raised 10% per year.

Lowering your assessment. The most important thing to know about your real estate taxes is that if you are over-assessed you can get the assessment lowered. In August each year the property appraisers send out a Truth In Millage (TRIM) Notice to each property owner listing the assessed value and the taxes from each taxing district. The notice gives a date by which you must file any protest of the value, and lists the dates of meeting of the taxing boards if you want to protest the tax rate.

Most counties provide detailed instructions on how to petition to lower your assessment. In most cases you need to research similar properties to show why your value is over-stated.

There are many companies that will file a petition for you for free and only get paid by a percentage of the taxes that they save you. I have put together a list of some of these on my web site at: www.warda.net/Resources.html

Taxes on Rental Income

Normally, when owning a rental property with a mortgage, an investor would have little or no taxes to pay on the rental income. This is because the deductible interest, repairs and maintenance, taxes, insurance and depreciation are usually close to the amount of the rent. Ideally you will have some extra profit, but in some markets your rentals can run at a loss every year, and yet still be good long term investments.

Running at a break-even or small tax loss is normally not a bad thing with rental property because each year you are paying down your mortgage, and hopefully inflation is raising the value of your property a few percent each year. So theoretically, you could put $20,000 down on a $100,000 property with a 20 year mortgage, and at the end of the twenty years of breaking even on the rents have a $200,000 property that you own free and clear.

When reporting your income and expenses for rental property you will use IRS "Schedule E." On this form there is a list of fourteen categories of deductible expenses on lines 5 through 18. They are:

Advertising
Auto and Travel
Cleaning and Maintenance
Commissions
Insurance
Legal and other professional fees
Management fees
Mortgage interest paid to banks, etc.
Other interest
Repairs
Supplies
Taxes
Utilities
Other

When you are keeping the financial records for your property, you should keep these in mind and categorize them as you record them. This way it will be quicker and easier to do the taxes when the time comes.

Mileage is something east to forget to deduct. Every trip to the property, to pick up parts for repairs, to landlord club meetings, is deductible. Keeping a mileage log book in the car is a good way to remember and provide proof in case of an audit.

Taxes on Sale of the Property

When selling a rental property there are several ways to lower the taxes you must pay. But there are some rules that can make the taxes higher than you expected. Careful planning can give you optimum profits.

Long term capital gains. To encourage people to invest their money in ways that will grow the economy, the tax code gives lower taxes on investments that are held for more than 12 months. So if you buy a house, fix it up and sell it in a few months, your profit is taxed like ordinary income (up to 25%, 33%, etc., depending on your tax bracket) but if you hold it for more than 12 months as an investment, you only pay 15% tax on the profit.

One thing to be careful of in this regard is if you do both kinds of investments, short term and long term, you need to separate them, ideally in different LLCs or corporations, to get the benefits.

If you are an investor, who has another job, and normally holds real estate for a long term, you get the long term capital gains rate on your profits, but if you are in the real estate business, and buy and sell for a living, then you pay ordinary income rates, even on long term holdings. This is so that people in the real estate business do not pay less taxes than those in other businesses.

So, if you want to do both short-term deals and long term investments you should set up a company, such as an LLC, for the short term deals. Then the long term holdings can either be in your own name (not the best plan) or in a separate LLC.

The way that your profit will be calculated on your sale of a property is usually roughly as follows:

You take the net proceeds that you receive from selling the property and then subtract your original purchase price, plus other purchase costs that were not deductible, plus improvements you paid for since you bought it, less the depreciation that you claimed over the years. The net profit is then your capital gain.

However, the government doesn't want you to pay low capital gains rates on depreciation that, over the years you deducted from your ordinary income, so they came up with a rule called "depreciation recapture" in which you pay your ordinary income tax rate on all amounts that you deducted for depreciation over the years.

After getting hit with this once you might decide that it is not worth taking the depreciation over the years if you will end up paying it all back later at a tax rate that might be even higher. But that's not allowed! Even if you didn't take depreciation over the years, you have to pay depreciation recapture on the depreciation you "could have taken" over the years but didn't!

Some Important Rules and Tips

It is always good to know the tax rules before you begin a venture so that you are not surprised at the end of the year by the taxes that are owed. Here are a few important things to know.

➲ If you rent your property to a family member you can lose the right to deduct your expenses.

➲ The tax advantages you would get from a home office is usually not worth the trouble and the risk of getting audited.

➲ If you have only long term investments and not actively turning properties you are limited in the amount of *passive losses* you can deduct in a year to $25,000. However, if you have more than this amount you can carry them over to the next year.

➲ If you make an arrangement with a "qualified intermediary" to hold the proceeds of your sale of real estate, you can use it to buy another property and not pay any tax on the profit. This is called a 1031 exchange and you must find a property within 45 days of selling and close the deal within 180 days.

➲ You can buy real estate that you manage yourself in your IRA or Roth IRA. What you need to do is set up a "self-directed IRA" account with a company that specializes in these.

➲ While "improvements" are supposed to be amortized over several years rather than deducted in one year, you can often break out the cost of repairs from the overall cost of an improvement.

For more information see *Every Landlord's Tax Deduction Guide* by Stephen Fishman (Nolo).

Appendix A

Florida Statutes

This appendix contains Florida Statutes relating to landlord issues current through January, 2012. The Florida legislature meets each year, usually in March through May, and the bills that are signed into law by the governor are usually known by mid June. The following laws are included:

Section 51.011, Summary Procedure

Section 57.105, Attorney's fee; sanctions for raising unsupported claims or defenses

Chapter 83, Landlord and Tenant

Section 212.03, Transient rentals tax; rate, procedure, enforcement, exemptions

Section 212.031, Tax on rental or license fee for use of real property

Section 713.691, Landlord's lien for rent; exemptions

Section 715.07, Vehicles or vessels parked on private property; towing

Section 715.10, Disposition of Personal Property Landlord and Tenant Act

You can find the most recent laws here:

http://www.leg.state.fl.us/statutes/

51.011 Summary procedure.—The procedure in this section applies only to those actions specified by statute or rule. Rules of procedure apply to this section except when this section or the statute or rule prescribing this section provides a different procedure. If there is a difference between the time period prescribed in a rule and in this section, this section governs.

(1) PLEADINGS.—Plaintiff's initial pleading shall contain the matters required by the statute or rule prescribing this section or, if none is so required, shall state a cause of action. All defenses of law or fact shall be contained in defendant's answer which shall be filed within 5 days after service of process. If the answer incorporates a counterclaim, plaintiff shall include all defenses of law or fact in his or her answer to the counterclaim and shall serve it within 5 days after service of the counterclaim. No other pleadings are permitted. All defensive motions, including motions to quash, shall be heard by the court prior to trial.

(2) DISCOVERY.—Depositions on oral examination may be taken by any party at any time. Other discovery and admissions may be had only on order of court setting the time for compliance. No discovery postpones the time for trial except for good cause shown or by stipulation of the parties.

(3) JURY.—If a jury trial is authorized by law, any party may demand it in any pleading or by a separate paper served not later than 5 days after the action comes to issue. When a jury is in attendance at the close of pleading or the time of demand for jury trial, the action may be tried immediately; otherwise, the court shall order a special venire to be summoned immediately. If a special venire be summoned, the party demanding the jury shall deposit sufficient money with the clerk to pay the jury fees which shall be taxed as costs if he or she prevails.

(4) NEW TRIAL.—Motion for new trial shall be filed and served within 5 days after verdict, if a jury trial was had, or after entry of judgment, if trial was by the court. A reserved motion for directed verdict shall be renewed within the period for moving for a new trial.

(5) APPEAL.—Notice of appeal shall be filed and served within 30 days from the rendition of the judgment appealed from.

History.—s. 7, ch. 67-254; s. 23, ch. 73-333; s. 5, ch. 87-405; s. 292, ch. 95-147.

57.105 Attorney's fee; sanctions for raising unsupported claims or defenses; service of motions; damages for delay of litigation.—

(1) Upon the court's initiative or motion of any party, the court shall award a reasonable attorney's fee to be paid to the prevailing party in equal amounts by the losing party and the losing party's attorney on any claim or defense at any time during a civil proceeding or action in which the court finds that the losing party or the losing party's attorney knew or should have known that a claim or defense when initially presented to the court or at any time before trial:

(a) Was not supported by the material facts necessary to establish the claim or defense; or

(b) Would not be supported by the application of then-existing law to those material facts.

However, the losing party's attorney is not personally responsible if he or she has acted in good faith, based on the representations of his or her client as to the existence of those material facts. If the court awards attorney's fees to a claimant pursuant to this subsection, the court shall also award prejudgment interest.

(2) Paragraph (1)(b) does not apply if the court determines that the claim or defense was initially presented to the court as a good faith argument for the extension, modification, or reversal of existing law or the establishment of new law, as it applied to the material facts, with a reasonable expectation of success.

(3) At any time in any civil proceeding or action in which the moving party proves by a preponderance of the evidence that any action taken by the opposing party, including, but not limited to, the filing of any pleading or part thereof, the assertion of or response to any discovery demand, the assertion of any claim or defense, or the response to any request by any other party, was taken primarily for the purpose of unreasonable delay, the court shall award damages to the moving party for its reasonable expenses incurred in obtaining the order, which may include attorney's fees, and other loss resulting from the improper delay.

(4) A motion by a party seeking sanctions under this section must be served but may not be filed with or presented to the court unless, within 21 days after service of the motion, the challenged paper, claim, defense, contention, allegation, or denial is not withdrawn or appropriately corrected.

(5) In administrative proceedings under chapter 120, an administrative law judge shall award a reasonable attorney's fee and damages to be paid to the prevailing party in equal amounts by the losing party and a losing party's attorney or qualified representative in the same manner and upon the same basis as provided in subsections (1)-(4). Such award shall be a final order subject to judicial review pursuant to s. 120.68. If the losing party is an agency as defined in s. 120.52(1), the award to the prevailing party shall be against and paid by the agency. A voluntary dismissal by a nonprevailing party does not divest the administrative law judge of jurisdiction to make the award described in this subsection.

(6) The provisions of this section are supplemental to other sanctions or remedies available under law or under court rules.

(7) If a contract contains a provision allowing attorney's fees to a party when he or she is required to take any action to enforce the contract, the court may also allow reasonable attorney's fees to the other party when that party prevails in any action, whether as plaintiff or defendant, with respect to the contract. This subsection applies to any contract entered into on or after October 1, 1988.

History.—s. 1, ch. 78-275; s. 61, ch. 86-160; ss. 1, 2, ch. 88-160; s. 1, ch. 90-300; s. 316, ch. 95-147; s. 4, ch. 99-225; s. 1, ch. 2002-77; s. 9, ch. 2003-94.

CHAPTER 83 LANDLORD AND TENANT
PART I - NONRESIDENTIAL TENANCIES (ss. 83.001-83.251)
PART II - RESIDENTIAL TENANCIES (ss. 83.40-83.682)
PART III - SELF-SERVICE STORAGE SPACE (ss. 83.801-83.809)

PART I NONRESIDENTIAL TENANCIES

83.001 Application.—This part applies to nonresidential tenancies and all tenancies not governed by part II of this chapter.
History.—s. 1, ch. 73-330.

83.01 Unwritten lease tenancy at will; duration.—Any lease of lands and tenements, or either, made shall be deemed and held to be a tenancy at will unless it shall be in writing signed by the lessor. Such tenancy shall be from year to year, or quarter to quarter, or month to month, or week to week, to be determined by the periods at which the rent is payable. If the rent is payable weekly, then the tenancy shall be from week to week; if payable monthly, then from month to month; if payable quarterly, then from quarter to quarter; if payable yearly, then from year to year.

History.—ss. 1, 2, ch. 5441, 1905; RGS 3567, 3568; CGL 5431, 5432; s. 34, ch. 67-254.

83.02 Certain written leases tenancies at will; duration.—Where any tenancy has been created by an instrument in writing from year to year, or quarter to quarter, or month to month, or week to week, to be determined by the periods at which the rent is payable, and the term of which tenancy is unlimited, the tenancy shall be a tenancy at will. If the rent is payable weekly, then the tenancy shall be from week to week; if payable monthly, then the tenancy shall be from month to month; if payable quarterly, then from quarter to quarter; if payable yearly, then from year to year.

History.—s. 2, ch. 5441, 1905; RGS 3568; CGL 5432; s. 2, ch. 15057, 1931; s. 34, ch. 67-254.

83.03 Termination of tenancy at will; length of notice.—A tenancy at will may be terminated by either party giving notice as follows:

(1)   Where the tenancy is from year to year, by giving not less than 3 months' notice prior to the end of any annual period;

(2)   Where the tenancy is from quarter to quarter, by giving not less than 45 days' notice prior to the end of any quarter;

(3)   Where the tenancy is from month to month, by giving not less than 15 days' notice prior to the end of any monthly period; and

(4)   Where the tenancy is from week to week, by giving not less than 7 days' notice prior to the end of any weekly period.
History.—s. 3, ch. 5441, 1905; RGS 3569; CGL 5433; s. 34, ch. 67-254; s. 3, ch. 2003-5.

83.04 Holding over after term, tenancy at sufferance, etc.—When any tenancy created by an instrument in writing, the term of which is limited, has expired and the tenant holds over in the possession of said premises without renewing the lease by some further instrument in writing then such holding over shall be construed to be a tenancy at sufferance. The mere payment or acceptance of rent shall not be construed to be a renewal of the term, but if the holding over be continued with the written consent of the lessor then the tenancy shall become a tenancy at will under the provisions of this law.
History.—s. 4, ch. 5441, 1905; RGS 3570; CGL 5434; s. 3, ch. 15057, 1931; s. 34, ch. 67-254.

83.05 Right of possession upon default in rent; determination of right of possession in action or surrender or abandonment of premises.—

(1)   If any person leasing or renting any land or premises other than a dwelling unit fails to pay the rent at the time it becomes due, the lessor has the right to obtain possession of the premises as provided by law.

(2)   The landlord shall recover possession of rented premises only:

(a)   In an action for possession under s. 83.20, or other civil action in which the issue of right of possession is determined;

(b)   When the tenant has surrendered possession of the rented premises to the landlord; or

(c)   When the tenant has abandoned the rented premises.

(3)   In the absence of actual knowledge of abandonment, it shall be presumed for purposes of paragraph (2)(c) that the tenant has abandoned the rented premises if:

(a)   The landlord reasonably believes that the tenant has been absent from the rented premises for a period of 30 consecutive days;

(b)   The rent is not current; and

(c)   A notice pursuant to s. 83.20(2) has been served and 10 days have elapsed since service of such notice.

However, this presumption does not apply if the rent is current or the tenant has notified the landlord in writing of an intended absence.

History.—s. 5, Nov. 21, 1828; RS 1750; GS 2226; RGS 3534; CGL 5398; s. 34, ch. 67-254; s. 1, ch. 83-151.

83.06   Right to demand double rent upon refusal to deliver possession.—

(1)   When any tenant refuses to give up possession of the premises at the end of the tenant's lease, the landlord, the landlord's agent, attorney, or legal representatives, may demand of such tenant double the monthly rent, and may recover the same at the expiration of every month, or in the same proportion for a longer or shorter time by distress, in the manner pointed out hereinafter.

(2)   All contracts for rent, verbal or in writing, shall bear interest from the time the rent becomes due, any law, usage or custom to the contrary notwithstanding.

History.—ss. 4, 6, Nov. 21, 1828; RS 1759; GS 2235; RGS 3554; CGL 5418; s. 34, ch. 67-254; s. 427, ch. 95-147.

83.07   Action for use and occupation.—Any landlord, the landlord's heirs, executors, administrators or assigns may recover reasonable damages for any house, lands, tenements, or hereditaments held or occupied by any person by the landlord's permission in an action on the case for the use and occupation of the lands, tenements, or hereditaments when they are not held, occupied by or under agreement or demise by deed; and if on trial of any action, any demise or agreement (not being by deed) whereby a certain rent was reserved is given in evidence, the plaintiff shall not be dismissed but may make use thereof as an evidence of the quantum of damages to be recovered.

History.—s. 7, Nov. 21, 1828; RS 1760; GS 2236; RGS 3555; CGL 5419; s. 34, ch. 67-254; s. 428, ch. 95-147.

83.08   Landlord's lien for rent.—Every person to whom rent may be due, the person's heirs, executors, administrators or assigns, shall have a lien for such rent upon the property found upon or off the premises leased or rented, and in the possession of any person, as follows:

(1)   Upon agricultural products raised on the land leased or rented for the current year. This lien shall be superior to all other liens, though of older date.

(2)   Upon all other property of the lessee or his or her sublessee or assigns, usually kept on the premises. This lien shall be superior to any lien acquired subsequent to the bringing of the property on the premises leased.

(3)   Upon all other property of the defendant. This lien shall date from the levy of the distress warrant hereinafter provided.

History.—ss. 1, 9, 10, ch. 3131, 1879; RS 1761; GS 2237; RGS 3556; CGL 5420; s. 34, ch. 67-254; s. 429, ch. 95-147.

83.09   Exemptions from liens for rent.—No property of any tenant or lessee shall be exempt from distress and sale for rent, except beds, bedclothes and wearing apparel.

History.—s. 6, Feb. 14, 1835; RS 1762; GS 2238; RGS 3557; CGL 5421; s. 34, ch. 67-254.

83.10   Landlord's lien for advances.—Landlords shall have a lien on the crop grown on rented land for advances made in money or other things of value, whether made directly by them or at their instance and requested by another person, or for which they have assumed a legal responsibility, at or before the time at which such advances were made, for the sustenance or well-being of the tenant or the tenant's family, or for preparing the ground for cultivation, or for cultivating, gathering, saving, handling, or preparing the crop for market. They shall have a lien also upon each and every article advanced, and upon all property purchased with money advanced, or obtained, by barter or exchange for any articles advanced, for the aggregate value or price of all the property or articles so advanced. The liens upon the crop shall be of equal dignity with liens for rent, and upon the articles advanced shall be paramount to all other liens.

History.—s. 2, ch. 3247, 1879; RS 1763; GS 2239; RGS 3558; CGL 5422; s. 34, ch. 67-254; s. 430, ch. 95-147.

83.11   Distress for rent; complaint.—Any person to whom any rent or money for advances is due or the person's agent or attorney may file an action in the court in the county where the land lies having jurisdiction of the amount claimed, and the court shall have jurisdiction to order the relief provided in this part. The complaint shall be verified and shall allege the name and relationship of the defendant to the plaintiff, how the obligation for rent arose, the amount or quality and value of the rent due for such land, or the advances, and whether payable in money, an agricultural product, or any other thing of value.

History.—s. 2, ch. 3131, 1879; RS 1764; GS 2240; RGS 3559; CGL 5423; s. 34, ch. 67-254; s. 1, ch. 80-282; s. 431, ch. 95-147.

83.12   Distress writ.—A distress writ shall be issued by a judge of the court which has jurisdiction of the amount claimed. The writ shall enjoin the defendant from damaging, disposing of, secreting, or removing any property liable to distress from the rented real property after the time of service of the writ until the sheriff levies on the property, the writ is vacated, or the court otherwise orders. A violation of the command of the writ may be punished as a contempt of court. If the defendant does not move for dissolution of the writ as provided in s. 83.135, the sheriff shall, pursuant to a further order of the court, levy on the property liable to distress forthwith after the time for answering the complaint has expired. Before the writ issues, the plaintiff or the plaintiff's agent or attorney shall file a bond with surety to be approved by the clerk payable to defendant in at least double the sum demanded or, if property, in double the value of the property sought to be levied on, conditioned to pay all costs and damages which defendant sustains in consequence of plaintiff's improperly suing out the distress.

History.—s. 2, ch. 3131, 1879; RS 1765; GS 2241; s. 10, ch. 7838, 1919; RGS 3560; CGL 5424; s. 34, ch. 67-254; s. 2, ch. 80-282; s. 432, ch. 95-147.

83.13 Levy of writ.—The sheriff shall execute the writ by service on defendant and, upon the order of the court, by levy on property distrainable for rent or advances, if found in the sheriff's jurisdiction. If the property is in another jurisdiction, the party who had the writ issued shall deliver the writ to the sheriff in the other jurisdiction; and that sheriff shall execute the writ, upon order of the court, by levying on the property and delivering it to the sheriff of the county in which the action is pending, to be disposed of according to law, unless he or she is ordered by the court from which the writ emanated to hold the property and dispose of it in his or her jurisdiction according to law. If the plaintiff shows by a sworn statement that the defendant cannot be found within the state, the levy on the property suffices as service on the defendant.

History.—s. 3, ch. 3721, 1887; RS 1765; GS 2241; RGS 3560; CGL 5424; s. 34, ch. 67-254; s. 3, ch. 80-282; s. 15, ch. 82-66; s. 8, ch. 83-255; s. 433, ch. 95-147; s. 5, ch. 2004-273.

83.135 Dissolution of writ.—The defendant may move for dissolution of a distress writ at any time. The court shall hear the motion not later than the day on which the sheriff is authorized under the writ to levy on property liable under distress. If the plaintiff proves a prima facie case, or if the defendant defaults, the court shall order the sheriff to proceed with the levy.

History.—s. 4, ch. 80-282.

83.14 Replevy of distrained property.—The property distrained may be restored to the defendant at any time on the defendant's giving bond with surety to the sheriff levying the writ. The bond shall be approved by such sheriff; made payable to plaintiff in double the value of the property levied on, with the value to be fixed by the sheriff; and conditioned for the forthcoming of the property restored to abide the final order of the court. It may be also restored to defendant on defendant's giving bond with surety to be approved by the sheriff making the levy conditioned to pay the plaintiff the amount or value of the rental or advances which may be adjudicated to be payable to plaintiff. Judgment may be entered against the surety on such bonds in the manner and with like effect as provided in s. 76.31.

History.—s. 3, ch. 3131, 1879; RS 1766; s. 1, ch. 4408, 1895; RGS 3561; CGL 5425; s. 34, ch. 67-254; s. 16, ch. 82-66; s. 9, ch. 83-255; s. 434, ch. 95-147.

83.15 Claims by third persons.—Any third person claiming any property so distrained may interpose and prosecute his or her claim for it in the same manner as is provided in similar cases of claim to property levied on under execution.

History.—s. 7, ch. 3131, 1879; RS 1770; GS 2246; RGS 3565; CGL 5429; s. 34, ch. 67-254; s. 17, ch. 82-66; s. 435, ch. 95-147.

83.18 Distress for rent; trial; verdict; judgment.—If the verdict or the finding of the court is for plaintiff, judgment shall be rendered against defendant for the amount or value of the rental or advances, including interest and costs, and against the surety on defendant's bond as provided for in s. 83.14, if the property has been restored to defendant, and execution shall issue. If the verdict or the finding of the court is for defendant, the action shall be dismissed and defendant shall have judgment and execution against plaintiff for costs.

History.—RS 1768; s. 3, ch. 4408, 1895; GS 2244; RGS 3563; CGL 5427; s. 14, ch. 63-559; s. 34, ch. 67-254; s. 18, ch. 82-66.

83.19 Sale of property distrained.—

(1) If the judgment is for plaintiff and the property in whole or in part has not been replevied, it, or the part not restored to the defendant, shall be sold and the proceeds applied on the payment of the execution. If the rental or any part of it is due in agricultural products and the property distrained, or any part of it, is of a similar kind to that claimed in the complaint, the property up to a quantity to be adjudged of by the officer holding the execution (not exceeding that claimed), may be delivered to the plaintiff as a payment on the plaintiff's execution at his or her request.

(2) When any property levied on is sold, it shall be advertised two times, the first advertisement being at least 10 days before the sale. All property so levied on shall be sold at the location advertised in the notice of sheriff's sale.

(3) Before the sale if defendant appeals and obtains supersedeas and pays all costs accrued up to the time that the supersedeas becomes operative, the property shall be restored to defendant and there shall be no sale.

(4) In case any property is sold to satisfy any rent payable in cotton or other agricultural product or thing, the officer shall settle with the plaintiff at the value of the rental at the time it became due.

History.—ss. 5, 6, ch. 3131, 1879; RS 1769; GS 2245; RGS 3564; CGL 5428; s. 34, ch. 67-254; s. 19, ch. 82-66; s. 10, ch. 83-255; s. 436, ch. 95-147.

83.20 Causes for removal of tenants.—Any tenant or lessee at will or sufferance, or for part of the year, or for one or more years, of any houses, lands or tenements, and the assigns, under tenants or legal representatives of such tenant or lessee, may be removed from the premises in the manner hereinafter provided in the following cases:

(1) Where such person holds over and continues in the possession of the demised premises, or any part thereof, after the expiration of the person's time, without the permission of the person's landlord.

(2) Where such person holds over without permission as aforesaid, after any default in the payment of rent pursuant to the agreement under which the premises are held, and 3 days' notice in writ-

ing requiring the payment of the rent or the possession of the premises has been served by the person entitled to the rent on the person owing the same. The service of the notice shall be by delivery of a true copy thereof, or, if the tenant is absent from the rented premises, by leaving a copy thereof at such place.

(3)   Where such person holds over without permission after failing to cure a material breach of the lease or oral agreement, other than nonpayment of rent, and when 15 days' written notice requiring the cure of such breach or the possession of the premises has been served on the tenant. This subsection applies only when the lease is silent on the matter or when the tenancy is an oral one at will. The notice may give a longer time period for cure of the breach or surrender of the premises. In the absence of a lease provision prescribing the method for serving notices, service must be by mail, hand delivery, or, if the tenant is absent from the rental premises or the address designated by the lease, by posting.

History.—s. 1, ch. 3248, 1881; RS 1751; GS 2227; RGS 3535; CGL 5399; s. 34, ch. 67-254; s. 20, ch. 77-104; s. 2, ch. 88-379; s. 1, ch. 93-70; s. 437, ch. 95-147.

83.201   Notice to landlord of failure to maintain or repair, rendering premises wholly untenantable; right to withhold rent.— When the lease is silent on the procedure to be followed to effect repair or maintenance and the payment of rent relating thereto, yet affirmatively and expressly places the obligation for same upon the landlord, and the landlord has failed or refused to do so, rendering the leased premises wholly untenantable, the tenant may withhold rent after notice to the landlord. The tenant shall serve the landlord, in the manner prescribed by s. 83.20(3), with a written notice declaring the premises to be wholly untenantable, giving the landlord at least 20 days to make the specifically described repair or maintenance, and stating that the tenant will withhold the rent for the next rental period and thereafter until the repair or maintenance has been performed. The lease may provide for a longer period of time for repair or maintenance. Once the landlord has completed the repair or maintenance, the tenant shall pay the landlord the amounts of rent withheld. If the landlord does not complete the repair or maintenance in the allotted time, the parties may extend the time by written agreement or the tenant may abandon the premises, retain the amounts of rent withheld, terminate the lease, and avoid any liability for future rent or charges under the lease. This section is cumulative to other existing remedies, and this section does not prevent any tenant from exercising his or her other remedies.

History.—s. 2, ch. 93-70; s. 438, ch. 95-147.

83.202   Waiver of right to proceed with eviction claim.—The landlord's acceptance of the full amount of rent past due, with knowledge of the tenant's breach of the lease by nonpayment, shall be considered a waiver of the landlord's right to proceed with an eviction claim for nonpayment of that rent. Acceptance of the rent includes conduct by the landlord concerning any tender of the rent by the tenant which is inconsistent with reasonably prompt return of the payment to the tenant.

History.—s. 3, ch. 93-70.

83.21   Removal of tenant.—The landlord, the landlord's attorney or agent, applying for the removal of any tenant, shall file a com-

plaint stating the facts which authorize the removal of the tenant, and describing the premises in the proper court of the county where the premises are situated and is entitled to the summary procedure provided in s. 51.011.

History.—s. 2, ch. 3248, 1881; RS 1752; GS 2228; RGS 3536; CGL 5400; s. 1, ch. 61-318; s. 34, ch. 67-254; s. 439, ch. 95-147.

83.22   Removal of tenant; service.—

(1)   After at least two attempts to obtain service as provided by law, if the defendant cannot be found in the county in which the action is pending and either the defendant has no usual place of abode in the county or there is no person 15 years of age or older residing at the defendant's usual place of abode in the county, the sheriff shall serve the summons by attaching it to some part of the premises involved in the proceeding. The minimum time delay between the two attempts to obtain service shall be 6 hours.

(2)   If a landlord causes, or anticipates causing, a defendant to be served with a summons and complaint solely by attaching them to some conspicuous part of the premises involved in the proceeding, the landlord shall provide the clerk of the court with two additional copies of the complaint and two prestamped envelopes addressed to the defendant. One envelope shall be addressed to such address or location as has been designated by the tenant for receipt of notice in a written lease or other agreement or, if none has been designated, to the residence of the tenant, if known. The second envelope shall be addressed to the last known business address of the tenant. The clerk of the court shall immediately mail the copies of the summons and complaint by first-class mail, note the fact of mailing in the docket, and file a certificate in the court file of the fact and date of mailing. Service shall be effective on the date of posting or mailing, whichever occurs later; and at least 5 days from the date of service must have elapsed before a judgment for final removal of the defendant may be entered.

History.—s. 2, ch. 3248, 1881; RS 1753; GS 2229; RGS 3537; CGL 5401; s. 1, ch. 22731, 1945; s. 34, ch. 67-254; s. 2, ch. 83-151; s. 3, ch. 84-339; s. 440, ch. 95-147.

83.231   Removal of tenant; judgment.—If the issues are found for plaintiff, judgment shall be entered that plaintiff recover possession of the premises. If the plaintiff expressly and specifically sought money damages in the complaint, in addition to awarding possession of the premises to the plaintiff, the court shall also direct, in an amount which is within its jurisdictional limitations, the entry of a money judgment in favor of the plaintiff and against the defendant for the amount of money found due, owing, and unpaid by the defendant, with costs. However, no money judgment shall be entered unless service of process has been effected by personal service or, where authorized by law, by certified or registered mail, return receipt, or in any other manner prescribed by law or the rules of the court, and no money judgment may be entered except in compliance with the Florida Rules of Civil Procedure. Where otherwise authorized by law, the plaintiff in the judgment for possession and money damages may also be awarded attorney's fees and costs. If the issues are found for defendant, judgment shall be entered dismissing the action.

History.—s. 8, ch. 6463, 1913; RGS 3549; CGL 5413; s. 34, ch. 67-254; s. 1, ch. 87-195; s. 4, ch. 93-70; s. 441, ch. 95-147.
Note.—Former s. 83.34.

83.232 Rent paid into registry of court.—

(1) In an action by the landlord which includes a claim for possession of real property, the tenant shall pay into the court registry the amount alleged in the complaint as unpaid, or if such amount is contested, such amount as is determined by the court, and any rent accruing during the pendency of the action, when due, unless the tenant has interposed the defense of payment or satisfaction of the rent in the amount the complaint alleges as unpaid. Unless the tenant disputes the amount of accrued rent, the tenant must pay the amount alleged in the complaint into the court registry on or before the date on which his or her answer to the claim for possession is due. If the tenant contests the amount of accrued rent, the tenant must pay the amount determined by the court into the court registry on the day that the court makes its determination. The court may, however, extend these time periods to allow for later payment, upon good cause shown. Even though the defense of payment or satisfaction has been asserted, the court, in its discretion, may order the tenant to pay into the court registry the rent that accrues during the pendency of the action, the time of accrual being as set forth in the lease. If the landlord is in actual danger of loss of the premises or other hardship resulting from the loss of rental income from the premises, the landlord may apply to the court for disbursement of all or part of the funds so held in the court registry.

(2) If the tenant contests the amount of money to be placed into the court registry, any hearing regarding such dispute shall be limited to only the factual or legal issues concerning:

(a) Whether the tenant has been properly credited by the landlord with any and all rental payments made; and

(b) What properly constitutes rent under the provisions of the lease.

(3) The court, on its own motion, shall notify the tenant of the requirement that rent be paid into the court registry by order, which shall be issued immediately upon filing of the tenant's initial pleading, motion, or other paper.

(4) The filing of a counterclaim for money damages does not relieve the tenant from depositing rent due into the registry of the court.

(5) Failure of the tenant to pay the rent into the court registry pursuant to court order shall be deemed an absolute waiver of the tenant's defenses. In such case, the landlord is entitled to an immediate default for possession without further notice or hearing thereon.

History.—s. 5, ch. 93-70; s. 442, ch. 95-147.

83.241 Removal of tenant; process.—After entry of judgment in favor of plaintiff the clerk shall issue a writ to the sheriff describing the premises and commanding the sheriff to put plaintiff in possession.

History.—s. 9, ch. 6463, 1913; RGS 3550; CGL 5414; s. 34, ch. 67-254; s. 1, ch. 70-360; s. 5, ch. 94-170; s. 1371, ch. 95-147.
Note.—Former s. 83.35.

83.251 Removal of tenant; costs.—The prevailing party shall have judgment for costs and execution shall issue therefor.

History.—s. 11, ch. 6463, 1913; RGS 3552; CGL 5416; s. 34, ch. 67-254.
Note.—Former s. 83.37.

PART II RESIDENTIAL TENANCIES

83.40 Short title.—This part shall be known as the "Florida Residential Landlord and Tenant Act."
History.—s. 2, ch. 73-330.

83.41 Application.—This part applies to the rental of a dwelling unit.
History.—s. 2, ch. 73-330; ss. 2, 20, ch. 82-66.

83.42 Exclusions from application of part.—This part does not apply to:

(1) Residency or detention in a facility, whether public or private, when residence or detention is incidental to the provision of medical, geriatric, educational, counseling, religious, or similar services.

(2) Occupancy under a contract of sale of a dwelling unit or the property of which it is a part.

(3) Transient occupancy in a hotel, condominium, motel, roominghouse, or similar public lodging, or transient occupancy in a mobile home park.

(4) Occupancy by a holder of a proprietary lease in a cooperative apartment.

(5) Occupancy by an owner of a condominium unit.

History.—s. 2, ch. 73-330.

83.43 Definitions.—As used in this part, the following words and terms shall have the following meanings unless some other meaning is plainly indicated:

(1) "Building, housing, and health codes" means any law, ordinance, or governmental regulation concerning health, safety, sanitation or fitness for habitation, or the construction, maintenance, operation, occupancy, use, or appearance, of any dwelling unit.

(2) "Dwelling unit" means:

(a) A structure or part of a structure that is rented for use as a home, residence, or sleeping place by one person or by two or more persons who maintain a common household.

(b) A mobile home rented by a tenant.

(c) A structure or part of a structure that is furnished, with or without rent, as an incident of employment for use as a home, residence, or sleeping place by one or more persons.

(3) "Landlord" means the owner or lessor of a dwelling unit.

(4) "Tenant" means any person entitled to occupy a dwelling unit under a rental agreement.

(5) "Premises" means a dwelling unit and the structure of which it is a part and a mobile home lot and the appurtenant facilities and grounds, areas, facilities, and property held out for the use of tenants generally.

(6) "Rent" means the periodic payments due the landlord from the tenant for occupancy under a rental agreement and any other payments due the landlord from the tenant as may be designated as rent in a written rental agreement.

(7) "Rental agreement" means any written agreement, including amendments or addenda, or oral agreement for a duration of less than 1 year, providing for use and occupancy of premises.

(8) "Good faith" means honesty in fact in the conduct or transaction concerned.

(9) "Advance rent" means moneys paid to the landlord to be applied to future rent payment periods, but does not include rent paid in advance for a current rent payment period.

(10) "Transient occupancy" means occupancy when it is the intention of the parties that the occupancy will be temporary.

(11) "Deposit money" means any money held by the landlord on behalf of the tenant, including, but not limited to, damage deposits, security deposits, advance rent deposit, pet deposit, or any contractual deposit agreed to between landlord and tenant either in writing or orally.

(12) "Security deposits" means any moneys held by the landlord as security for the performance of the rental agreement, including, but not limited to, monetary damage to the landlord caused by the tenant's breach of lease prior to the expiration thereof.

(13) "Legal holiday" means holidays observed by the clerk of the court.

(14) "Servicemember" shall have the same meaning as provided in s. 250.01.

(15) "Active duty" shall have the same meaning as provided in s. 250.01.

(16) "State active duty" shall have the same meaning as provided in s. 250.01.

(17) "Early termination fee" means any charge, fee, or forfeiture that is provided for in a written rental agreement and is assessed to a tenant when a tenant elects to terminate the rental agreement, as provided in the agreement, and vacates a dwelling unit before the end of the rental agreement. An early termination fee does not include:

(a) Unpaid rent and other accrued charges through the end of the month in which the landlord retakes possession of the dwelling unit.

(b) Charges for damages to the dwelling unit.

(c) Charges associated with a rental agreement settlement, release, buy-out, or accord and satisfaction agreement.

History.—s. 2, ch. 73-330; s. 1, ch. 74-143; s. 1, ch. 81-190; s. 3, ch. 83-151; s. 17, ch. 94-170; s. 2, ch. 2003-72; s. 1, ch. 2008-131.

83.44 Obligation of good faith.—Every rental agreement or duty within this part imposes an obligation of good faith in its performance or enforcement.

History.—s. 2, ch. 73-330.

83.45 Unconscionable rental agreement or provision.—

(1) If the court as a matter of law finds a rental agreement or any provision of a rental agreement to have been unconscionable at the time it was made, the court may refuse to enforce the rental agreement, enforce the remainder of the rental agreement without the unconscionable provision, or so limit the application of any unconscionable provision as to avoid any unconscionable result.

(2) When it is claimed or appears to the court that the rental agreement or any provision thereof may be unconscionable, the parties shall be afforded a reasonable opportunity to present evidence as to meaning, relationship of the parties, purpose, and effect to aid the court in making the determination.

History.—s. 2, ch. 73-330.

83.46 Rent; duration of tenancies.—

(1) Unless otherwise agreed, rent is payable without demand or notice; periodic rent is payable at the beginning of each rent payment period; and rent is uniformly apportionable from day to day.

(2) If the rental agreement contains no provision as to duration of the tenancy, the duration is determined by the periods for which the rent is payable. If the rent is payable weekly, then the tenancy is from week to week; if payable monthly, tenancy is from month to month; if payable quarterly, tenancy is from quarter to quarter; if payable yearly, tenancy is from year to year.

(3) If the dwelling unit is furnished without rent as an incident of employment and there is no agreement as to the duration of the tenancy, the duration is determined by the periods for which wages are payable. If wages are payable weekly or more frequently, then the tenancy is from week to week; and if wages are payable monthly or no wages are payable, then the tenancy is from month to month. In the event that the employee ceases employment, the employer shall be entitled to rent for the period from the day after the employee ceases employment until the day that the dwelling unit is vacated at a rate equivalent to the rate charged for similarly situated residences in the area. This subsection shall not apply to an employee or a resident manager of an apartment house or an apartment complex when there is a written agreement to the contrary.

History.—s. 2, ch. 73-330; s. 2, ch. 81-190; s. 2, ch. 87-195; s. 2, ch. 90-133; s. 1, ch. 93-255.

83.47 Prohibited provisions in rental agreements.—

(1) A provision in a rental agreement is void and unenforceable to the extent that it:

(a) Purports to waive or preclude the rights, remedies, or requirements set forth in this part.

(b) Purports to limit or preclude any liability of the landlord to the tenant or of the tenant to the landlord, arising under law.

(2) If such a void and unenforceable provision is included in a rental agreement entered into, extended, or renewed after the effective date of this part and either party suffers actual damages as a result of the inclusion, the aggrieved party may recover those damages sustained after the effective date of this part.

History.—s. 2, ch. 73-330.

83.48 Attorney's fees.—In any civil action brought to enforce the provisions of the rental agreement or this part, the party in whose favor a judgment or decree has been rendered may recover reasonable court costs, including attorney's fees, from the nonprevailing party.

History.—s. 2, ch. 73-330; s. 4, ch. 83-151.

83.49 Deposit money or advance rent; duty of landlord and tenant.—

(1) Whenever money is deposited or advanced by a tenant on a rental agreement as security for performance of the rental agreement or as advance rent for other than the next immediate rental period, the landlord or the landlord's agent shall either:

(a) Hold the total amount of such money in a separate non-interest-bearing account in a Florida banking institution for the benefit of the tenant or tenants. The landlord shall not commingle such moneys with any other funds of the landlord or hypothecate, pledge, or in any other way make use of such moneys until such moneys are actually due the landlord;

(b) Hold the total amount of such money in a separate interest-bearing account in a Florida banking institution for the benefit of the tenant or tenants, in which case the tenant shall receive and collect interest in an amount of at least 75 percent of the annualized average interest rate payable on such account or interest at the rate of 5 percent per year, simple interest, whichever the landlord elects. The landlord shall not commingle such moneys with any other funds of the landlord or hypothecate, pledge, or in any other way make use of such moneys until such moneys are actually due the landlord; or

(c) Post a surety bond, executed by the landlord as principal and a surety company authorized and licensed to do business in the state as surety, with the clerk of the circuit court in the county in which the dwelling unit is located in the total amount of the security deposits and advance rent he or she holds on behalf of the tenants or $50,000, whichever is less. The bond shall be conditioned upon the faithful compliance of the landlord with the provisions of this section and shall run to the Governor for the benefit of any tenant injured by the landlord's violation of the provisions of this section. In addition to posting the surety bond, the landlord shall pay to the tenant interest at the rate of 5 percent per year, simple interest. A landlord, or the landlord's agent, engaged in the renting of dwelling units in five or more counties, who holds deposit moneys or advance rent and who is otherwise subject to the provisions of this section, may, in lieu of posting a surety bond in each county, elect to post a surety bond in the form and manner provided in this paragraph with the office of the Secretary of State. The bond shall be in the total amount of the security deposit or advance rent held on behalf of tenants or in the amount of $250,000, whichever is less. The bond shall be conditioned upon the faithful compliance of the landlord with the provisions of this section and shall run to the Governor for the benefit of any tenant injured by the landlord's violation of this section. In addition to posting a surety bond, the landlord shall pay to the tenant interest on the security deposit or advance rent held on behalf of that tenant at the rate of 5 percent per year simple interest.

(2) The landlord shall, within 30 days of receipt of advance rent or a security deposit, notify the tenant in writing of the manner in which the landlord is holding the advance rent or security deposit and the rate of interest, if any, which the tenant is to receive and the time of interest payments to the tenant. Such written notice shall:

(a) Be given in person or by mail to the tenant.

(b) State the name and address of the depository where the advance rent or security deposit is being held, whether the advance rent or security deposit is being held in a separate account for the benefit of the tenant or is commingled with other funds of the landlord, and, if commingled, whether such funds are deposited in an interest-bearing account in a Florida banking institution.

(c)   Include a copy of the provisions of subsection (3).

Subsequent to providing such notice, if the landlord changes the manner or location in which he or she is holding the advance rent or security deposit, he or she shall notify the tenant within 30 days of the change according to the provisions herein set forth. This subsection does not apply to any landlord who rents fewer than five individual dwelling units. Failure to provide this notice shall not be a defense to the payment of rent when due.

(3)(a)   Upon the vacating of the premises for termination of the lease, if the landlord does not intend to impose a claim on the security deposit, the landlord shall have 15 days to return the security deposit together with interest if otherwise required, or the landlord shall have 30 days to give the tenant written notice by certified mail to the tenant's last known mailing address of his or her intention to impose a claim on the deposit and the reason for imposing the claim. The notice shall contain a statement in substantially the following form:

This is a notice of my intention to impose a claim for damages in the amount of _____ upon your security deposit, due to _____. It is sent to you as required by s. 83.49(3), Florida Statutes. You are hereby notified that you must object in writing to this deduction from your security deposit within 15 days from the time you receive this notice or I will be authorized to deduct my claim from your security deposit. Your objection must be sent to   (landlord's address) .

If the landlord fails to give the required notice within the 30-day period, he or she forfeits the right to impose a claim upon the security deposit.

(b)   Unless the tenant objects to the imposition of the landlord's claim or the amount thereof within 15 days after receipt of the landlord's notice of intention to impose a claim, the landlord may then deduct the amount of his or her claim and shall remit the balance of the deposit to the tenant within 30 days after the date of the notice of intention to impose a claim for damages.

(c)   If either party institutes an action in a court of competent jurisdiction to adjudicate the party's right to the security deposit, the prevailing party is entitled to receive his or her court costs plus a reasonable fee for his or her attorney. The court shall advance the cause on the calendar.

(d)   Compliance with this section by an individual or business entity authorized to conduct business in this state, including Florida-licensed real estate brokers and sales associates, shall constitute compliance with all other relevant Florida Statutes pertaining to security deposits held pursuant to a rental agreement or other landlord-tenant relationship. Enforcement personnel shall look solely to this section to determine compliance. This section prevails over any conflicting provisions in chapter 475 and in other sections of the Florida Statutes, and shall operate to permit licensed real estate brokers to disburse security deposits and deposit money without having to comply with the notice and settlement procedures contained in s. 475.25(1)(d).

(4)   The provisions of this section do not apply to transient rentals by hotels or motels as defined in chapter 509; nor do they apply in those instances in which the amount of rent or deposit, or both, is regulated by law or by rules or regulations of a public body, including public housing authorities and federally administered or regulated housing programs including s. 202, s. 221(d)(3) and (4), s. 236, or s. 8 of the National Housing Act, as amended, other than for rent stabilization. With the exception of subsections (3), (5), and (6), this section is not applicable to housing authorities or public housing agencies created pursuant to chapter 421 or other statutes.

(5)   Except when otherwise provided by the terms of a written lease, any tenant who vacates or abandons the premises prior to the expiration of the term specified in the written lease, or any tenant who vacates or abandons premises which are the subject of a tenancy from week to week, month to month, quarter to quarter, or year to year, shall give at least 7 days' written notice by certified mail or personal delivery to the landlord prior to vacating or abandoning the premises which notice shall include the address where the tenant may be reached. Failure to give such notice shall relieve the landlord of the notice requirement of paragraph (3)(a) but shall not waive any right the tenant may have to the security deposit or any part of it.

(6)   For the purposes of this part, a renewal of an existing rental agreement shall be considered a new rental agreement, and any security deposit carried forward shall be considered a new security deposit.

(7)   Upon the sale or transfer of title of the rental property from one owner to another, or upon a change in the designated rental agent, any and all security deposits or advance rents being held for the benefit of the tenants shall be transferred to the new owner or agent, together with any earned interest and with an accurate accounting showing the amounts to be credited to each tenant account. Upon the transfer of such funds and records as stated herein, and upon transmittal of a written receipt therefor, the transferor shall be free from the obligation imposed in subsection (1) to hold such moneys on behalf of the tenant. However, nothing herein shall excuse the landlord or agent for a violation of the provisions of this section while in possession of such deposits.

(8)   Any person licensed under the provisions of s. 509.241, unless excluded by the provisions of this part, who fails to comply with the provisions of this part shall be subject to a fine or to the suspension or revocation of his or her license by the Division of Hotels and Restaurants of the Department of Business and Professional Regulation in the manner provided in s. 509.261.

(9)   In those cases in which interest is required to be paid to the tenant, the landlord shall pay directly to the tenant, or credit against the current month's rent, the interest due to the tenant at least once annually. However, no interest shall be due a tenant who wrongfully terminates his or her tenancy prior to the end of the rental term.

History.—s. 1, ch. 69-282; s. 3, ch. 70-360; s. 1, ch. 72-19; s. 1, ch. 72-43; s. 5, ch. 73-330; s. 1, ch. 74-93; s. 3, ch. 74-146; ss. 1, 2, ch. 75-133; s. 1, ch. 76-15; s. 1, ch. 77-445; s. 20, ch. 79-400; s. 21, ch. 82-66; s. 5, ch. 83-151; s. 13, ch. 83-217; s. 3, ch. 87-195; s. 1, ch. 87-369; s. 3, ch. 88-379; s. 2, ch. 93-255; s. 5, ch. 94-218; s. 1372, ch. 95-147; s. 1, ch. 96-146; s. 1, ch. 2001-179; s. 53, ch. 2003-164.

Note.—Former s. 83.261.

83.50 Disclosure.—

(1)   The landlord, or a person authorized to enter into a rental agreement on the landlord's behalf, shall disclose in writing to the tenant, at or before the commencement of the tenancy, the name and address of the landlord or a person authorized to receive notices and demands in the landlord's behalf. The person so authorized to receive notices and demands retains authority until the tenant is notified otherwise. All notices of such names and addresses or changes thereto shall be delivered to the tenant's residence or, if specified in writing by the tenant, to any other address.

(2)   The landlord or the landlord's authorized representative, upon completion of construction of a building exceeding three stories in height and containing dwelling units, shall disclose to the tenants initially moving into the building the availability or lack of availability of fire protection.

History.—s. 2, ch. 73-330; s. 443, ch. 95-147.

83.51 Landlord's obligation to maintain premises.—

(1)   The landlord at all times during the tenancy shall:

(a)   Comply with the requirements of applicable building, housing, and health codes; or

(b)   Where there are no applicable building, housing, or health codes, maintain the roofs, windows, screens, doors, floors, steps, porches, exterior walls, foundations, and all other structural components in good repair and capable of resisting normal forces and loads and the plumbing in reasonable working condition. However, the landlord shall not be required to maintain a mobile home or other structure owned by the tenant.

The landlord's obligations under this subsection may be altered or modified in writing with respect to a single-family home or duplex.

(2)(a)   Unless otherwise agreed in writing, in addition to the requirements of subsection (1), the landlord of a dwelling unit other than a single-family home or duplex shall, at all times during the tenancy, make reasonable provisions for:

1.   The extermination of rats, mice, roaches, ants, wood-destroying organisms, and bedbugs. When vacation of the premises is required for such extermination, the landlord shall not be liable for damages but shall abate the rent. The tenant shall be required to temporarily vacate the premises for a period of time not to exceed 4 days, on 7 days' written notice, if necessary, for extermination pursuant to this subparagraph.

2.   Locks and keys.

3.   The clean and safe condition of common areas.

4.   Garbage removal and outside receptacles therefor.

5.   Functioning facilities for heat during winter, running water, and hot water.

(b)   Unless otherwise agreed in writing, at the commencement of the tenancy of a single-family home or duplex, the landlord shall install working smoke detection devices. As used in this paragraph, the term "smoke detection device" means an electrical or battery-operated device which detects visible or invisible particles of combustion and which is listed by Underwriters Laboratories, Inc., Factory Mutual Laboratories, Inc., or any other nationally recognized testing laboratory using nationally accepted testing standards.

(c)   Nothing in this part authorizes the tenant to raise a noncompliance by the landlord with this subsection as a defense to an action for possession under s. 83.59.

(d)   This subsection shall not apply to a mobile home owned by a tenant.

(e)   Nothing contained in this subsection prohibits the landlord from providing in the rental agreement that the tenant is obligated to pay costs or charges for garbage removal, water, fuel, or utilities.

(3)   If the duty imposed by subsection (1) is the same or greater than any duty imposed by subsection (2), the landlord's duty is determined by subsection (1).

(4)   The landlord is not responsible to the tenant under this section for conditions created or caused by the negligent or wrongful act or omission of the tenant, a member of the tenant's family, or other person on the premises with the tenant's consent.

History.—s. 2, ch. 73-330; s. 22, ch. 82-66; s. 4, ch. 87-195; s. 1, ch. 90-133; s. 3, ch. 93-255; s. 444, ch. 95-147; s. 8, ch. 97-95.

83.52 Tenant's obligation to maintain dwelling unit.—The tenant at all times during the tenancy shall:

(1)   Comply with all obligations imposed upon tenants by applicable provisions of building, housing, and health codes.

(2)   Keep that part of the premises which he or she occupies and uses clean and sanitary.

(3)   Remove from the tenant's dwelling unit all garbage in a clean and sanitary manner.

(4)   Keep all plumbing fixtures in the dwelling unit or used by the tenant clean and sanitary and in repair.

(5)   Use and operate in a reasonable manner all electrical, plumbing, sanitary, heating, ventilating, air-conditioning and other facilities and appliances, including elevators.

(6) Not destroy, deface, damage, impair, or remove any part of the premises or property therein belonging to the landlord nor permit any person to do so.

(7) Conduct himself or herself, and require other persons on the premises with his or her consent to conduct themselves, in a manner that does not unreasonably disturb the tenant's neighbors or constitute a breach of the peace.

History.—s. 2, ch. 73-330; s. 445, ch. 95-147.

83.53 Landlord's access to dwelling unit.—

(1) The tenant shall not unreasonably withhold consent to the landlord to enter the dwelling unit from time to time in order to inspect the premises; make necessary or agreed repairs, decorations, alterations, or improvements; supply agreed services; or exhibit the dwelling unit to prospective or actual purchasers, mortgagees, tenants, workers, or contractors.

(2) The landlord may enter the dwelling unit at any time for the protection or preservation of the premises. The landlord may enter the dwelling unit upon reasonable notice to the tenant and at a reasonable time for the purpose of repair of the premises. "Reasonable notice" for the purpose of repair is notice given at least 12 hours prior to the entry, and reasonable time for the purpose of repair shall be between the hours of 7:30 a.m. and 8:00 p.m. The landlord may enter the dwelling unit when necessary for the further purposes set forth in subsection (1) under any of the following circumstances:

(a) With the consent of the tenant;

(b) In case of emergency;

(c) When the tenant unreasonably withholds consent; or

(d) If the tenant is absent from the premises for a period of time equal to one-half the time for periodic rental payments. If the rent is current and the tenant notifies the landlord of an intended absence, then the landlord may enter only with the consent of the tenant or for the protection or preservation of the premises.

(3) The landlord shall not abuse the right of access nor use it to harass the tenant.

History.—s. 2, ch. 73-330; s. 5, ch. 87-195; s. 4, ch. 93-255; s. 446, ch. 95-147.

83.535 Flotation bedding system; restrictions on use.—No landlord may prohibit a tenant from using a flotation bedding system in a dwelling unit, provided the flotation bedding system does not violate applicable building codes. The tenant shall be required to carry in the tenant's name flotation insurance as is standard in the industry in an amount deemed reasonable to protect the tenant and owner against personal injury and property damage to the dwelling units. In any case, the policy shall carry a loss payable clause to the owner of the building.

History.—s. 7, ch. 82-66; s. 5, ch. 93-255.

83.54 Enforcement of rights and duties; civil action.—Any right or duty declared in this part is enforceable by civil action.

History.—s. 2, ch. 73-330.

83.55 Right of action for damages.—If either the landlord or the tenant fails to comply with the requirements of the rental agreement or this part, the aggrieved party may recover the damages caused by the noncompliance.

History.—s. 2, ch. 73-330.

83.56 Termination of rental agreement.—

(1) If the landlord materially fails to comply with s. 83.51(1) or material provisions of the rental agreement within 7 days after delivery of written notice by the tenant specifying the noncompliance and indicating the intention of the tenant to terminate the rental agreement by reason thereof, the tenant may terminate the rental agreement. If the failure to comply with s. 83.51(1) or material provisions of the rental agreement is due to causes beyond the control of the landlord and the landlord has made and continues to make every reasonable effort to correct the failure to comply, the rental agreement may be terminated or altered by the parties, as follows:

(a) If the landlord's failure to comply renders the dwelling unit untenantable and the tenant vacates, the tenant shall not be liable for rent during the period the dwelling unit remains uninhabitable.

(b) If the landlord's failure to comply does not render the dwelling unit untenantable and the tenant remains in occupancy, the rent for the period of noncompliance shall be reduced by an amount in proportion to the loss of rental value caused by the noncompliance.

(2) If the tenant materially fails to comply with s. 83.52 or material provisions of the rental agreement, other than a failure to pay rent, or reasonable rules or regulations, the landlord may:

(a) If such noncompliance is of a nature that the tenant should not be given an opportunity to cure it or if the noncompliance constitutes a subsequent or continuing noncompliance within 12 months of a written warning by the landlord of a similar violation, deliver a written notice to the tenant specifying the noncompliance and the landlord's intent to terminate the rental agreement by reason thereof. Examples of noncompliance which are of a nature that the tenant should not be given an opportunity to cure include, but are not limited to, destruction, damage, or misuse of the landlord's or other tenants' property by intentional act or a subsequent or continued unreasonable disturbance. In such event, the landlord may terminate the rental agreement, and the tenant shall have 7 days from the date that the notice is delivered to vacate the premises. The notice shall be adequate if it is in substantially the following form:

You are advised that your lease is terminated effective immediately. You shall have 7 days from the delivery of this letter to vacate the premises. This action is taken because   (cite the noncompliance) .

(b) If such noncompliance is of a nature that the tenant should be given an opportunity to cure it, deliver a written notice to the tenant specifying the noncompliance, including a notice that, if the noncompliance is not corrected within 7 days from the date the written notice is delivered, the landlord shall terminate the rental agreement by reason thereof. Examples of such noncompliance include, but are not limited to, activities in contravention of the lease or this act such as having or permitting unauthorized pets, guests, or vehicles; parking in an unauthorized manner or permitting such parking; or failing to keep the premises clean and sanitary. The notice shall be adequate if it is in substantially the following form:

You are hereby notified that (cite the noncompliance) . Demand is hereby made that you remedy the noncompliance within 7 days of receipt of this notice or your lease shall be deemed terminated and you shall vacate the premises upon such termination. If this same conduct or conduct of a similar nature is repeated within 12 months, your tenancy is subject to termination without your being given an opportunity to cure the noncompliance.

(3)   If the tenant fails to pay rent when due and the default continues for 3 days, excluding Saturday, Sunday, and legal holidays, after delivery of written demand by the landlord for payment of the rent or possession of the premises, the landlord may terminate the rental agreement. Legal holidays for the purpose of this section shall be court-observed holidays only. The 3-day notice shall contain a statement in substantially the following form:

You are hereby notified that you are indebted to me in the sum of _____ dollars for the rent and use of the premises (address of leased premises, including county) , Florida, now occupied by you and that I demand payment of the rent or possession of the premises within 3 days (excluding Saturday, Sunday, and legal holidays) from the date of delivery of this notice, to wit: on or before the _____ day of _____, (year) .

(landlord's name, address and phone number)

(4)   The delivery of the written notices required by subsections (1), (2), and (3) shall be by mailing or delivery of a true copy thereof or, if the tenant is absent from the premises, by leaving a copy thereof at the residence.

(5)   If the landlord accepts rent with actual knowledge of a noncompliance by the tenant or accepts performance by the tenant of any other provision of the rental agreement that is at variance with its provisions, or if the tenant pays rent with actual knowledge of a noncompliance by the landlord or accepts performance by the landlord of any other provision of the rental agreement that is at variance with its provisions, the landlord or tenant waives his or her right to terminate the rental agreement or to bring a civil action for that noncompliance, but not for any subsequent or continuing noncompliance. Any tenant who wishes to defend against an action by the landlord for possession of the unit for noncompliance of the rental agreement or of relevant statutes shall comply with the provisions in s. 83.60(2). The court may not set a date for mediation or trial unless the provisions of s. 83.60(2) have been met, but shall enter a default judgment for removal of the tenant with a writ of possession to issue immediately if the tenant fails to comply with s. 83.60(2). This subsection does not apply to that portion of rent subsidies received from a local, state, or national government or an agency of local, state, or national government; however, waiver will occur if an action has not been instituted within 45 days of the non-

compliance.

(6)   If the rental agreement is terminated, the landlord shall comply with s. 83.49(3).

History.—s. 2, ch. 73-330; s. 23, ch. 82-66; s. 6, ch. 83-151; s. 14, ch. 83-217; s. 6, ch. 87-195; s. 6, ch. 93-255; s. 6, ch. 94-170; s. 1373, ch. 95-147; s. 5, ch. 99-6.

83.57   Termination of tenancy without specific term.—A tenancy without a specific duration, as defined in s. 83.46(2) or (3), may be terminated by either party giving written notice in the manner provided in s. 83.56(4), as follows:

(1)   When the tenancy is from year to year, by giving not less than 60 days' notice prior to the end of any annual period;

(2)   When the tenancy is from quarter to quarter, by giving not less than 30 days' notice prior to the end of any quarterly period;

(3)   When the tenancy is from month to month, by giving not less than 15 days' notice prior to the end of any monthly period; and

(4)   When the tenancy is from week to week, by giving not less than 7 days' notice prior to the end of any weekly period.

History.—s. 2, ch. 73-330; s. 3, ch. 81-190; s. 15, ch. 83-217.

83.575   Termination of tenancy with specific duration.—

(1)   A rental agreement with a specific duration may contain a provision requiring the tenant to notify the landlord before vacating the premises at the end of the rental agreement; however, a rental agreement may not require more than 60 days' notice before vacating the premises.

(2)   A rental agreement with a specific duration may provide that if a tenant fails to give the required notice before vacating the premises at the end of the rental agreement, the tenant may be liable for liquidated damages as specified in the rental agreement if the landlord provides written notice to the tenant specifying the tenant's obligations under the notification provision contained in the lease and the date the rental agreement is terminated. The landlord must provide such written notice to the tenant within 15 days before the start of the notification period contained in the lease. The written notice shall list all fees, penalties, and other charges applicable to the tenant under this subsection.

(3)   If the tenant remains on the premises with the permission of the landlord after the rental agreement has terminated and fails to give notice required under s. 83.57(3), the tenant is liable to the landlord for an additional 1 month's rent.

History.—s. 3, ch. 2003-30; s. 1, ch. 2004-375.

83.58   Remedies; tenant holding over.—If the tenant holds over and continues in possession of the dwelling unit or any part thereof after the expiration of the rental agreement without the permission of the landlord, the landlord may recover possession of the dwelling unit in the manner provided for in s. 83.59 [F.S. 1973]. The landlord may also recover double the amount of rent due on the dwelling unit, or any part thereof, for the period during which the tenant refuses to surrender possession.

History.—s. 2, ch. 73-330.

83.59 Right of action for possession.—

(1) If the rental agreement is terminated and the tenant does not vacate the premises, the landlord may recover possession of the dwelling unit as provided in this section.

(2) A landlord, the landlord's attorney, or the landlord's agent, applying for the removal of a tenant shall file in the county court of the county where the premises are situated a complaint describing the dwelling unit and stating the facts that authorize its recovery. A landlord's agent is not permitted to take any action other than the initial filing of the complaint, unless the landlord's agent is an attorney. The landlord is entitled to the summary procedure provided in s. 51.011 [F.S. 1971], and the court shall advance the cause on the calendar.

(3) The landlord shall not recover possession of a dwelling unit except:

(a) In an action for possession under subsection (2) or other civil action in which the issue of right of possession is determined;

(b) When the tenant has surrendered possession of the dwelling unit to the landlord;

(c) When the tenant has abandoned the dwelling unit. In the absence of actual knowledge of abandonment, it shall be presumed that the tenant has abandoned the dwelling unit if he or she is absent from the premises for a period of time equal to one-half the time for periodic rental payments. However, this presumption does not apply if the rent is current or the tenant has notified the landlord, in writing, of an intended absence; or

(d) When the last remaining tenant of a dwelling unit is deceased, personal property remains on the premises, rent is unpaid, at least 60 days have elapsed following the date of death, and the landlord has not been notified in writing of the existence of a probate estate or of the name and address of a personal representative. This paragraph does not apply to a dwelling unit used in connection with a federally administered or regulated housing program, including programs under s. 202, s. 221(d)(3) and (4), s. 236, or s. 8 of the National Housing Act, as amended.

(4) The prevailing party is entitled to have judgment for costs and execution therefor.

History.—s. 2, ch. 73-330; s. 1, ch. 74-146; s. 24, ch. 82-66; s. 1, ch. 92-36; s. 447, ch. 95-147; s. 1, ch. 2007-136.

83.595 Choice of remedies upon breach or early termination by tenant.—If the tenant breaches the rental agreement for the dwelling unit and the landlord has obtained a writ of possession, or the tenant has surrendered possession of the dwelling unit to the landlord, or the tenant has abandoned the dwelling unit, the landlord may:

(1) Treat the rental agreement as terminated and retake possession for his or her own account, thereby terminating any further liability of the tenant;

(2) Retake possession of the dwelling unit for the account of the tenant, holding the tenant liable for the difference between the rent stipulated to be paid under the rental agreement and what the landlord is able to recover from a reletting. If the landlord retakes possession, the landlord has a duty to exercise good faith in attempting to relet the premises, and any rent received by the landlord as a result of the reletting must be deducted from the balance of rent due from the tenant. For purposes of this subsection, the term "good faith in attempting to relet the premises" means that the landlord uses at least the same efforts to relet the premises as were used in the initial rental or at least the same efforts as the landlord uses in attempting to rent other similar rental units but does not require the landlord to give a preference in renting the premises over other vacant dwelling units that the landlord owns or has the responsibility to rent;

(3) Stand by and do nothing, holding the lessee liable for the rent as it comes due; or

(4) Charge liquidated damages, as provided in the rental agreement, or an early termination fee to the tenant if the landlord and tenant have agreed to liquidated damages or an early termination fee, if the amount does not exceed 2 months' rent, and if, in the case of an early termination fee, the tenant is required to give no more than 60 days' notice, as provided in the rental agreement, prior to the proposed date of early termination. This remedy is available only if the tenant and the landlord, at the time the rental agreement was made, indicated acceptance of liquidated damages or an early termination fee. The tenant must indicate acceptance of liquidated damages or an early termination fee by signing a separate addendum to the rental agreement containing a provision in substantially the following form:

[ ] I agree, as provided in the rental agreement, to pay $_____ (an amount that does not exceed 2 months' rent) as liquidated damages or an early termination fee if I elect to terminate the rental agreement, and the landlord waives the right to seek additional rent beyond the month in which the landlord retakes possession.

[ ] I do not agree to liquidated damages or an early termination fee, and I acknowledge that the landlord may seek damages as provided by law.

(a) In addition to liquidated damages or an early termination fee, the landlord is entitled to the rent and other charges accrued through the end of the month in which the landlord retakes possession of the dwelling unit and charges for damages to the dwelling unit.

(b) This subsection does not apply if the breach is failure to give notice as provided in s. 83.575.

History.—s. 2, ch. 87-369; s. 4, ch. 88-379; s. 448, ch. 95-147; s. 2, ch. 2008-131.

83.60 Defenses to action for rent or possession; procedure.—

(1)   In an action by the landlord for possession of a dwelling unit based upon nonpayment of rent or in an action by the landlord under s. 83.55 seeking to recover unpaid rent, the tenant may defend upon the ground of a material noncompliance with s. 83.51(1) [F.S. 1973], or may raise any other defense, whether legal or equitable, that he or she may have, including the defense of retaliatory conduct in accordance with s. 83.64. The defense of a material noncompliance with s. 83.51(1) [F.S. 1973] may be raised by the tenant if 7 days have elapsed after the delivery of written notice by the tenant to the landlord, specifying the noncompliance and indicating the intention of the tenant not to pay rent by reason thereof. Such notice by the tenant may be given to the landlord, the landlord's representative as designated pursuant to s. 83.50(1), a resident manager, or the person or entity who collects the rent on behalf of the landlord. A material noncompliance with s. 83.51(1) [F.S. 1973] by the landlord is a complete defense to an action for possession based upon nonpayment of rent, and, upon hearing, the court or the jury, as the case may be, shall determine the amount, if any, by which the rent is to be reduced to reflect the diminution in value of the dwelling unit during the period of noncompliance with s. 83.51(1) [F.S. 1973]. After consideration of all other relevant issues, the court shall enter appropriate judgment.

(2)   In an action by the landlord for possession of a dwelling unit, if the tenant interposes any defense other than payment, the tenant shall pay into the registry of the court the accrued rent as alleged in the complaint or as determined by the court and the rent which accrues during the pendency of the proceeding, when due. The clerk shall notify the tenant of such requirement in the summons. Failure of the tenant to pay the rent into the registry of the court or to file a motion to determine the amount of rent to be paid into the registry within 5 days, excluding Saturdays, Sundays, and legal holidays, after the date of service of process constitutes an absolute waiver of the tenant's defenses other than payment, and the landlord is entitled to an immediate default judgment for removal of the tenant with a writ of possession to issue without further notice or hearing thereon. In the event a motion to determine rent is filed, documentation in support of the allegation that the rent as alleged in the complaint is in error is required. Public housing tenants or tenants receiving rent subsidies shall be required to deposit only that portion of the full rent for which the tenant is responsible pursuant to federal, state, or local program in which they are participating.

History.—s. 2, ch. 73-330; s. 7, ch. 83-151; s. 7, ch. 87-195; s. 7, ch. 93-255; s. 7, ch. 94-170; s. 1374, ch. 95-147.

83.61 Disbursement of funds in registry of court; prompt final hearing.—When the tenant has deposited funds into the registry of the court in accordance with the provisions of s. 83.60(2) and the landlord is in actual danger of loss of the premises or other personal hardship resulting from the loss of rental income from the premises, the landlord may apply to the court for disbursement of all or part of the funds or for prompt final hearing. The court shall advance the cause on the calendar. The court, after preliminary hearing, may award all or any portion of the funds on deposit to the landlord or may proceed immediately to a final resolution of the cause.

History.—s. 2, ch. 73-330; s. 2, ch. 74-146.

83.62 Restoration of possession to landlord.—

(1)   In an action for possession, after entry of judgment in favor of the landlord, the clerk shall issue a writ to the sheriff describing the premises and commanding the sheriff to put the landlord in possession after 24 hours' notice conspicuously posted on the premises.

(2)   At the time the sheriff executes the writ of possession or at any time thereafter, the landlord or the landlord's agent may remove any personal property found on the premises to or near the property line. Subsequent to executing the writ of possession, the landlord may request the sheriff to stand by to keep the peace while the landlord changes the locks and removes the personal property from the premises. When such a request is made, the sheriff may charge a reasonable hourly rate, and the person requesting the sheriff to stand by to keep the peace shall be responsible for paying the reasonable hourly rate set by the sheriff. Neither the sheriff nor the landlord or the landlord's agent shall be liable to the tenant or any other party for the loss, destruction, or damage to the property after it has been removed.

History.—s. 2, ch. 73-330; s. 3, ch. 82-66; s. 5, ch. 88-379; s. 8, ch. 94-170; s. 1375, ch. 95-147; s. 2, ch. 96-146.

83.625 Power to award possession and enter money judgment.—
In an action by the landlord for possession of a dwelling unit based upon nonpayment of rent, if the court finds the rent is due, owing, and unpaid and by reason thereof the landlord is entitled to possession of the premises, the court, in addition to awarding possession of the premises to the landlord, shall direct, in an amount which is within its jurisdictional limitations, the entry of a money judgment with costs in favor of the landlord and against the tenant for the amount of money found due, owing, and unpaid by the tenant to the landlord. However, no money judgment shall be entered unless service of process has been effected by personal service or, where authorized by law, by certified or registered mail, return receipt, or in any other manner prescribed by law or the rules of the court; and no money judgment may be entered except in compliance with the Florida Rules of Civil Procedure. The prevailing party in the action may also be awarded attorney's fees and costs.

History.—s. 1, ch. 75-147; s. 8, ch. 87-195; s. 6, ch. 88-379.

83.63   Casualty damage.—If the premises are damaged or destroyed other than by the wrongful or negligent acts of the tenant so that the enjoyment of the premises is substantially impaired, the tenant may terminate the rental agreement and immediately vacate the premises. The tenant may vacate the part of the premises rendered unusable by the casualty, in which case the tenant's liability for rent shall be reduced by the fair rental value of that part of the premises damaged or destroyed. If the rental agreement is terminated, the landlord shall comply with s. 83.49(3) [F.S. 1973].

History.—s. 2, ch. 73-330; s. 449, ch. 95-147.

83.64   Retaliatory conduct.—

(1)   It is unlawful for a landlord to discriminatorily increase a tenant's rent or decrease services to a tenant, or to bring or threaten to

bring an action for possession or other civil action, primarily because the landlord is retaliating against the tenant. In order for the tenant to raise the defense of retaliatory conduct, the tenant must have acted in good faith. Examples of conduct for which the landlord may not retaliate include, but are not limited to, situations where:

(a)   The tenant has complained to a governmental agency charged with responsibility for enforcement of a building, housing, or health code of a suspected violation applicable to the premises;

(b)   The tenant has organized, encouraged, or participated in a tenants' organization;

(c)   The tenant has complained to the landlord pursuant to s. 83.56(1); or

(d)   The tenant is a servicemember who has terminated a rental agreement pursuant to s. 83.682.

(2)   Evidence of retaliatory conduct may be raised by the tenant as a defense in any action brought against him or her for possession.

(3)   In any event, this section does not apply if the landlord proves that the eviction is for good cause. Examples of good cause include, but are not limited to, good faith actions for nonpayment of rent, violation of the rental agreement or of reasonable rules, or violation of the terms of this chapter.

(4)   "Discrimination" under this section means that a tenant is being treated differently as to the rent charged, the services rendered, or the action being taken by the landlord, which shall be a prerequisite to a finding of retaliatory conduct.

History.—s. 8, ch. 83-151; s. 450, ch. 95-147; s. 3, ch. 2003-72.

83.67 Prohibited practices.—

(1)   A landlord of any dwelling unit governed by this part shall not cause, directly or indirectly, the termination or interruption of any utility service furnished the tenant, including, but not limited to, water, heat, light, electricity, gas, elevator, garbage collection, or refrigeration, whether or not the utility service is under the control of, or payment is made by, the landlord.

(2)   A landlord of any dwelling unit governed by this part shall not prevent the tenant from gaining reasonable access to the dwelling unit by any means, including, but not limited to, changing the locks or using any bootlock or similar device.

(3)   A landlord of any dwelling unit governed by this part shall not discriminate against a servicemember in offering a dwelling unit for rent or in any of the terms of the rental agreement.

(4)   A landlord shall not prohibit a tenant from displaying one portable, removable, cloth or plastic United States flag, not larger than 4 and 1/2 feet by 6 feet, in a respectful manner in or on the dwelling unit regardless of any provision in the rental agreement dealing with flags or decorations. The United States flag shall be displayed in accordance with s. 83.52(6). The landlord is not liable for damages caused by a United States flag displayed by a tenant. Any United

States flag may not infringe upon the space rented by any other tenant.

(5)   A landlord of any dwelling unit governed by this part shall not remove the outside doors, locks, roof, walls, or windows of the unit except for purposes of maintenance, repair, or replacement; and the landlord shall not remove the tenant's personal property from the dwelling unit unless such action is taken after surrender, abandonment, recovery of possession of the dwelling unit due to the death of the last remaining tenant in accordance with s. 83.59(3)(d), or a lawful eviction. If provided in the rental agreement or a written agreement separate from the rental agreement, upon surrender or abandonment by the tenant, the landlord is not required to comply with s. 715.104 and is not liable or responsible for storage or disposition of the tenant's personal property; if provided in the rental agreement, there must be printed or clearly stamped on such rental agreement a legend in substantially the following form:

BY SIGNING THIS RENTAL AGREEMENT, THE TENANT AGREES THAT UPON SURRENDER, ABANDONMENT, OR RECOVERY OF POSSESSION OF THE DWELLING UNIT DUE TO THE DEATH OF THE LAST REMAINING TENANT, AS PROVIDED BY CHAPTER 83, FLORIDA STATUTES, THE LANDLORD SHALL NOT BE LIABLE OR RESPONSIBLE FOR STORAGE OR DISPOSITION OF THE TENANT'S PERSONAL PROPERTY.

For the purposes of this section, abandonment shall be as set forth in s. 83.59(3)(c).

(6)   A landlord who violates any provision of this section shall be liable to the tenant for actual and consequential damages or 3 months' rent, whichever is greater, and costs, including attorney's fees. Subsequent or repeated violations that are not contemporaneous with the initial violation shall be subject to separate awards of damages.

(7)   A violation of this section constitutes irreparable harm for the purposes of injunctive relief.

(8)   The remedies provided by this section are not exclusive and do not preclude the tenant from pursuing any other remedy at law or equity that the tenant may have. The remedies provided by this section shall also apply to a servicemember who is a prospective tenant who has been discriminated against under subsection (3).

History.—s. 3, ch. 87-369; s. 7, ch. 88-379; s. 3, ch. 90-133; s. 3, ch. 96-146; s. 2, ch. 2001-179; s. 2, ch. 2003-30; s. 4, ch. 2003-72; s. 1, ch. 2004-236; s. 2, ch. 2007-136.

83.681 Orders to enjoin violations of this part.—

(1)   A landlord who gives notice to a tenant of the landlord's intent to terminate the tenant's lease pursuant to s. 83.56(2)(a), due to the tenant's intentional destruction, damage, or misuse of the landlord's property may petition the county or circuit court for an injunction prohibiting the tenant from continuing to violate any of the provisions of that part.

(2)   The court shall grant the relief requested pursuant to subsection (1) in conformity with the principles that govern the granting of injunctive relief from threatened loss or damage in other civil cases.

(3)   Evidence of a tenant's intentional destruction, damage, or misuse of the landlord's property in an amount greater than twice the value of money deposited with the landlord pursuant to s. 83.49 or $300, whichever is greater, shall constitute irreparable harm for the purposes of injunctive relief.

History.—s. 8, ch. 93-255; s. 451, ch. 95-147.

83.682   Termination of rental agreement by a servicemember.—

(1)   Any servicemember may terminate his or her rental agreement by providing the landlord with a written notice of termination to be effective on the date stated in the notice that is at least 30 days after the landlord's receipt of the notice if any of the following criteria are met:

(a)   The servicemember is required, pursuant to a permanent change of station orders, to move 35 miles or more from the location of the rental premises;

(b)   The servicemember is prematurely or involuntarily discharged or released from active duty or state active duty;

(c)   The servicemember is released from active duty or state active duty after having leased the rental premises while on active duty or state active duty status and the rental premises is 35 miles or more from the servicemember's home of record prior to entering active duty or state active duty;

(d)   After entering into a rental agreement, the servicemember receives military orders requiring him or her to move into government quarters or the servicemember becomes eligible to live in and opts to move into government quarters;

(e)   The servicemember receives temporary duty orders, temporary change of station orders, or state active duty orders to an area 35 miles or more from the location of the rental premises, provided such orders are for a period exceeding 60 days; or

(f)   The servicemember has leased the property, but prior to taking possession of the rental premises, receives a change of orders to an area that is 35 miles or more from the location of the rental premises.

(2)   The notice to the landlord must be accompanied by either a copy of the official military orders or a written verification signed by the servicemember's commanding officer.

(3)   In the event a servicemember dies during active duty, an adult member of his or her immediate family may terminate the servicemember's rental agreement by providing the landlord with a written notice of termination to be effective on the date stated in the notice that is at least 30 days after the landlord's receipt of the notice. The notice to the landlord must be accompanied by either a copy of the official military orders showing the servicemember was

on active duty or a written verification signed by the servicemember's commanding officer and a copy of the servicemember's death certificate.

(4)   Upon termination of a rental agreement under this section, the tenant is liable for the rent due under the rental agreement prorated to the effective date of the termination payable at such time as would have otherwise been required by the terms of the rental agreement. The tenant is not liable for any other rent or damages due to the early termination of the tenancy as provided for in this section. Notwithstanding any provision of this section to the contrary, if a tenant terminates the rental agreement pursuant to this section 14 or more days prior to occupancy, no damages or penalties of any kind will be assessable.

(5)   The provisions of this section may not be waived or modified by the agreement of the parties under any circumstances.

History.—s. 6, ch. 2001-179; s. 1, ch. 2002-4; s. 1, ch. 2003-30; s. 5, ch. 2003-72.

PART III

SELF-SERVICE STORAGE SPACE

83.801   Short title.

83.803   Definitions.

83.805   Lien.

83.8055   Withholding access to personal property upon nonpayment of rent.

83.806   Enforcement of lien.

83.808   Contractual liens.

83.809   Application of act.

83.801   Short title.—Sections 83.801-83.809 shall be known and may be cited as the "Self-storage Facility Act."

History.—s. 1, ch. 79-404; s. 1, ch. 82-151.

83.803   Definitions.—As used in ss. 83.801-83.809:

(1)   "Self-service storage facility" means any real property designed and used for the purpose of renting or leasing individual storage space to tenants who are to have access to such space for the purpose of storing and removing personal property. No individual storage space may be used for residential purposes. A self-service storage facility is not a "warehouse" as that term is used in chapter 677. If an owner issues any warehouse receipt, bill of lading, or other document of title for the personal property stored, the owner and the tenant shall be subject to the provisions of chapter 677, and the provisions of this act shall not apply.

(2)   "Self-contained storage unit" means any unit not less than 200 cubic feet in size, including, but not limited to, a trailer, box, or

other shipping container, which is leased by a tenant primarily for use as storage space whether the unit is located at a facility owned or operated by the owner or at another location designated by the tenant.

(3) "Owner" means the owner, operator, lessor, or sublessor of a self-service storage facility or self-contained storage unit or his or her agent or any other person authorized by him or her to manage the facility or to receive rent from a tenant under a rental agreement.

(4) "Tenant" means a person or the person's sublessee, successor, or assign entitled to the use of storage space at a self-service storage facility or in a self-contained unit, under a rental agreement, to the exclusion of others.

(5) "Rental agreement" means any agreement or lease which establishes or modifies terms, conditions, rules, or any other provisions concerning the use and occupancy of a self-service storage facility or use of a self-contained storage unit.

(6) "Last known address" means that address provided by the tenant in the latest rental agreement or the address provided by the tenant by hand delivery or certified mail in a subsequent written notice of a change of address.

History.—s. 1, ch. 79-404; s. 2, ch. 82-151; s. 2, ch. 92-36; s. 1, ch. 93-238; s. 452, ch. 95-147; s. 1, ch. 2006-4.

83.805 Lien.—The owner of a self-service storage facility or self-contained storage unit and the owner's heirs, executors, administrators, successors, and assigns have a lien upon all personal property, whether or not owned by the tenant, located at a self-service storage facility or in a self-contained storage unit for rent, labor charges, or other charges, present or future, in relation to the personal property and for expenses necessary for its preservation or expenses reasonably incurred in its sale or other disposition pursuant to ss. 83.801-83.809. The lien provided for in this section attaches as of the date that the personal property is brought to the self-service storage facility or as of the date the tenant takes possession of the self-contained storage unit, and the priority of this lien shall be the same as provided in s. 83.08; however, in the event of default, the owner must give notice to persons who hold perfected security interests under the Uniform Commercial Code in which the tenant is named as the debtor.

History.—s. 1, ch. 79-404; s. 3, ch. 82-151; s. 19, ch. 83-217; s. 2, ch. 93-238; s. 453, ch. 95-147.

83.8055 Withholding access to personal property upon nonpayment of rent.—Upon the failure of a tenant to pay the rent when it becomes due, the owner may, without notice, after 5 days from the date the rent is due, deny the tenant access to the personal property located in the self-service storage facility or self-contained storage unit. In denying the tenant access to personal property contained in the self-contained storage unit, the owner may proceed without judicial process, if this can be done without breach of the peace, or may proceed by action.

History.—s. 4, ch. 82-151; s. 3, ch. 93-238.

83.806 Enforcement of lien.—An owner's lien as provided in s. 83.805 may be satisfied as follows:

(1) The tenant shall be notified by written notice delivered in person or by certified mail to the tenant's last known address and conspicuously posted at the self-service storage facility or on the self-contained storage unit.

(2) The notice shall include:

(a) An itemized statement of the owner's claim, showing the sum due at the time of the notice and the date when the sum became due.

(b) The same description, or a reasonably similar description, of the personal property as provided in the rental agreement.

(c) A demand for payment within a specified time not less than 14 days after delivery of the notice.

(d) A conspicuous statement that, unless the claim is paid within the time stated in the notice, the personal property will be advertised for sale or other disposition and will be sold or otherwise disposed of at a specified time and place.

(e) The name, street address, and telephone number of the owner whom the tenant may contact to respond to the notice.

(3) Any notice given pursuant to this section shall be presumed delivered when it is deposited with the United States Postal Service, registered, and properly addressed with postage prepaid.

(4) After the expiration of the time given in the notice, an advertisement of the sale or other disposition shall be published once a week for 2 consecutive weeks in a newspaper of general circulation in the area where the self-service storage facility or self-contained storage unit is located. Inasmuch as any sale may involve property of more than one tenant, a single advertisement may be used to dispose of property at any one sale.

(a) The advertisement shall include:

1. A brief and general description of what is believed to constitute the personal property contained in the storage unit, as provided in paragraph (2)(b).

2. The address of the self-service storage facility or the address where the self-contained storage unit is located and the name of the tenant.

3. The time, place, and manner of the sale or other disposition. The sale or other disposition shall take place not sooner than 15 days after the first publication.

(b) If there is no newspaper of general circulation in the area where the self-service storage facility or self-contained storage unit is located, the advertisement shall be posted at least 10 days before the date of the sale or other disposition in not fewer than three conspicuous places in the neighborhood where the self-service storage facility or self-contained storage unit is located.

(5) Any sale or other disposition of the personal property shall conform to the terms of the notification as provided for in this section and shall be conducted in a commercially reasonable manner, as that term is used in s. 679.610.

(6) Before any sale or other disposition of personal property pursuant to this section, the tenant may pay the amount necessary to satisfy the lien and the reasonable expenses incurred under this section and thereby redeem the personal property. Upon receipt of such payment, the owner shall return the property to the tenant and thereafter shall have no liability to any person with respect to such personal property. If the tenant fails to redeem the personal property or satisfy the lien, including reasonable expenses, he or she will be deemed to have unjustifiably abandoned the self-service storage facility or self-contained storage unit, and the owner may resume possession of the premises for himself or herself.

(7) A purchaser in good faith of the personal property sold to satisfy a lien provided for in s. 83.805 takes the property free of any claims, except those interests provided for in s. 83.808, despite noncompliance by the owner with the requirements of this section.

(8) In the event of a sale under this section, the owner may satisfy his or her lien from the proceeds of the sale, provided the owner's lien has priority over all other liens in the personal property. The lien rights of secured lienholders are automatically transferred to the remaining proceeds of the sale. The balance, if any, shall be held by the owner for delivery on demand to the tenant. A notice of any balance shall be delivered by the owner to the tenant in person or by certified mail to the last known address of the tenant. If the tenant does not claim the balance of the proceeds within 2 years of the date of sale, the proceeds shall be deemed abandoned, and the owner shall have no further obligation with regard to the payment of the balance. In the event that the owner's lien does not have priority over all other liens, the sale proceeds shall be held for the benefit of the holders of those liens having priority. A notice of the amount of the sale proceeds shall be delivered by the owner to the tenant or secured lienholders in person or by certified mail to their last known addresses. If the tenant or the secured lienholders do not claim the sale proceeds within 2 years of the date of sale, the proceeds shall be deemed abandoned, and the owner shall have no further obligation with regard to the payment of the proceeds.

History.—s. 1, ch. 79-404; s. 5, ch. 82-151; s. 3, ch. 92-36; s. 4, ch. 93-238; s. 454, ch. 95-147; s. 15, ch. 2002-1.

83.808 Contractual liens.—Nothing in ss. 83.801-83.809 shall be construed as in any manner impairing or affecting the right of parties to create liens by special contract or agreement nor shall it in any manner impair or affect any other lien arising at common law, in equity, or by any statute of this state or any other lien not provided for in s. 83.805.

History.—s. 6, ch. 82-151.

83.809 Application of act.—

(1) Nothing in this act shall be construed as in any manner impairing or affecting the right of parties to create additional rights, duties, and obligations in and by virtue of a rental agreement. The provisions of ss. 83.801-83.809 shall be in addition to all other rights allowed by law in a creditor-debtor or landlord-tenant relationship.

(2) Chapter 82-151, Laws of Florida, shall apply to all rental agreements entered into, extended, or renewed after July 1, 1982.

History.—ss. 7, 10, ch. 82-151.

212.03 Transient rentals tax; rate, procedure, enforcement, exemptions.—

1(1)(a) It is hereby declared to be the legislative intent that every person is exercising a taxable privilege who engages in the business of renting, leasing, letting, or granting a license to use any living quarters or sleeping or housekeeping accommodations in, from, or a part of, or in connection with any hotel, apartment house, roominghouse, tourist or trailer camp, mobile home park, recreational vehicle park, condominium, or timeshare resort. However, any person who rents, leases, lets, or grants a license to others to use, occupy, or enter upon any living quarters or sleeping or housekeeping accommodations in any apartment house, roominghouse, tourist camp, trailer camp, mobile home park, recreational vehicle park, condominium, or timeshare resort and who exclusively enters into a bona fide written agreement for continuous residence for longer than 6 months in duration at such property is not exercising a taxable privilege. For the exercise of such taxable privilege, a tax is hereby levied in an amount equal to 6 percent of and on the total rental charged for such living quarters or sleeping or housekeeping accommodations by the person charging or collecting the rental. Such tax shall apply to hotels, apartment houses, roominghouses, tourist or trailer camps, mobile home parks, recreational vehicle parks, condominiums, or timeshare resorts, whether or not these facilities have dining rooms, cafes, or other places where meals or lunches are sold or served to guests.

(b)1. Tax shall be due on the consideration paid for occupancy in the county pursuant to a regulated short-term product, as defined in s. 721.05, or occupancy in the county pursuant to a product that would be deemed a regulated short-term product if the agreement to purchase the short-term right was executed in this state. Such tax shall be collected on the last day of occupancy within the county unless such consideration is applied to the purchase of a timeshare estate. The occupancy of an accommodation of a timeshare resort pursuant to a timeshare plan, a multisite timeshare plan, or an exchange transaction in an exchange program, as defined in s. 721.05, by the owner of a timeshare interest or such owner's guest, which guest is not paying monetary consideration to the owner or to a third party for the benefit of the owner, is not a privilege subject to taxation under this section. A membership or transaction fee paid by a timeshare owner that does not provide the timeshare owner with the right to occupy any specific timeshare unit but merely provides the timeshare owner with the opportunity to exchange a timeshare interest through an exchange program is a service charge and not subject to taxation under this section.

2. Consideration paid for the purchase of a timeshare license in a timeshare plan, as defined in s. 721.05, is rent subject to taxation under this section.

(2) The tax provided for herein shall be in addition to the total amount of the rental, shall be charged by the lessor or person receiving the rent in and by said rental arrangement to the lessee or person paying the rental, and shall be due and payable at the time of the receipt of such rental payment by the lessor or person, as defined in this chapter, who receives said rental or payment. The owner, lessor, or person receiving the rent shall remit the tax to the department at the times and in the manner hereinafter provided for dealers to remit taxes under this chapter. The same duties imposed by this chap-

ter upon dealers in tangible personal property respecting the collection and remission of the tax; the making of returns; the keeping of books, records, and accounts; and the compliance with the rules and regulations of the department in the administration of this chapter shall apply to and be binding upon all persons who manage or operate hotels, apartment houses, roominghouses, tourist and trailer camps, and the rental of condominium units, and to all persons who collect or receive such rents on behalf of such owner or lessor taxable under this chapter.

(3) When rentals are received by way of property, goods, wares, merchandise, services, or other things of value, the tax shall be at the rate of 6 percent of the value of the property, goods, wares, merchandise, services, or other things of value.

(4) The tax levied by this section shall not apply to, be imposed upon, or collected from any person who shall have entered into a bona fide written lease for longer than 6 months in duration for continuous residence at any one hotel, apartment house, roominghouse, tourist or trailer camp, or condominium, or to any person who shall reside continuously longer than 6 months at any one hotel, apartment house, roominghouse, tourist or trailer camp, or condominium and shall have paid the tax levied by this section for 6 months of residence in any one hotel, roominghouse, apartment house, tourist or trailer camp, or condominium. Notwithstanding other provisions of this chapter, no tax shall be imposed upon rooms provided guests when there is no consideration involved between the guest and the public lodging establishment. Further, any person who, on the effective date of this act, has resided continuously for 6 months at any one hotel, apartment house, roominghouse, tourist or trailer camp, or condominium, or, if less than 6 months, has paid the tax imposed herein until he or she shall have resided continuously for 6 months, shall thereafter be exempt, so long as such person shall continuously reside at such location. The Department of Revenue shall have the power to reform the rental contract for the purposes of this chapter if the rental payments are collected in other than equal daily, weekly, or monthly amounts so as to reflect the actual consideration to be paid in the future for the right of occupancy during the first 6 months.

(5) The tax imposed by this section shall constitute a lien on the property of the lessee or rentee of any sleeping accommodations in the same manner as and shall be collectible as are liens authorized and imposed by ss. 713.68 and 713.69.

(6) It is the legislative intent that every person is engaging in a taxable privilege who leases or rents parking or storage spaces for motor vehicles in parking lots or garages, who leases or rents docking or storage spaces for boats in boat docks or marinas, or who leases or rents tie-down or storage space for aircraft at airports. For the exercise of this privilege, a tax is hereby levied at the rate of 6 percent on the total rental charged.

(7)(a) Full-time students enrolled in an institution offering postsecondary education and military personnel currently on active duty who reside in the facilities described in subsection (1) shall be exempt from the tax imposed by this section. The department shall be empowered to determine what shall be deemed acceptable proof of full-time enrollment. The exemption contained in this subsection shall apply irrespective of any other provisions of this section. The tax levied by this section shall not apply to or be imposed upon or collected on the basis of rentals to any person who resides in any building or group of buildings intended primarily for lease or rent to persons as their permanent or principal place of residence.

(b)   It is the intent of the Legislature that this subsection provide tax relief for persons who rent living accommodations rather than own their homes, while still providing a tax on the rental of lodging facilities that primarily serve transient guests.

(c)   The rental of facilities, as defined in s. 212.02(10)(f), which are intended primarily for rental as a principal or permanent place of residence is exempt from the tax imposed by this chapter. The rental of such facilities that primarily serve transient guests is not exempt by this subsection. In the application of this law, or in making any determination against the exemption, the department shall consider the facility as primarily serving transient guests unless the facility owner makes a verified declaration on a form prescribed by the department that more than half of the total rental units available are occupied by tenants who have a continuous residence in excess of 3 months. The owner of a facility declared to be exempt by this paragraph must make a determination of the taxable status of the facility at the end of the owner's accounting year using any consecutive 3-month period at least one month of which is in the accounting year. The owner must use a selected consecutive 3-month period during each annual redetermination. In the event that an exempt facility no longer qualifies for exemption by this paragraph, the owner must notify the department on a form prescribed by the department by the 20th day of the first month of the owner's next succeeding accounting year that the facility no longer qualifies for such exemption. The tax levied by this section shall apply to the rental of facilities that no longer qualify for exemption under this paragraph beginning the first day of the owner's next succeeding accounting year. The provisions of this paragraph do not apply to mobile home lots regulated under chapter 723.

(d)   The rental of living accommodations in migrant labor camps is not taxable under this section. "Migrant labor camps" are defined as one or more buildings or structures, tents, trailers, or vehicles, or any portion thereof, together with the land appertaining thereto, established, operated, or used as living quarters for seasonal, temporary, or migrant workers.

History.—s. 3, ch. 26319, 1949; s. 4, ch. 26871, 1951; ss. 2, 3, ch. 29883, 1955; ss. 2, 7, ch. 63-526; s. 7, ch. 63-253; s. 5, ch. 65-371; s. 2, ch. 65-420; s. 3, ch. 68-27; s. 2, ch. 68-119; ss. 4, 5, ch. 69-222; s. 15, ch. 69-353; ss. 21, 35, ch. 69-106; s. 1, ch. 71-986; s. 2, ch. 79-359; s. 1, ch. 82-154; s. 70, ch. 83-217; s. 59, ch. 85-342; s. 2, ch. 87-548; s. 1, ch. 89-362; s. 4, ch. 89-529; s. 7, ch. 94-353; s. 1492, ch. 95-147; s. 2, ch. 98-140; s. 3, ch. 2009-133.

1Note.—Section 5, ch. 2009-133, provides that "[t]he amendments to sections 125.0104, 125.0108, 212.03, and 212.0305, Florida Statutes, made by this act are intended to be clarifying and remedial in nature and do not provide a basis for assessments of tax, or refunds of tax, for periods prior to July 1, 2009."

212.031   Tax on rental or license fee for use of real property.—

(1)(a)   It is declared to be the legislative intent that every person is exercising a taxable privilege who engages in the business of renting, leasing, letting, or granting a license for the use of any real property unless such property is:

1.   Assessed as agricultural property under s. 193.461.

2.   Used exclusively as dwelling units.

3.   Property subject to tax on parking, docking, or storage spaces under s. 212.03(6).

4.   Recreational property or the common elements of a condominium when subject to a lease between the developer or owner thereof and the condominium association in its own right or as agent for the owners of individual condominium units or the owners of individual condominium units. However, only the lease payments on such property shall be exempt from the tax imposed by this chapter, and any other use made by the owner or the condominium association shall be fully taxable under this chapter.

5.   A public or private street or right-of-way and poles, conduits, fixtures, and similar improvements located on such streets or rights-of-way, occupied or used by a utility or provider of communications services, as defined by s. 202.11, for utility or communications or television purposes. For purposes of this subparagraph, the term "utility" means any person providing utility services as defined in s. 203.012. This exception also applies to property, wherever located, on which the following are placed: towers, antennas, cables, accessory structures, or equipment, not including switching equipment, used in the provision of mobile communications services as defined in s. 202.11. For purposes of this chapter, towers used in the provision of mobile communications services, as defined in s. 202.11, are considered to be fixtures.

6.   A public street or road which is used for transportation purposes.

7.   Property used at an airport exclusively for the purpose of aircraft landing or aircraft taxiing or property used by an airline for the purpose of loading or unloading passengers or property onto or from aircraft or for fueling aircraft.

8.a.   Property used at a port authority, as defined in s. 315.02(2), exclusively for the purpose of oceangoing vessels or tugs docking, or such vessels mooring on property used by a port authority for the purpose of loading or unloading passengers or cargo onto or from such a vessel, or property used at a port authority for fueling such vessels, or to the extent that the amount paid for the use of any property at the port is based on the charge for the amount of tonnage actually imported or exported through the port by a tenant.

b.   The amount charged for the use of any property at the port in excess of the amount charged for tonnage actually imported or exported shall remain subject to tax except as provided in sub-sub-paragraph a.

9.   Property used as an integral part of the performance of qualified production services. As used in this subparagraph, the term "quali-

fied production services" means any activity or service performed directly in connection with the production of a qualified motion picture, as defined in s. 212.06(1)(b), and includes:

a.   Photography, sound and recording, casting, location managing and scouting, shooting, creation of special and optical effects, animation, adaptation (language, media, electronic, or otherwise), technological modifications, computer graphics, set and stage support (such as electricians, lighting designers and operators, greensmen, prop managers and assistants, and grips), wardrobe (design, preparation, and management), hair and makeup (design, production, and application), performing (such as acting, dancing, and playing), designing and executing stunts, coaching, consulting, writing, scoring, composing, choreographing, script supervising, directing, producing, transmitting dailies, dubbing, mixing, editing, cutting, looping, printing, processing, duplicating, storing, and distributing;

b.   The design, planning, engineering, construction, alteration, repair, and maintenance of real or personal property including stages, sets, props, models, paintings, and facilities principally required for the performance of those services listed in sub-subparagraph a.; and

c.   Property management services directly related to property used in connection with the services described in sub-subparagraphs a. and b.

This exemption will inure to the taxpayer upon presentation of the certificate of exemption issued to the taxpayer under the provisions of s. 288.1258.

10.   Leased, subleased, licensed, or rented to a person providing food and drink concessionaire services within the premises of a convention hall, exhibition hall, auditorium, stadium, theater, arena, civic center, performing arts center, publicly owned recreational facility, or any business operated under a permit issued pursuant to chapter 550. A person providing retail concessionaire services involving the sale of food and drink or other tangible personal property within the premises of an airport shall be subject to tax on the rental of real property used for that purpose, but shall not be subject to the tax on any license to use the property. For purposes of this subparagraph, the term "sale" shall not include the leasing of tangible personal property.

11.   Property occupied pursuant to an instrument calling for payments which the department has declared, in a Technical Assistance Advisement issued on or before March 15, 1993, to be nontaxable pursuant to rule 12A-1.070(19)(c), Florida Administrative Code; provided that this subparagraph shall only apply to property occupied by the same person before and after the execution of the subject instrument and only to those payments made pursuant to such instrument, exclusive of renewals and extensions thereof occurring after March 15, 1993.

12.   Rented, leased, subleased, or licensed to a concessionaire by a convention hall, exhibition hall, auditorium, stadium, theater, arena, civic center, performing arts center, or publicly owned recreational facility, during an event at the facility, to be used by the concessionaire to sell souvenirs, novelties, or other event-related products. This subparagraph applies only to that portion of the rental, lease, or license payment which is based on a percentage of sales and not based on a fixed price. This subparagraph is repealed July 1, 2009.

13.   Property used or occupied predominantly for space flight business purposes. As used in this subparagraph, "space flight business" means the manufacturing, processing, or assembly of a space facility, space propulsion system, space vehicle, satellite, or station of any kind possessing the capacity for space flight, as defined by s. 212.02(23), or components thereof, and also means the following activities supporting space flight: vehicle launch activities, flight operations, ground control or ground support, and all administrative activities directly related thereto. Property shall be deemed to be used or occupied predominantly for space flight business purposes if more than 50 percent of the property, or improvements thereon, is used for one or more space flight business purposes. Possession by a landlord, lessor, or licensor of a signed written statement from the tenant, lessee, or licensee claiming the exemption shall relieve the landlord, lessor, or licensor from the responsibility of collecting the tax, and the department shall look solely to the tenant, lessee, or licensee for recovery of such tax if it determines that the exemption was not applicable.

(b)   When a lease involves multiple use of real property wherein a part of the real property is subject to the tax herein, and a part of the property would be excluded from the tax under subparagraph (a)1., subparagraph (a)2., subparagraph (a)3., or subparagraph (a)5., the department shall determine, from the lease or license and such other information as may be available, that portion of the total rental charge which is exempt from the tax imposed by this section. The portion of the premises leased or rented by a for-profit entity providing a residential facility for the aged will be exempt on the basis of a pro rata portion calculated by combining the square footage of the areas used for residential units by the aged and for the care of such residents and dividing the resultant sum by the total square footage of the rented premises. For purposes of this section, the term "residential facility for the aged" means a facility that is licensed or certified in whole or in part under chapter 400, chapter 429, or chapter 651; or that provides residences to the elderly and is financed by a mortgage or loan made or insured by the United States Department of Housing and Urban Development under s. 202, s. 202 with a s. 8 subsidy, s. 221(d)(3) or (4), s. 232, or s. 236 of the National Housing Act; or other such similar facility that provides residences primarily for the elderly.

(c)   For the exercise of such privilege, a tax is levied in an amount equal to 6 percent of and on the total rent or license fee charged for such real property by the person charging or collecting the rental or license fee. The total rent or license fee charged for such real property shall include payments for the granting of a privilege to use or occupy real property for any purpose and shall include base rent, percentage rents, or similar charges. Such charges shall be included in the total rent or license fee subject to tax under this section whether or not they can be attributed to the ability of the lessor's or licensor's property as used or operated to attract customers. Payments for intrinsically valuable personal property such as franchises, trademarks, service marks, logos, or patents are not subject to tax under this section. In the case of a contractual arrangement that provides for both payments taxable as total rent or license fee and payments not subject to tax, the tax shall be based on a reasonable allocation of such payments and shall not apply to that portion which is for the nontaxable payments.

(d)   When the rental or license fee of any such real property is paid by way of property, goods, wares, merchandise, services, or other thing of value, the tax shall be at the rate of 6 percent of the value of the property, goods, wares, merchandise, services, or other thing of value.

(2)(a)   The tenant or person actually occupying, using, or entitled to the use of any property from which the rental or license fee is subject to taxation under this section shall pay the tax to his or her immediate landlord or other person granting the right to such tenant or person to occupy or use such real property.

(b)   It is the further intent of this Legislature that only one tax be collected on the rental or license fee payable for the occupancy or use of any such property, that the tax so collected shall not be pyramided by a progression of transactions, and that the amount of the tax due the state shall not be decreased by any such progression of transactions.

(3)   The tax imposed by this section shall be in addition to the total amount of the rental or license fee, shall be charged by the lessor or person receiving the rent or payment in and by a rental or license fee arrangement with the lessee or person paying the rental or license fee, and shall be due and payable at the time of the receipt of such rental or license fee payment by the lessor or other person who receives the rental or payment. Notwithstanding any other provision of this chapter, the tax imposed by this section on the rental, lease, or license for the use of a convention hall, exhibition hall, auditorium, stadium, theater, arena, civic center, performing arts center, or publicly owned recreational facility to hold an event of not more than 7 consecutive days' duration shall be collected at the time of the payment for that rental, lease, or license but is not due and payable to the department until the first day of the month following the last day that the event for which the payment is made is actually held, and becomes delinquent on the 21st day of that month. The owner, lessor, or person receiving the rent or license fee shall remit the tax to the department at the times and in the manner hereinafter provided for dealers to remit taxes under this chapter. The same duties imposed by this chapter upon dealers in tangible personal property respecting the collection and remission of the tax; the making of returns; the keeping of books, records, and accounts; and the compliance with the rules and regulations of the department in the administration of this chapter shall apply to and be binding upon all persons who manage any leases or operate real property, hotels, apartment houses, roominghouses, or tourist and trailer camps and all persons who collect or receive rents or license fees taxable under this chapter on behalf of owners or lessors.

(4)   The tax imposed by this section shall constitute a lien on the property of the lessee or licensee of any real estate in the same manner as, and shall be collectible as are, liens authorized and imposed by ss. 713.68 and 713.69.

(5)   When space is subleased to a convention or industry trade show in a convention hall, exhibition hall, or auditorium, whether publicly or privately owned, the sponsor who holds the prime lease is subject to tax on the prime lease and the sublease is exempt.

(6)   The lease or rental of land or a hall or other facilities by a fair association subject to the provisions of chapter 616 to a show promoter or prime operator of a carnival or midway attraction is exempt from the tax imposed by this section; however, the sublease of land or a hall or other facilities by the show promoter or prime operator is not exempt from the provisions of this section.

(7)   Utility charges subject to sales tax which are paid by a tenant to the lessor and which are part of a payment for the privilege or right to use or occupy real property are exempt from tax if the lessor has paid sales tax on the purchase of such utilities and the charges billed by the lessor to the tenant are separately stated and at the same or a lower price than those paid by the lessor.

(8)   Charges by lessors to a lessee to cancel or terminate a lease agreement are presumed taxable if the lessor records such charges as rental income in its books and records. This presumption can be overcome by the provision of sufficient documentation by either the lessor or the lessee that such charges were other than for the rental of real property.

(9)   The rental, lease, sublease, or license for the use of a skybox, luxury box, or other box seats for use during a high school or college football game is exempt from the tax imposed by this section when the charge for such rental, lease, sublease, or license is imposed by a nonprofit sponsoring organization which is qualified as nonprofit pursuant to s. 501(c)(3) of the Internal Revenue Code.

1(10)   Separately stated charges imposed by a convention hall, exhibition hall, auditorium, stadium, theater, arena, civic center, performing arts center, or publicly owned recreational facility upon a lessee or licensee for food, drink, or services required or available in connection with a lease or license to use real property, including charges for laborers, stagehands, ticket takers, event staff, security personnel, cleaning staff, and other event-related personnel, advertising, and credit card processing, are exempt from the tax imposed by this section.

History.—s. 6, ch. 69-222; ss. 21, 35, ch. 69-106; s. 3, ch. 71-986; s. 2, ch. 77-194; s. 1, ch. 78-107; s. 95, ch. 79-400; s. 2, ch. 82-154; s. 1, ch. 82-207; s. 71, ch. 83-217; s. 4, ch. 83-297; s. 2, ch. 85-310; s. 66, ch. 86-152; ss. 2, 8, ch. 86-166; ss. 8, 25, ch. 87-6; s. 10, ch. 87-101; ss. 3, 4, ch. 87-548; s. 92, ch. 90-132; s. 57, ch. 92-348; s. 4, ch. 93-86; s. 1108, ch. 95-147; s. 2, ch. 95-391; s. 20, ch. 96-397; s. 4, ch. 97-221; s. 3, ch. 98-140; s. 1, ch. 99-238; s. 1, ch. 99-270; s. 1, ch. 99-363; s. 2, ch. 2000-182; s. 1, ch. 2000-183; s. 53, ch. 2000-260; ss. 1, 3, ch. 2000-345; ss. 26, 27, ch. 2001-140; s. 55, ch. 2002-218; ss. 1, 2, ch. 2006-101; s. 10, ch. 2006-197.

713.691 Landlord's lien for rent; exemptions.—

(1) With regard to a residential tenancy, the landlord has a lien on all personal property of the tenant located on the premises for accrued rent due to the landlord under the rental agreement. This lien shall be in addition to any other liens upon such property which the landlord may acquire by law and may be modified or waived, in whole or in part, by the provisions of a written rental agreement. The landlord's lien for rent shall attach to the tenant's personal property at the time the sheriff gives the landlord possession of the premises, but it is not required that the tenant's property be removed in order to give the landlord possession of the premises.

(2) When the tenant is the head of a family, personal property owned by her or him in the value of $1,000 is exempt from the lien provided by this section. This subsection does not authorize an exemption any greater than that which may be available to the tenant in s. 4, Art. X of the State Constitution.

(3) The remedy of distress for rent is abolished with regard to residential tenancies.

History.—s. 3, ch. 73-330; s. 9, ch. 87-195; s. 8, ch. 88-379; s. 826, ch. 97-102.

715.07 Vehicles or vessels parked on private property; towing.—

(1) As used in this section, the term:

(a) "Vehicle" means any mobile item which normally uses wheels, whether motorized or not.

(b) "Vessel" means every description of watercraft, barge, and airboat used or capable of being used as a means of transportation on water, other than a seaplane or a "documented vessel" as defined in s. 327.02(9).

(2) The owner or lessee of real property, or any person authorized by the owner or lessee, which person may be the designated representative of the condominium association if the real property is a condominium, may cause any vehicle or vessel parked on such property without her or his permission to be removed by a person regularly engaged in the business of towing vehicles or vessels, without liability for the costs of removal, transportation, or storage or damages caused by such removal, transportation, or storage, under any of the following circumstances:

(a) The towing or removal of any vehicle or vessel from private property without the consent of the registered owner or other legally authorized person in control of that vehicle or vessel is subject to strict compliance with the following conditions and restrictions:

1.a. Any towed or removed vehicle or vessel must be stored at a site within a 10-mile radius of the point of removal in any county of 500,000 population or more, and within a 15-mile radius of the point of removal in any county of less than 500,000 population. That site must be open for the purpose of redemption of vehicles on any day that the person or firm towing such vehicle or vessel is open for towing purposes, from 8:00 a.m. to 6:00 p.m., and, when closed, shall have prominently posted a sign indicating a telephone

number where the operator of the site can be reached at all times. Upon receipt of a telephoned request to open the site to redeem a vehicle or vessel, the operator shall return to the site within 1 hour or she or he will be in violation of this section.

b. If no towing business providing such service is located within the area of towing limitations set forth in sub-subparagraph a., the following limitations apply: any towed or removed vehicle or vessel must be stored at a site within a 20-mile radius of the point of removal in any county of 500,000 population or more, and within a 30-mile radius of the point of removal in any county of less than 500,000 population.

2. The person or firm towing or removing the vehicle or vessel shall, within 30 minutes after completion of such towing or removal, notify the municipal police department or, in an unincorporated area, the sheriff, of such towing or removal, the storage site, the time the vehicle or vessel was towed or removed, and the make, model, color, and license plate number of the vehicle or description and registration number of the vessel and shall obtain the name of the person at that department to whom such information was reported and note that name on the trip record.

3. A person in the process of towing or removing a vehicle or vessel from the premises or parking lot in which the vehicle or vessel is not lawfully parked must stop when a person seeks the return of the vehicle or vessel. The vehicle or vessel must be returned upon the payment of a reasonable service fee of not more than one-half of the posted rate for the towing or removal service as provided in subparagraph 6. The vehicle or vessel may be towed or removed if, after a reasonable opportunity, the owner or legally authorized person in control of the vehicle or vessel is unable to pay the service fee. If the vehicle or vessel is redeemed, a detailed signed receipt must be given to the person redeeming the vehicle or vessel.

4. A person may not pay or accept money or other valuable consideration for the privilege of towing or removing vehicles or vessels from a particular location.

5. Except for property appurtenant to and obviously a part of a single-family residence, and except for instances when notice is personally given to the owner or other legally authorized person in control of the vehicle or vessel that the area in which that vehicle or vessel is parked is reserved or otherwise unavailable for unauthorized vehicles or vessels and that the vehicle or vessel is subject to being removed at the owner's or operator's expense, any property owner or lessee, or person authorized by the property owner or lessee, prior to towing or removing any vehicle or vessel from private property without the consent of the owner or other legally authorized person in control of that vehicle or vessel, must post a notice meeting the following requirements:

a. The notice must be prominently placed at each driveway access or curb cut allowing vehicular access to the property, within 5 feet from the public right-of-way line. If there are no curbs or access barriers, the signs must be posted not less than one sign for each 25 feet of lot frontage.

b. The notice must clearly indicate, in not less than 2-inch high, light-reflective letters on a contrasting background, that unauthorized vehicles will be towed away at the owner's expense. The words "tow-away zone" must be included on the sign in not less than 4-inch high letters.

c.   The notice must also provide the name and current telephone number of the person or firm towing or removing the vehicles or vessels.

d.   The sign structure containing the required notices must be permanently installed with the words "tow-away zone" not less than 3 feet and not more than 6 feet above ground level and must be continuously maintained on the property for not less than 24 hours prior to the towing or removal of any vehicles or vessels.

e.   The local government may require permitting and inspection of these signs prior to any towing or removal of vehicles or vessels being authorized.

f.   A business with 20 or fewer parking spaces satisfies the notice requirements of this subparagraph by prominently displaying a sign stating "Reserved Parking for Customers Only Unauthorized Vehicles or Vessels Will be Towed Away At the Owner's Expense" in not less than 4-inch high, light-reflective letters on a contrasting background.

g.   A property owner towing or removing vessels from real property must post notice, consistent with the requirements in sub-subparagraphs a.-f., which apply to vehicles, that unauthorized vehicles or vessels will be towed away at the owner's expense.

A business owner or lessee may authorize the removal of a vehicle or vessel by a towing company when the vehicle or vessel is parked in such a manner that restricts the normal operation of business; and if a vehicle or vessel parked on a public right-of-way obstructs access to a private driveway the owner, lessee, or agent may have the vehicle or vessel removed by a towing company upon signing an order that the vehicle or vessel be removed without a posted tow-away zone sign.

6.   Any person or firm that tows or removes vehicles or vessels and proposes to require an owner, operator, or person in control of a vehicle or vessel to pay the costs of towing and storage prior to redemption of the vehicle or vessel must file and keep on record with the local law enforcement agency a complete copy of the current rates to be charged for such services and post at the storage site an identical rate schedule and any written contracts with property owners, lessees, or persons in control of property which authorize such person or firm to remove vehicles or vessels as provided in this section.

7.   Any person or firm towing or removing any vehicles or vessels from private property without the consent of the owner or other legally authorized person in control of the vehicles or vessels shall, on any trucks, wreckers as defined in s. 713.78(1)(c), or other vehicles used in the towing or removal, have the name, address, and telephone number of the company performing such service clearly printed in contrasting colors on the driver and passenger sides of the vehicle. The name shall be in at least 3-inch permanently affixed letters, and the address and telephone number shall be in at least 1-inch permanently affixed letters.

8.   Vehicle entry for the purpose of removing the vehicle or vessel shall be allowed with reasonable care on the part of the person or firm towing the vehicle or vessel. Such person or firm shall be liable for any damage occasioned to the vehicle or vessel if such entry is not in accordance with the standard of reasonable care.

9.   When a vehicle or vessel has been towed or removed pursuant to this section, it must be released to its owner or custodian within one hour after requested. Any vehicle or vessel owner or agent shall have the right to inspect the vehicle or vessel before accepting its return, and no release or waiver of any kind which would release the person or firm towing the vehicle or vessel from liability for damages noted by the owner or other legally authorized person at the time of the redemption may be required from any vehicle or vessel owner, custodian, or agent as a condition of release of the vehicle or vessel to its owner. A detailed, signed receipt showing the legal name of the company or person towing or removing the vehicle or vessel must be given to the person paying towing or storage charges at the time of payment, whether requested or not.

(b)   These requirements are minimum standards and do not preclude enactment of additional regulations by any municipality or county including the right to regulate rates when vehicles or vessels are towed from private property.

(3)   This section does not apply to law enforcement, firefighting, rescue squad, ambulance, or other emergency vehicles or vessels that are marked as such or to property owned by any governmental entity.

(4)   When a person improperly causes a vehicle or vessel to be removed, such person shall be liable to the owner or lessee of the vehicle or vessel for the cost of removal, transportation, and storage; any damages resulting from the removal, transportation, or storage of the vehicle or vessel; attorney's fees; and court costs.

(5)(a)   Any person who violates subparagraph (2)(a)2. or subparagraph (2)(a)6. commits a misdemeanor of the first degree, punishable as provided in s. 775.082 or s. 775.083.

(b)   Any person who violates subparagraph (2)(a)1., subparagraph (2)(a)3., subparagraph (2)(a)4., subparagraph (2)(a)7., or subparagraph (2)(a)9. commits a felony of the third degree, punishable as provided in s. 775.082, s. 775.083, or s. 775.084.

History.—s. 1, ch. 76-83; s. 221, ch. 77-104; s. 2, ch. 79-206; s. 2, ch. 79-271; s. 2, ch. 79-410; s. 1, ch. 83-330; s. 51, ch. 87-198; s. 3, ch. 88-240; s. 9, ch. 90-283; s. 839, ch. 97-102; s. 18, ch. 2001-64; s. 5, ch. 2005-137; s. 11, ch. 2006-172.

715.10 Disposition of Personal Property Landlord and Tenant Act; short title.—Sections 715.10-715.111 may be cited as the "Disposition of Personal Property Landlord and Tenant Act."

History.—s. 11, ch. 83-151.

715.101 Application of ss. 715.10-715.111.—

(1) Sections 715.10-715.111 apply to all tenancies to which part I or part II of chapter 83 are applicable, and to tenancies after a writ of possession has been issued pursuant to s. 723.062.

(2) Sections 715.10-715.111 provide an optional procedure for the disposition of personal property which remains on the premises after a tenancy has terminated or expired and the premises have been vacated by the tenant through eviction, surrender, abandonment, or otherwise.

(3) Sections 715.10-715.111 do not apply to property which exists for the purpose of providing utility services and is owned by a utility, whether or not such property is actually in operation to provide such utility services.

(4) If the requirements of ss. 715.10-715.111 are not satisfied, nothing in ss. 715.10-715.111 affects the rights and liabilities of the landlord, the former tenant, or any other person.

History.—s. 11, ch. 83-151; s. 4, ch. 2003-263.

715.102 Definitions of terms used in ss. 715.10-715.111.—As used in ss. 715.10-715.111, unless some other meaning is clearly indicated, the term:

(1) "Landlord" means any operator, keeper, lessor, or sublessor of furnished or unfurnished premises for rent, or her or his agent or successor-in-interest.

(2) "Owner" means any person other than the landlord who has any right, title, or interest in personal property.

(3) "Premises" includes any common areas associated therewith.

(4) "Reasonable belief" means the actual knowledge or belief a prudent person should have without making an investigation, including any investigation of public records; except that, when the landlord has specific information indicating that such an investigation would more probably than not reveal pertinent information and the cost of such an investigation would be reasonable in relation to the probable value of the personal property involved, the term "reasonable belief" includes the actual knowledge or belief a prudent person would have if such an investigation were made.

(5) "Tenant" includes any paying guest, lessee, or sublessee of any premises for rent, whether a dwelling unit or not.

History.—s. 11, ch. 83-151; s. 840, ch. 97-102.

715.103 Lost property.—Personal property which the landlord reasonably believes to have been lost shall be disposed of as otherwise provided by law. However, if the appropriate law enforcement agency or other government agency refuses to accept custody of property pursuant to chapter 705, the landlord may dispose of the property pursuant to ss. 715.10-715.111. The landlord is not liable to the owner of the property if she or he complies with this section and the other provisions of ss. 715.10-715.111.

History.—s. 11, ch. 83-151; s. 841, ch. 97-102.

715.104 Notification of former tenant of personal property remaining on premises after tenancy has terminated.—

(1) When personal property remains on the premises after a tenancy has terminated or expired and the premises have been vacated by the tenant, through eviction or otherwise, the landlord shall give written notice to such tenant and to any other person the landlord reasonably believes to be the owner of the property.

(2) The notice shall describe the property in a manner reasonably adequate to permit the owner of the property to identify it. The notice may describe all or a portion of the property, but the limitation of liability provided by s. 715.11 does not protect the landlord from any liability arising from the disposition of property not described in the notice, except that a trunk, valise, box, or other container which is locked, fastened, or tied in a manner which deters immediate access to its contents may be described as such without describing its contents. The notice shall advise the person to be notified that reasonable costs of storage may be charged before the property is returned, and the notice shall state where the property may be claimed and the date before which the claim must be made. The date specified in the notice shall be a date not fewer than 10 days after the notice is personally delivered or, if mailed, not fewer than 15 days after the notice is deposited in the mail.

(3) The notice shall be personally delivered or sent by first-class mail, postage prepaid, to the person to be notified at her or his last known address and, if there is reason to believe that the notice sent to that address will not be received by that person, also delivered or sent to such other address, if any, known to the landlord where such person may reasonably be expected to receive the notice.

History.—s. 11, ch. 83-151; s. 842, ch. 97-102.

715.105 Form of notice concerning abandoned property to former tenant.—

(1) A notice to the former tenant which is in substantially the following form satisfies the requirements of s. 715.104:

Notice of Right to Reclaim Abandoned Property

To: (Name of former tenant)
(Address of former tenant)

When you vacated the premises at (address of premises, including room or apartment number, if any) , the following personal property remained: (insert description of personal property) .

You may claim this property at (address where property may be claimed) .

Unless you pay the reasonable costs of storage and advertising, if any, for all the above-described property and take possession of the property which you claim, not later than (insert date not fewer than 10 days after notice is personally delivered or, if mailed, not fewer than 15 days after notice is deposited in the mail) , this property may be disposed of pursuant to s. 715.109.

(Insert here the statement required by subsection (2))

Dated:_____

(Signature of landlord)

(Type or print name of landlord)

(Telephone number)

(Address)

(2)   The notice set forth in subsection (1) shall also contain one of the following statements:

(a)   "If you fail to reclaim the property, it will be sold at a public sale after notice of the sale has been given by publication. You have the right to bid on the property at this sale. After the property is sold and the costs of storage, advertising, and sale are deducted, the remaining money will be paid over to the county. You may claim the remaining money at any time within 1 year after the county receives the money."

(b)   "Because this property is believed to be worth less than $500, it may be kept, sold, or destroyed without further notice if you fail to reclaim it within the time indicated above."

History.—s. 11, ch. 83-151; s. 3, ch. 2001-179.

715.106   Form of notice concerning abandoned property to owner other than former tenant.—

(1)   A notice which is in substantially the following form given to a person who is not the former tenant and whom the landlord reasonably believes to be the owner of any of the abandoned personal property satisfies the requirements of s. 715.104:

Notice of Right to Reclaim Abandoned Property

To: (Name)
  (Address)

When   (name of former tenant)   vacated the premises at   (address of premises, including room or apartment number, if any) , the following personal property remained: (insert description of personal property) .

If you own any of this property, you may claim it at   (address where property may be claimed) . Unless you pay the reasonable costs of storage and advertising, if any, and take possession of the property to which you are entitled, not later than   (insert date not fewer than 10 days after notice is personally delivered or, if mailed, not fewer than 15 days after notice is deposited in the mail) , this property may be disposed of pursuant to s. 715.109.

(Insert here the statement required by subsection (2))

Dated:_____

(Signature of landlord)

(Type or print name of landlord)

(Telephone number)

(Address)

(2)   The notice set forth in subsection (1) shall also contain one of the following statements:

(a)   "If you fail to reclaim the property, it will be sold at a public sale after notice of the sale has been given by publication. You have the right to bid on the property at this sale. After the property is sold and the costs of storage, advertising, and sale are deducted, the remaining money will be paid over to the county. You may claim the remaining money at any time within 1 year after the county receives the money."

(b)   "Because this property is believed to be worth less than $500, it may be kept, sold, or destroyed without further notice if you fail to reclaim it within the time indicated above."

History.—s. 11, ch. 83-151; s. 4, ch. 2001-179.

715.107   Storage of abandoned property.—The personal property described in the notice either shall be left on the vacated premises or be stored by the landlord in a place of safekeeping until the landlord either releases the property pursuant to s. 715.108 or disposes of the property pursuant to s. 715.109. The landlord shall exercise reasonable care in storing the property, but she or he is not liable to the tenant or any other owner for any loss unless caused by the landlord's deliberate or negligent act.

History.—s. 11, ch. 83-151; s. 843, ch. 97-102.

715.108   Release of personal property.—

(1)   The personal property described in the notice shall be released by the landlord to the former tenant or, at the landlord's option, to any person reasonably believed by the landlord to be its owner, if such tenant or other person pays the reasonable costs of storage and advertising and takes possession of the property not later than the date specified in the notice for taking possession.

(2)   Where personal property is not released pursuant to subsection (1) and the notice has stated that the personal property will be sold at a public sale, the landlord shall release the personal property to the former tenant if she or he claims it prior to the time it is sold and pays the reasonable costs of storage, advertising, and sale incurred prior to the time the property is withdrawn from sale.

History.—s. 11, ch. 83-151; s. 844, ch. 97-102.

715.109   Sale or disposition of abandoned property.—

(1)   If the personal property described in the notice is not released pursuant to s. 715.108, it shall be sold at public sale by competitive bidding. However, if the landlord reasonably believes that the total resale value of the property not released is less than $500, she or he may retain such property for her or his own use or dispose of it in any manner she or he chooses. Nothing in this section shall be construed to preclude the landlord or tenant from bidding on the

property at the public sale. The successful bidder's title is subject to ownership rights, liens, and security interests which have priority by law.

(2)   Notice of the time and place of the public sale shall be given by an advertisement of the sale published once a week for two consecutive weeks in a newspaper of general circulation where the sale is to be held. The sale must be held at the nearest suitable place to that where the personal property is held or stored. The advertisement must include a description of the goods, the name of the former tenant, and the time and place of the sale. The sale must take place at least 10 days after the first publication. If there is no newspaper of general circulation where the sale is to be held, the advertisement must be posted at least 10 days before the sale in not less than six conspicuous places in the neighborhood of the proposed sale. The last publication shall be at least 5 days before the sale is to be held. Notice of sale may be published before the last of the dates specified for taking possession of the property in any notice given pursuant to s. 715.104.

(3)   The notice of the sale shall describe the property to be sold in a manner reasonably adequate to permit the owner of the property to identify it. The notice may describe all or a portion of the property, but the limitation of liability provided by s. 715.11 does not protect the landlord from any liability arising from the disposition of property not described in the notice, except that a trunk, valise, box, or other container which is locked, fastened, or tied in a manner which deters immediate access to its contents may be described as such without describing its contents.

(4)   After deduction of the costs of storage, advertising, and sale, any balance of the proceeds of the sale which is not claimed by the former tenant or an owner other than such tenant shall be paid into the treasury of the county in which the sale took place not later than 30 days after the date of sale. The former tenant or other owner or other person having interest in the funds may claim the balance within 1 year from the date of payment to the county by making application to the county treasurer or other official designated by the county. If the county pays the balance or any part thereof to a claimant, neither the county nor any officer or employee thereof is liable to any other claimant as to the amount paid.

History.—s. 11, ch. 83-151; s. 845, ch. 97-102; s. 5, ch. 2001-179.

715.11   Nonliability of landlord after disposition of property.—

(1)   Notwithstanding the provisions of s. 715.101, after the landlord releases to the former tenant property which remains on the premises after a tenancy is terminated, the landlord is not liable with respect to that property to any person.

(2)   After the landlord releases property pursuant to s. 715.108 to a person who is not the former tenant and who is reasonably believed by the landlord to be the owner of the property, the landlord is not liable with respect to that property to:

(a)   Any person to whom notice was given pursuant to s. 715.104; or

(b)   Any person to whom notice was not given pursuant to s. 715.104

unless such person proves that, prior to releasing the property, the landlord believed or reasonably should have believed that such person had an interest in the property and also that the landlord knew or should have known upon reasonable investigation the address of such person.

(3)   Where property is disposed of pursuant to s. 715.109, the landlord is not liable with respect to that property to:

(a)   Any person to whom notice was given pursuant to s. 715.104; or

(b)   Any person to whom notice was not given pursuant to s. 715.104 unless such person proves that, prior to disposing of the property pursuant to s. 715.109, the landlord believed or reasonably should have believed that such person had an interest in the property and also that the landlord knew or should have known upon reasonable investigation the address of such person.

History.—s. 11, ch. 83-151.

715.111   Assessing costs of storage.—

(1)   Costs of storage for which payment may be required under ss. 715.10-715.111 shall be assessed in the following manner:

(a)   When a former tenant claims property pursuant to s. 715.108, she or he may be required to pay the reasonable costs of storage for all the personal property remaining on the premises at the termination of the tenancy, which costs are unpaid at the time the claim is made.

(b)   When an owner other than the former tenant claims property pursuant to s. 715.108, she or he may be required to pay the reasonable costs of storage for only the property in which she or he claims an interest.

(2)   In determining the costs to be assessed under subsection (1), the landlord may not charge more than one person for the same costs.

(3)   If the landlord stores the personal property on the premises, the costs of storage shall be the fair rental value of the space reasonably required for such storage for the term of the storage.

History.—s. 11, ch. 83-151; s. 846, ch. 97-102.

Appendix B

Evicting a Tenant

Since the only legal way to force a tenant out of a property is to get a Writ of Possession from a court, you may some day need to file an eviction action if you have a tenant who refuses to leave. As discussed earlier, while it may violate your sense of justice, sometimes giving a tenant a couple hundred bucks to get out today can save you thousands of dollars in lost rent, damage to the property and legal fees, not to mention months of stress.

But if that fails, this appendix should provide everything you need to go through a court action and obtain a Writ of Possession to your property. Fortunately, the eviction process usually works quite quickly in Florida. In some cases, tenants' lawyers have abused the system and allowed nonpaying tenants to remain in possession for months, but most of the time the system allows delinquent tenants to be removed quickly.

Unfortunately, budget cuts have raised the cost of filing an eviction to about $270 as this is written, and in addition, payment must be made for having a sheriff or process server deliver the eviction papers to the tenant ($25-$50 per person) and for the sheriff to deliver the Writ of Possession (about $100).

There are two main reasons for evictions, failure of the tenant to pay rent, and violation of the terms of the lease. The procedures you will need to follow to get the Writ of Possession are shown on the flow charts on the next two pages, the first is for nonpayment of rent and the second for violation of the lease. When evicting for failure to pay rent you must be sure you followed the proper procedures in serving the Three Day Notice *exactly right*. When evicting a tenant for violation of the lease, you must be sure you have properly terminated the tenancy by using a Seven Day Notice and a Notice of Termination, or just a Notice of Termination depending on whether the violation is "curable or "uncurable." See Chapter 8.

Terminating the Tenancy

It is an ancient rule of law that an eviction suit cannot be filed until the tenancy is legally terminated. There are cases from the 1500s in which evictions were dismissed because the landlord failed to properly terminate the tenancy. If you make the same mistake, do not expect the judge to overlook it. What the judges often do is order the landlord to pay the tenant's attorney's fees.

Termination for Cause. The tenancy may terminate by natural expiration or by action by the landlord. If you need to evict a tenant whose tenancy has not expired, then you should carefully read the previous chapter and follow the procedures to properly terminate the tenancy.

Termination by Expiration. If parties to a rental agreement do not agree to renew or extend the agreement, then it automatically ends at its expiration date. (This is different from some areas in which the lease is automatically renewed unless notice is given that it is not being renewed.)

Non-Tenant Situations

If the person in the property is not a tenant, such as a friend or relative you felt sorry for and let stay in your apartment for free, the situation might not be as easy as a tenant eviction.

Continued on page 161

Eviction Flowchart - Nonpayment of Rent

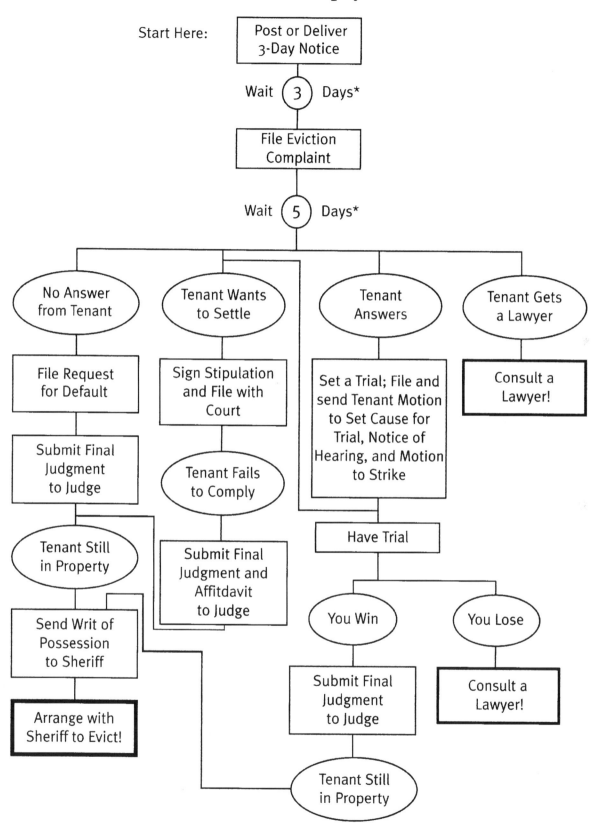

Start Here:

Post or Deliver
3-Day Notice

Wait (3) Days*

File Eviction
Complaint

Wait (5) Days*

No Answer from Tenant
- File Request for Default
- Submit Final Judgment to Judge
- Tenant Still in Property
- Send Writ of Possession to Sheriff
- **Arrange with Sheriff to Evict!**

Tenant Wants to Settle
- Sign Stipulation and File with Court
- Tenant Fails to Comply
- Submit Final Judgment and Affitdavit to Judge

Tenant Answers
- Set a Trial; File and send Tenant Motion to Set Cause for Trial, Notice of Hearing, and Motion to Strike
- Have Trial
  - You Win
    - Submit Final Judgment to Judge
    - Tenant Still in Property
  - You Lose
    - **Consult a Lawyer!**

Tenant Gets a Lawyer
- **Consult a Lawyer!**

*Excluding Saturdays, Sundays and legal holidays (see page 110)

Eviction Flowchart - Breach of Lease

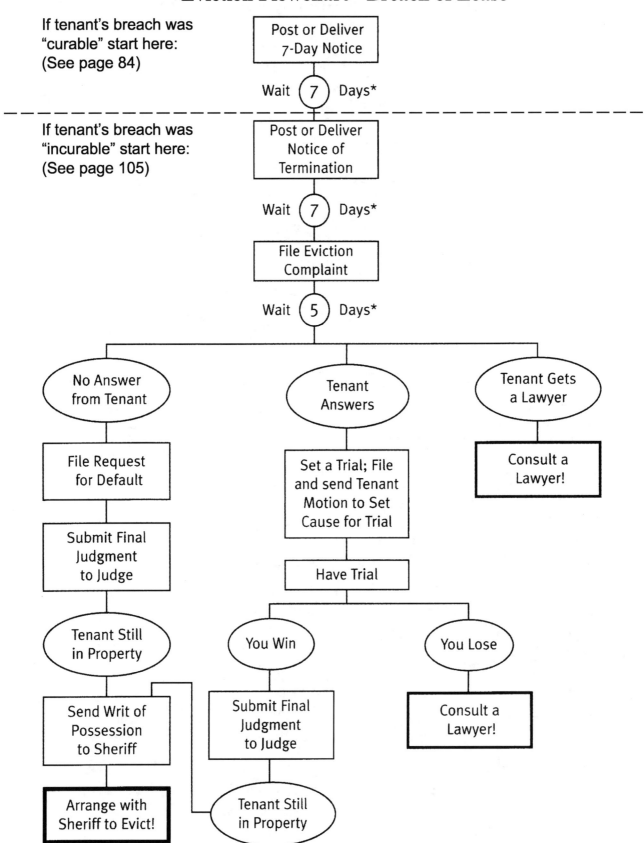

If tenant's breach was "curable" start here:
(See page 84)

Post or Deliver 7-Day Notice

Wait (7) Days*

If tenant's breach was "incurable" start here:
(See page 105)

Post or Deliver Notice of Termination

Wait (7) Days*

File Eviction Complaint

Wait (5) Days*

No Answer from Tenant

File Request for Default

Submit Final Judgment to Judge

Tenant Still in Property

Send Writ of Possession to Sheriff

Arrange with Sheriff to Evict!

Tenant Answers

Set a Trial; File and send Tenant Motion to Set Cause for Trial

Have Trial

You Win

Submit Final Judgment to Judge

Tenant Still in Property

You Lose

Consult a Lawyer!

Tenant Gets a Lawyer

Consult a Lawyer!

*Excluding Saturdays, Sundays and legal holidays (see page 110)

You might get lucky and the police might help you get them out, but if they can show they receive mail at your property the police might tell you that you need a court order, Since they are not technically a tenant you wouldn't use a tenant eviction, you would need something more complicated like an ejectment or an unlawful detainer lawsuit. If this is your situation check with an attorney. Again, it may violate your sense of justice, but giving they a few hundred dollars to leave may save you thousands of dollars in legal fees, time and aggravation.

Self-Help by Landlord

As explained in Chapter 8, self-help methods, such as shutting off electricity or changing locks, can result in thousands of dollars in fines against the landlord. Residential landlords are specifically forbidden to use self-help methods to evict tenants, even if the lease allows it. (Fla. Stat., Sec. 83.67.) As explained in the section "Retaliatory Conduct" on page 76, if a landlord directly or indirectly terminates utilities such as water, electricity, gas, elevators, lights, garbage collection, or refrigeration, or if the landlord locks up the unit or takes off the doors, windows, roofs, walls, etc., then the landlord is liable for damages of at least three months' rent plus court costs and attorney's fees.

A landlord posted a three-day notice and when the tenant was absent from the premises, he entered and removed her possessions. In a lawsuit, she testified that her possessions were all heirlooms and antiques and since the landlord had disposed of them, he could not prove otherwise. She was awarded $31,000.00 in damages. *Reynolds v. Towne Mgt. of Fla., Inc.,* 426 So.2d 1011 (Fla. 2 DCA 1983).

The potential for even greater damages exists, especially if the landlord's self-help actions result in punitive damages being awarded as well. A jury awarded the occupant $250,000 in punitive damages in a situation in which purchasers of a tax deed to property kept changing the locks on the property, nailing the door shut, and placing "for sale" signs on the property when the occupant was away.

Surrender or Abandonment

To surrender a dwelling, a tenant must tell the landlord that they are leaving or leave the keys. It can be presumed that a tenant abandoned the dwelling if the tenant has been absent for half of the rental term (unless the rent is current or notice is given). (Fla. Stat., Sec. 83-59(3)(c).) In some cases, such as when all of a tenant's possessions are gone and the electricity has been turned off, a landlord would be safe in assuming abandonment, but in the unlikely event that it went to court, the landlord may lose. If a tenant has died see page 108.

A landlord changed the locks the day after a lease expired and the tenant had moved most of his things out and had the utilities shut off. When the tenant sued saying he left a valuable Rolex on the premises, he lost. *Newman v. Gray, 4* FLW Supp. 271 (11th Cir. Dade 1996).

Using an Attorney

The landlord/tenant statutes provide that the loser in a landlord/tenant case can be charged with the winner's attorney's fees. Because of this, it is important to do an eviction carefully. In some cases, the tenant may just be waiting for the eviction notice before leaving the premises. In such a case, the landlord may regain the premises no matter what kind of papers he or she files. However, in other cases, tenants with no money and no defenses have gotten free lawyers, who find technical defects in the case. This can cause a delay in the eviction and cause the landlord to be ordered to pay the tenant's attorney's fees. A simple error in a landlord's court papers can cost him or her the case.

A landlord facing an eviction should consider the costs and benefits of using an attorney compared to doing it without one. One possibility is to file the case without an attorney and hope the tenant moves out. If the tenant stays and fights the case, an attorney can be hired to finish the case. Some landlords who prefer to do their evictions themselves start by paying a lawyer for a half-hour or hour of his or her time to review the facts of the case and point out problems. Whenever a tenant has an attorney, the landlord should also have one.

▤ In a suit by a cooperative association against a tenant for $191.33 in maintenance fees and to enforce the association rules, the tenant won the suit and was awarded $87,375 in attorney's fees. *Royal Saxon, Inc. v.Jaye,* 13 FLW 1809 (Fla. 4 DCA 1988).

▤ An argument that a legal aid organization was not entitled to attorney's fees did not win. The landlord had to pay $2,000 for twenty hours of the legal aid lawyer's time in having the case dismissed. *Beckwith v. Kesler, 2* FLW Supp. 82 (Broward Co. 1993).

Under Florida Statutes Section 59.46, the winner of the case is also entitled to attorney's fees for appeals that are made to a higher court. *Rose v. Gaglioti,* 49 Fla. Supp. 2d 6 (11th Cir. Dade 1991).

It is, of course, important to find an attorney who both knows landlord/tenant law and charges reasonable fees. There are many subtleties of the law that can be missed by someone without experience. Some attorneys who specialize in landlord/tenant cases charge very modest fees, to file the case and the same amount for a short hearing, unless the case gets complicated.

Others charge an hourly rate that can add up to thousands of dollars. You should check with other landlords or a local apartment association for names of good attorneys, or you might try calling the manager of a large apartment complex in the area.

If you get a security deposit at the beginning of the tenancy and start the eviction immediately upon a default, then the deposit should be nearly enough to cover the attorney's fee.

When an attorney represents a landlord in collecting rent, even for a bad check and even when following a state landlord/tenant law, some courts have held that the attorney must comply with the federal Fair Debt Collection Act. (U.S.C., Title 15, Sec. 1692.) This law requires that the debtor (the tenant) be given a specific notice and thirty days to dispute the debt. Fortunately, the Eleventh Circuit (in which Florida is located) ruled the other way. However, if in the future the court changes its ruling or the Supreme Court sides with the other courts, Florida attorneys will be required to follow this additional notice requirement. For this reason, demand letters are better sent by the landlords themselves.

Who Can Sue

An owner can represent him- or herself in court and does not need an attorney. (Fla. Stat., Sec. 454.18.) As a general rule, no one can represent another person in court except a licensed attorney. Only an attorney can represent a corporation. *Quill v. Orlando Housing Authority*, 385 So.2d 1167 (Fla. 5 DCA 1980)

Not even a corporate officer can represent a corporation, except in small claims court. It is a criminal offense for a non-lawyer to represent another party in court. In some cases, such as when a real estate agent or other agent of a landlord signed leases in his or her own name as rental agent, the agent can go to court without the owner of the property. This is because the agent is party to the contract. However, unless the agent is an attorney, the agent cannot take any action in the case other than filing the complaint. (Florida Statutes, Section 83.59.)

The Florida Supreme Court has approved simplified legal- forms for the use of those who are not attorneys. These forms include several for use in landlord/tenant matters, and the legend at the bottom indicates that they can be completed with the assistance of others who are not attorneys. In the case *The Florida Bar re Advisory Opinion—Nonlawyer Preparation of and Representation of Landlord in Uncontested Residential Evictions*, 605 So.2d 868 (Fla. 1993), the Florida Supreme Court granted the right to nonlawyer property managers to file eviction forms in cases in which only possession is sought (not damages) and the tenant does not contest the case. If the tenant contests the case, the property owner or an attorney must attend the hearing. *The Florida Bar re Advisory Opinion—Nonlawyer Preparation of and Representation of Landlord in Uncontested Residential Evictions*, 605 So.2d 868 (Fla. 1993).

In order to qualify to file an eviction for a landlord, a nonlawyer manager should have a written agreement with the landlord and should have the power to rent the property, to maintain the property, and to collect the rents. See the **PROPERTY MANAGEMENT AGREEMENT** (Form 26.)

If the landlord happens to die prior to when an eviction is necessary, the proper party to file the suit would be the personal representative of the landlord's estate (unless the property was inherited through joint tenancy or in a trust).

Court Procedures

An eviction is started by filing a *complaint* against the tenant in county court and paying the filing fee. An extra copy of the complaint must be provided for each defendant you are suing. The copies are *served* upon the tenants by the sheriff or by a private process server. A process server may cost a few dollars more than the sheriff but can often get service quicker and may be more likely to serve the papers personally, which will allow you to get a money judgment. In an eviction action, a landlord is entitled to a *summary procedure.* (Fla. Stat., Sec. 51.011.) This procedure is designed to speed up the normal court process and allow a landlord to remove a tenant quickly. This summary procedure is not related to the *Rules of Summary Procedure* used in small claims court.

County court is not like small claims court. The procedures are different and sometimes a judge will not be sympathetic to a landlord without a lawyer. But many landlords successfully handle their own cases. To see the steps of the eviction process, see the eviction flowcharts on pages 159-160.

Forms. Because judges may be more comfortable with Supreme Court approved forms, and to allow nonlawyers to use this book, all of the approved forms have been incorporated into this book. The format of the author's original forms have also been changed to make them look more like approved forms, therefore making them more acceptable to judges. However, nonlawyers, other than landlords, are not authorized to use the court forms that do not have the legend, "Approved for use under rule 10-2.1(a) of the Rules Regulating the Florida Bar" at the bottom.

Local forms. Some counties now have their own local forms. Check with your Clerk of the Circuit Court and if yours does have these forms, using them may help your case move along more quickly.

Be sure to read all of the text explaining evictions and to follow each step carefully.

NOTE: *Occasionally someone will write to the author and say that they followed this book but the judge gave the tenants extra time to move or let them speak without posting the rent into the court. Remember, most times a case will go smoothly, but judges do make mistakes. If your case gets complicated, you should invest in an experienced landlord/tenant attorney that can finish your case quickly.*

Complaint. To begin an eviction, you must prepare a COMPLAINT and file it with the clerk of the county court. You must attach a copy of the notice and also a copy of the lease or rental agreement if there is one. Along with the original, you must provide two copies for each defendant in the case. You should also keep a copy. (See Forms 36-39 for eviction complaints.)

You cannot be granted a judgment unless you swear that your complaint is true. Usually this is done by notarizing the complaint, but for some reason the Florida Bar did not put a place for notarizing the eviction complaints. Therefore, you should attach a verification form (see Form 40) to your complaint and have it notarized. This form also states that the defendants are not in the military service of the United States, because if they are, there will be a delay in granting your eviction.

The Florida Bar has a separate form of NONMILITARY AFFIDAVIT that is also included in this book in case some judges require it. (see Form 48) An eviction cannot proceed against a person who has provided a written notice that he or she is on active military service. (Fla. Stat., Sec. 250.5202.)

If you get to know your tenants you will be aware if they are or are not serving in the military. If you are not sure you can find out if a person is serving in the military by going to the Department of Defense web site. You will need their social security number and birth date (which you should have on their tenant application.) The web site is:

https://www.dmdc.osd.mil/appj/scra/scraHome.do

NOTE: *If your tenant is in the military service, you should consult an attorney.*

Attaching Lease. If there is a lease and a signed copy is not attached, the Complaint may be dismissed, but the landlord should be allowed to amend the Complaint to add a copy. *Weiner v. Lozman and Weinberg, P.A.*, 340 So.2d 1247 (1976).

Attaching Three-Day Notice. If the three-day notice is not attached or is faulty, some courts have dismissed the case (and awarded attorney's fees to the tenant) but some recent cases have allowed the landlord to amend the Complaint. *Miller v. Colon*, 2 FLW Supp. 243 (Dade Co. 1994). *Levenshon Emerald Park Partners, Ltd. v. Walantus*, 3 FLW Supp. 556 (Broward Co. 1995).

Lost Lease. If the lease has been lost or destroyed or if the tenant has the only copy, then the landlord can still sue, but these facts must be spelled out in the Complaint along with a statement of the terms of the lease. *Sachsa v. Tampa Music Co.*, 262 So.2d 17 (1972).

Venue. In some counties, such as Miami-Dade, there are several county court districts, and a landlord/tenant case is supposed to be filed in the district where the property is located. However, if you file in the wrong district and no one objects, the eviction will still be valid. *Meruelo v. Robinson*, 426 So.2d 1164 (Fla. 3 DCA 1983).

Filing the eviction in a court far from the rental property might make it less likely that the tenant will fight the eviction. If the tenant does object to the court, then the case should be quickly transferred to the correct district.

Seeking Damages. More information about obtaining a money judgment against the tenant is contained later in this chapter. However, you should read that section before filing your eviction since some of the forms in the eviction will be different.

Public Housing. In Section 8 housing, under the Code of Federal Regulations, Section 882.215(c)(4), the local housing authority must be notified in writing before the tenant can be served with the eviction. *Barkley v. Handy,* 1 FLW Supp. 57 (Pinellas Co. 1993).

Service of Process. Once the Complaint has been filed, the copies must be served on the tenants along with a summons. A summons is a legal document that tells the tenant that he or she must reply to your Complaint or have a judgment entered against him or her. In an eviction, a tenant has five days to answer. If you are also asking for back rent, the tenant has twenty days to respond to that portion of the Complaint. In some counties the SUMMONS is prepared by the clerk of the court but in others the landlord must prepare it. The forms approved by the Florida Supreme Court include two Summons forms, one for possession and one for damages, (see Forms 41 and 42.) If your clerk's office has its own Summons available, use that instead of the forms in this book.

Service of process can be done by either the sheriff or a process server. In some areas where the sheriff will be unable to handle the service for several days, a private process server can offer the advantage of quick service. A process server can be found by checking with the clerk or looking in the phone book under "Process Servers" or "Detective Agencies." The sheriff's fee for serving process is about $40.

The Summons and Complaint must be handed to the tenant or to a resident of the unit who is over 15 years of age. If after two attempts at least six hours apart the tenant has not been served, the papers may be served by posting them on the premises. If the tenant is served by posting, then a copy must also be mailed to the tenant by the clerk. If you anticipate service by posting, then extra copies and stamped envelopes with return addresses should be given to the clerk at the time the suit is filed. If you wish to obtain a money judgment, then the tenant must be personally served with the summons. Some landlords feel it is more important to get the tenant out quickly than to get a worthless judgment, so they instruct the sheriff or process server to post the summons.

⊟ A five-day summons is sufficient for a suit for both possession and money damages. When a court said that both a five- and a twenty-day summons had to be served, it was reversed by the appeals court. *Stein v. Hubbs,* 439 So.2d 1005 (Fla. 5 DCA 1983).

⊟ If the tenant does not read English, then the summons may not be valid if it is not in his or her language. Although there is no translation of the eviction summons provided by the court rules, at least one court held an eviction invalid when the landlord and tenant corresponded in Spanish and the lease was in Spanish. *Estevez v. Olarte,* 47 Fla. Supp. 2d 86 (Co.Ct. Dade 1991).

⊟ The summons cannot be served on a Sunday unless the landlord is afraid that the tenant is planning to escape from the state and files an affidavit so stating. (Fla. Stat., Sec. 48.20.) *Beckwith v. Kesler,* 1 FLW Supp. 494 (Broward Co. 1993).

⊟ In one case, a public housing authority obtained a tenant's signature on a stipulation that agreed to a default without needing service of process. The court found this was contrary to federal law. *Housing Authority of the City of Ft. Lauderdale v. Vinson,* 6 FLW Supp. 299 (17th Cir. App. Div. 1999). Such a waiver would probably be held illegal even in non-public housing.

⊟ If a tenant was not personally served, the court cannot enter a money judgment for the costs of the case. *Springbrook Commons, Ltd. v. Brown,* 761 So.2d 1192 (Fla. 4 DCA 2000).

Wait Five Days. After the papers have been served upon the tenants, they have five days (excluding Saturdays, Sundays, and legal holidays) in which to file an answer or else to vacate the premises. Most tenants leave at this point.

Default. If the tenants have not vacated the premises and have not filed any answer with the court within the five days, you must file a MOTION FOR CLERK'S DEFAULT (see Form 43) and then ask the judge in the case to sign a FINAL JUDGMENT. (see Form 49)

A few years ago the clerks in some counties required the landlord to wait more than five days before entering the default in case an answer was mailed. However, Florida Statutes, Section 51.011 makes it clear that the tenant must have the answer filed within five days.

Mediation. In recent years, to remedy overcrowded court calendars, more and more counties have started requiring or allowing parties in tenant eviction cases to participate in mediation. The net result of these is usually just to let the tenant stay in the unit longer without paying rent.

The tenant should be required to pay the pending rent into the registry of the court during mediation, but different counties and different judges use different procedures and there is not much you can do to fight it.

Hearing. If the tenants have filed any answer, even a postcard stating something nonsensical, you must have a hearing before the judge. If the tenant has a lawyer, you should also get one because a small mistake by you could cost you the case and you will have to pay the tenant's attorney's fees, possibly thousands of dollars.

NOTE: *You may feel that you cannot afford attorney's fees, but an occasional bad tenant is a risk of investing in real property. The cost should be factored into your return. Next time, screen your tenant better or get a bigger deposit.*

If the tenant filed an answer, then you should check with the clerk or the judge's secretary to set a hearing. Mention that this is a *summary proceeding* landlord/tenant case and that you need ten or fifteen minutes. You should be able to get a hearing within a week or ten days. If they want to schedule it a month or two away, state that you want a quick hearing under Florida Statutes, Section 51.011. When their calendars are crowded, some judges say a thirty-day wait for a hearing is reasonable. More sympathetic judges will squeeze you in for ten minutes early in the morning. If nothing is available, ask if the case might be transferred to a judge who has more time. If that does not help, check with an attorney.

If you are evicting for nonpayment of rent and the tenant has not deposited the rent into the registry of the court, you should file a MOTION TO STRIKE and a NOTICE OF HEARING (see Form 52 and Form 51), and send copies by regular mail to the tenants.

Some judges require that a trial be set at the same time, and in different counties they use either a MOTION TO SET CAUSE FOR TRIAL or a PLAINTIFF'S NOTICE FOR TRIAL, (see Form 55, or Form 56.) If you use the MOTION TO SET CAUSE FOR TRIAL, copies of the Motion for Trial (with only the top filled in by you) must be sent to the tenants by regular mail, and extra copies for each tenant and the landlord must be given to the judge along with stamped, addressed envelopes. If you use the PLAINTIFF'S NOTICE FOR TRIAL, send a copy to the tenant, keep a copy, and file the original with the court. If this sounds complicated, ask the judge's assistant exactly what is required of you.

If you are evicting for breach of the lease or if the tenant deposits the rent into the registry of the court, then you will need to go right to the trial instead of using the MOTION TO STRIKE. Use the MOTION TO SET CAUSE FOR TRIAL (form 55), or a PLAINTIFF'S NOTICE FOR TRIAL (Form 56) as explained in the previous paragraph.

If no one shows up at the hearing except you, then you should present to the judge your MOTION FOR DEFAULT FINAL JUDGMENT and FINAL JUDGMENT (see Form 45, and Form

49) along with extra copies for yourself and all tenants and stamped envelopes addressed to the tenants.

If the tenants show up, they should not be able to present any defenses unless they have deposited rent with the clerk of the court. (Fla. Stat., Sec. 83.60(2).) Even if they want to talk about building code violations, they should not be allowed to bring up the subject, unless they gave written notice to the landlord that they would withhold rent unless the premises were repaired within seven days. (Fla. Stat., Sec. 83.60(1).)

The judge should enter a default. Section 83.56(5) states: *The court may not set a date for mediation or trial unless the provisions of Section 83.60(2) have been met, but shall enter a default judgment for removal of the tenant with a writ of possession to issue immediately if the tenant fails to comply with Section 83.60(2).* You should be granted a FINAL JUDGMENT at this hearing if you did everything right. If not, you should consult an attorney who can move your case to judgment quickly. If the tenant wishes to dispute the amount of rent claimed in the COMPLAINT, he or she must file a *Motion to Determine the Amount of Rent to be Paid into the Registry* within five days of receiving the summons (excluding Saturdays, Sundays, and legal holidays). This action by the tenant can delay the eviction. However, the tenant must also attach to the motion some documentary evidence that the Complaint is in error. (Fla. Stat., Sec. 83.60(2).)

In the past, tenants were allowed to file a *Motion to Dismiss* without paying the rent into the court to contest the sufficiency of the three-day notice. Today this should not be allowed. *Johnson and McGee v. Francois*, 6 FLW Supp. 585 (9th Cir. App. Div. 1999). However, if the tenant's Motion to Dismiss is allowed, you will probably have to re-file your case. However, in a recent case, a landlord was allowed to deliver a proper notice without re-filing (and paying another filing fee). *Levenshon Emerald Park Partners, Ltd. v. Walantus*, 3 FLW Supp. 556 (Broward Co. 1995).

▤ In another case, the court ruled that if the case is dismissed because of a procedural error rather than on the merits of the case, the tenant is not entitled to attorney's fees. *Paramount v. P.R.D. Holding,* 4 FLW Supp. 683 (Cir. Ct. Dade 1997).

▤ If it is denied, the judge may grant your judgment or may schedule another hearing a few days later. An explanation of this situation can be found in the case *Cook v. Arrowhead Mobile Home Community,* 50 Fla. Supp. 2d 26 (3rd Cir. Columbia 1991).

If the tenant shows up with an attorney and you were not told previously, you should ask the judge for a continuance to get your own attorney. If you make a mistake and lose, you may have to pay the tenant's attorney's fees. If the tenant pays the rent into the registry of the court, then a trial will be held.

In a trial, you would need to go through each paragraph of your complaint and prove it was true. This would be done by sworn testimony by you or a witness. You would also need to present evidence to the court such as an original lease and a copy of the three-day notice that you served on the tenant. After you present your side, the tenant is able to rebut your case with testimony and evidence such as cancelled checks. The judge may make a ruling immediately after a trial or may take the case *under advisement* and mail out a judgment a few days later.

Depositions and Subpoenas. It is possible to take depositions of the parties and to subpoena their records. This means they are called before a court reporter, asked questions under oath, and required to show their records. The answers are then used in court to contradict what the party might say to the judge. (Legal aides sometimes use this to complicate the case for landlords.)

▤ When a landlord failed to show up for a deposition, he was ordered to pay $228.50 in attorney's fees and go to jail for three days unless he appeared at the next scheduled deposition. *(Jacobs v. Mobely,* 9 FLW Supp. 403 (Brevard Co. 2002).)

Mediation. Failure to show up at mediation can result in having the case dismissed and being ordered to pay the tenants attorney's fees. In some areas, mediation services are recommended or required before trial. At a mediation, the parries are encouraged to resolve their differences. This may mean a planned date of departure for the tenant or perhaps allowing the tenant to stay in the premises with a timetable for paying the back rent. In some cases damage to the premises or animosity between the parties may make it impossible to continue the tenancy. If a settlement is reached, then it should be in the form of a *stipulation* that is filed with the court. If you merely dismiss your case as part of the settlement, then you will have to start all over from scratch if the tenant again defaults.

Stipulation. Whether or not mediation is used, the parties may be able to resolve the matter without going through a hearing. This will allow the landlord to recover some back rent and avoid the hassle of cleaning and re-renting the unit. If you wish to settle with the tenant and come to an agreement in which the rent will be paid over time, then you can enter into a stipulation to delay the case. You should never accept any rent from the tenant once the case is filed without signing a stipulation.

Some counties have their own forms, but a STIPULATION form is included in this book in case your county does not provide one. (See Form 54.)

Basically, the STIPULATION is an agreement that the tenant will pay the back rent in installments and keep current in the rent and that the landlord will not proceed in the case. If the tenant fails to pay as agreed, the landlord can go to the judge without a hearing and get a WRIT OF POSSESSION upon presentation of a sworn, notarized statement that the tenant has defaulted on the STIPULATION. Be sure that any STIPULATION you sign says exactly when and how much rent the tenant must pay and that you are entitled to a default judgment in the event of default. A poorly worded STIPULATION can cause the landlord to lose the eviction. *Hodgson v. Jones*, 6 FLW Supp. 759 (17th Cir. App. Div. 1999).

Writ of Possession. Once your FINAL JUDGMENT has been signed by the judge, if the tenant has still not vacated the premises, you must take a WRIT OF POSSESSION and one extra copy of it to the clerk and pay the sheriff's fee for the eviction, (see form 47, p.261.) Recent laws provide that the landlord has the choice of changing the locks on the premises and asserting his or her lien on the tenant's possessions or moving the tenant's possessions out to the street. (Fla. Stat., Sec. 83.625 and Sec. 713.691.) The landlord is not liable for what happens to the tenant's possessions if put out on the street. (Fla. Stat., Sec. 83.625.) *McReady v. Booth*, 389 So.2d 1000 (Fla. 5 DCA 1981).

Regaining Possession. Different counties have different procedures for removing a tenant's possessions. Check with your local sheriff. In some cases, the sheriff stands by while the landlord moves the property out. In such a case, the landlord would in effect be acting as a deputy sheriff and would be protected by law from the tenant. (Fla. Stat., Sec. 843.01-.02.) The law now allows the sheriff to charge an hourly fee for such service. With some tenants and some property, it is not worth the trouble of attempting to claim a landlord's lien on the personal property left in the premises. The first $1000 in value is exempt from the lien and some tenants may break into the premises to retrieve their possessions. In many cases, it is just better to put the property on the street and hope you never hear from the tenant again.

The landlord can remove the tenant's possessions at the time the sheriff executes the WRIT OF POSSESSION or at any time thereafter. (Fla. Stat., Sec. 83.62.) If the personal property left on the premises appears to have been abandoned, then it should be treated as explained in Chapter 9.

Money Damages and Back Rent

Procedures for collecting money damages and back rent from a tenant are explained in Chapter 9.

Tenant's Possible Defenses

A tenant who is behind in rent usually has one objective—to stay in the property rent-free as long as possible. Tenants and the lawyers provided to them at no charge by legal aid clinics sometimes come up with creative, though ridiculous, defenses. Below is case law, with some cases dating back several years, showing how long these arguments have been blocked. Remember, the tenant should not be able to bring up any defenses unless he or she has paid the rent alleged to be due into the registry of the court.

Constitutionality. If a tenant or the tenant's attorney attempts to delay an eviction by using an argument without factual or legal basis, Section 57.105 allows the court to award attorney's fees and sanctions and can require the tenant's attorney to pay. (See Appendix A for the full statute.)

A tenant claims it is unconstitutional to have a quick eviction procedure and to require the tenant to pay the rent into the court before he or she is allowed to present any defenses. The U.S. Supreme Court says that such procedures can be constitutional. *Lindsey v. Normet*, 465 US 56 (1972).

In 1988, a Florida appellate court held Florida's law to be constitutional. *Karstetter v. Graham Companies,* 521 So.2d 298 (Fla. 3 DCA 1988).

Security Deposit. A tenant says that he or she is not in default because the landlord has a security deposit that covers the default. That is wrong. A security deposit is for a specific purpose at the end of the tenancy and does *not* cover current rent. *6701 Realty, Inc., v. Deauville Ent., Inc.* 84 So.2d 325 (Fla. 1955).

Amount Incorrect. A tenant disputes the amount of rent due. This is not a defense because if any rent is due, then the landlord is entitled to eviction. However, if the amount stated in the three-day notice is wrong, the case may be dismissed. *Helga Skin Therapy v. Dead River Prop., Inc.*, 478 So.2d 95 (Fla. 2 DCA 1985).

Title. A tenant claims that the landlord has not proved he or she has good title to the property. But a tenant who has entered into a rental agreement with a landlord is *estopped* (prevented) from denying that the landlord has good title. *Avila South Condo Assoc, Inc. v. Kappa Corp.*, 347 So.2d 599 (1977).

Fictitious Name. A tenant says that the landlord is using a fictitious name that has not been registered with the county. If the landlord actually is using an unregistered name, the case is abated until he or she complies with the statute. However, in order to use this defense, the tenant must raise the issue no later than in the written answer to the complaint. *Cor-Gal Builders, Inc., v. Southard*, 136 So.2d 244 (Fla. 3 DCA 1962).

Corporation is Dissolved. Under Florida corporate law, a court action may not be maintained by a corporation that is not in good standing with the Florida Department of State. If your corporation has been dissolved for nonpayment of fees, it can be reinstated by paying previous year's fees and a penalty. There are companies in Tallahassee that will hand carry your payment to the Division of Corporations and send you a certificate of good standing immediately.

Corporation Not Represented by Attorney. If the landlord is a corporation, it is required to be represented by an attorney. If not, the suit may be dismissed. While not all courts have agreed, the court in one case ruled that the pleadings could be made valid by amending them to add an attorney's signature. This would avoid filing a new case. *J.A.R. Inc., v. Universal American Rty. Corp.*, 485 So.2d 467 (Fla. 3 DCA 1986).03

Waiver by Refusal. A tenant says that because the landlord refused the rent after the three days were up, that it is a waiver of the rent. Wrong again. While the landlord does have to give the tenant three days to pay all past due rent, he or she does not have to accept rent after the three-day grace period expires. *Helga Skin Therapy, Inc. v. Dead River Properties, Inc.*, 478 So.2d 95 (Fla. 2 DCA 1985). *Multach v. Adams*, 418 So.2d 1254 (Fla. 4 DCA 1982).

Waiver by Acceptance of Rent. Usually, if a landlord accepts rent after serving a notice or filing suit, then he or she waives the right to continue and must serve a new notice or file a new suit. (Fla. Stat., Sec. 83.56(5).)

◫ When the tenant placed a check through the landlord's mail slot and the landlord immediately returned it by certified mail, this was not acceptance of rent by the landlord or a waiver. *Gene B. Glick Co., Inc. v. Oliver,* 36 Fla. Supp. 2d 208 (Co.Ct. Brevard Co. 1989).

◫ When the evidence indicated that the landlords did not know of an assignment of the lease when they accepted rent, such acceptance did not constitute a waiver of their rights. *El Prado Restaurant, Inc. v. Weaver,* 268 So.2d 382 (Fla. 3 DCA 1972).

◫ When a landlord accepted rent after giving tenants notice to vacate, a court found there was no waiver because the landlord only accepted past due rent and refused current rent. *Russo v. Manfredo,* 35 Fla. Supp. 2d 23 (Cir.Ct. Citrus Co. 1989).

◫ When a landlord accepted late payments without protest and never at any time notified the tenant that it was in default, this was a waiver of the landlord's right to claim a default on the part of the tenant even though the lease contained an *anti-waiver* clause. *Protean Investors Inc. v. Travel, Etc., Inc.,* 499 So.2d 49 (Fla. 3 DCA 1986).

Reg. Z. A tenant says that the landlord has not complied with *Reg. Z,* in the Code of Federal Regulations, which is a truth-in-lending requirement, but this federal regulation does not apply to the rental of property (C.F.R., Title 12, Sec. 226.1(c)(1).)

Unconscionability of Rent. A tenant claims that rent is unconscionable, but this is a legal conclusion and a tenant must state facts that would prove to the court that the rent is unconscionable. *State v. DeAnza Corp.,* 416 So.2d 1173 (Fla. 5 DCA 1982).

Insufficient Complaint. A tenant says that the landlord's complaint is not drawn properly and does not state a cause of action. The complaints included in this book include all elements necessary. Forms 36, 37, and 38 are Florida Supreme Court approved forms, and form 39 is a modified version of them.

Maintenance of Premises. *A* tenant says that the landlord has not complied with Florida Statutes, Section 83.51(1), and that the tenant is withholding rent. This defense may not be raised unless seven days have elapsed between when written notice was sent to the landlord and when the tenant withheld the rent. (Fla. Stat., Sec. 83.60(1).)

In a case in which the tenant did not raise the issue of the condition of the premises until after he had received the three-day notice, the tenant was not allowed to use this defense. *Lakeway Management Co. of Fla., Inc. v. Stolowilsky,* 13 FLW 1576 (1988).

The notice may be given by the tenant to the landlord, the landlord's representative, a resident manager, or anyone who collects rent for the landlord. (Fla. Stat., Sec. 83.60(1).)

The violation must be a material violation of the building code. Minor problems should not be allowed as defenses for withholding rent. Also, the tenant must attach a copy of the seven-day notice to his or her answer, and the tenant must attach a copy of the code that the landlord has allegedly violated and request the court to take judicial notice of it. If the tenant does not do all these things, then he or she should not be able to use this defense.

There is a good argument that this statute is unconstitutional. The statute does not set certain standards, but lets any and all housing authorities throughout the state set the standards. This may be an unconstitutional delegation of legislative authority under Article II, Section 3 of the Florida constitution. *Askew v. Cross Key Waterways,* 372 So.2d 913 (Fla. 1979).

Equitable Defenses. There is a general rule that only circuit court can hear *equitable matters.* Tenants sometimes try to raise *equitable defenses* in an eviction case in order to delay it by transferring it to circuit court. But courts have ruled that in a landlord/tenant dispute, the county court has exclusive jurisdiction and may consider all defenses. *Palm Corp. v. 183rd St. Theatre Corp.*, 344 So.2d 252 (Fla. 3 DCA 1977).

Retaliatory Conduct. *A* tenant says that he or she is being evicted in retaliation for some lawful action and that this is illegal under Florida Statutes, Section 83.64. This defense does not apply if the landlord is evicting the tenant for good cause— such as nonpayment of rent, violation of the lease or reasonable rules, or violation of the landlord/tenant law.

Discovery. A tenant wants more time in order to take *discovery,* which means to ask questions of the landlord and any witnesses under oath before a court reporter. This should not delay the case. The discovery should be done quickly in order to comply with Florida Statutes, Section 51.011, which applies to an eviction suit under Florida Statutes, Section 83.59.

Jury Trial. If a tenant makes a request for a jury trial, then he or she should be required to first post the past rent and any rent that comes due during the pendency of the suit. If there is a jury presently impaneled, then it should go to that jury, and if not, one should be immediately summoned. The tenant must pay the costs of the jury. If the tenant requests a jury, the landlord should file a *Preliminary Motion to Summon a Jury and Determine Fees.* This can be found in a civil procedure form book in the courthouse law library.

Attorney Busy or Unprepared. The tenant's attorney may say that he or she just got on the case and needs time to prepare or has a busy schedule and is not available for trial for a month or so. This should not delay the case. The landlord has a right to a quick procedure under Florida Statutes, Section 51.01. If the tenant's attorney is unavailable, he or she should not have taken the case. If the tenant has a lawyer, the landlord should have one too.

Attorney's Fees for Dismissal. When a tenant moves out of the property, the landlord sometimes dismisses his or her case.

In some cases, the tenants have then claimed that they should have their attorney's fees paid because they were the *prevailing party* in the case. But, if the landlord dismisses his or her case as moot, this does not make the tenant the prevailing party. *The Colony II Assoc, Ltd. v. Crocki*, 37 Fla. Supp. 2d 138 (Co.Ct. Palm Beach 1989).

If a landlord is handling his or her own eviction, then the landlord should not dismiss the case after the tenant moves out. He or she should proceed to judgment at least for the court costs and to be officially granted possession. If the landlord is represented by an attorney, then he or she will have to weigh the costs.

Grievance Procedure. In federally subsidized housing, the regulations require that tenants be given a *grievance procedure* in some evictions. However, when the tenant is a threat to the health and safety of other tenants or employees, the Code of Federal Regulations, Tide 24, Chapter 9, Section 966.51(a) states such a hearing is not required. *Housing Authority of St. Petersburg v. Wilcox*, 50 Fla. Supp. 2d 110 (Co.Ct. Pinellas 1991).

Right to Possession. One court dismissed a suit because the landlord did not "prove he had a right to possession." The appellate court reversed, stating that he did not need to prove so. *Ferrante v. Schirm*, FLW Supp. 209 (Hernando Co. 1995).

Bad Faith. A mere claim of *bad faith* was not enough to state a cause of action under the mobile home section of the Landlord-Tenant Act as to entitle the state attorney to seek an injunction. *State v. DeAnza Corp.*, 416 So.2d 1173 (1982).

Tenant's Possible Countersuits

Another way tenants try to delay things is by filing a countersuit. This should not delay the eviction.

Exceeding Jurisdiction. Since county court can only hear cases of amounts under $ 15,000, tenants sometimes try to claim over $15,000 in damages against the landlords. This way they hope to transfer the case to circuit court where it will drag out for a long time.

➲ In most cases, a claim of over $15,000 is clearly ridiculous and obviously intended as a delaying tactic. In such cases a MOTION TO STRIKE (see Form 52) should be filed along with the MOTION FOR DEFAULT, (see Form 53) *Pearce v. Parsons*, 414 So.2d 296 (Fla. 2 DCA 1982).

➲ If the tenant does submit a legitimate claim for over $15,000, then he or she must also pay the additional filing fee for transfer of the case. (Rule 1.170(j), Florida Rules of Civil Procedure.)

➲ One way to speed things along is to request that the circuit court designate the county court judge as an acting circuit judge for the purpose of hearing your action. *A-One Coin Laundry v. Waterside Towers*, 561 So.2d 590 (Fla. 3 DCA 1990).

Negligence. A landlord's failure to maintain the premises may be a breach of contract, but alone it is not actionable negligence. *K.D. Lewis Ent. Corp., Inc. v. Smith*, 445 So.2d 1032 (Fla. 5 DCA 1984).

Malicious Prosecution. *A malicious prosecution* action cannot be brought in the same case being complained. It is a separate suit that can be brought if the landlord loses the original suit. *Blue v. Weinstein*, 381 So.2d 308 (Fla. 3 DCA 1980).

Punitive Damages. There is no such thing as *punitive damages* in a case regarding a contract. *Club Eden Roc, Inc. v. Fortune Cookie Restaurant, Inc.*, 490 So.2d 210 (Fla. 3 DCA 1986). In order for a party to be entitled to punitive damages, there must be a tort committed by the landlord and there must be proof of "fraud, actual malice, deliberate violence, or oppression or such gross negligence as to indicate wanton disregard for the rights of others." *KD.Lewis Ent. Corp., Inc., v. Smith*, 445 So.2d 1032 (Fla. 5 DCA 1984). Even when a landlord wrongfully overcharged tenants and lied to a federal agency, he could not be charged with punitive damages because it was merely a breach of contract. *Guthartz v. Lewis*, 408 So.2d 600 (Fla. 3 DCA 1981).

Moving Expenses. Tenants are not entitled to moving expenses after a lawful eviction. *Bruce v. Stork's Nest, Inc.*, 477 So.2d 51 (Fla. 2 DCA 1985).

Harassment. There is no such thing as an *action for harassment* in Florida. *Kamhi v. Waterview Towers Condominium Association, Inc.*, 793 So.2d 1033 (Fla. 4 DCA 2001).

Class Action. Since the claims of each tenant will in most cases be different, they probably cannot counterclaim as a *class action suit* on behalf of all tenants in the building. *K.D. Lewis Ent. Corp., Inc. v. Smith*, 445 So.2d 1032 (Fla. 5 DCA 1984).

Civil Theft. Tenants have claimed that failing to return a security deposit and removing belongings were *civil theft,* which would entitle them to triple damages. However, courts have held that the tenant must prove that the landlord had criminal intent, and this is difficult. *Globe Communications Corp. v. 2112 Congress Assoc. Ltd.*, 538 So.2d 949 (Fla. 4 DCA 1989), *Pelletier v. Cutler*, 543 So.2d 406 (Fla. 4 DCA 1989).

Withdrawal of Rent Money from the Court

If the tenant actually has paid any rent money into the registry of the court, it will in most cases be awarded to the landlord at some point in the case. This is done by filing a MOTION TO DISBURSE FUNDS FROM THE COURT REGISTRY (see Form 58) and having the judge sign an ORDER DISBURSING FUNDS FROM THE COURT REGISTRY, (see Form 59.) If the landlord is in danger of losing the premises or has some other hardship, he or she can do this during the pendency of the case by setting a special hearing for this purpose. (This would only be necessary if the tenant has been successful in delaying the case with a motion or appeal.)

Abandonment after Dismissal

In some cases, the tenant will fight the eviction, have it dismissed on a technicality, and then move out. In such a situation, if you have been given the right to re-file the case to correct the error, you should do so. *Beckwith v. Kesler*, 1 FLW Supp. 82 (Broward Co. 1993), *Levenshon Emerald Park Partners, Ltd. v. Walantus*, 3 FLW Supp. 556 (Broward Co. 1995). Otherwise the tenant might later seek attorney's fees saying you never had a good case to begin with.

Tenant's Appeal

A tenant has thirty days in which to file a notice of appeal, but since the WRIT OF POSSESSION gives the tenant twenty-four hours to vacate the property, the tenant will have to act immediately if he or she wants to stop the eviction. The eviction should not be halted by filing a notice of appeal. If the tenant files a notice of appeal, then the landlord should immediately file a *Motion to Set a Supersedeas Bond.* (Rule 9.310, Florida Rules of Appellate Procedure.) The amount of the bond will have to be decided by a judge and should be done at a hearing with both parties present. Palm Beach Hts. Dv. & Sales Corp. v. Decillis, 385 So.2d 1170 (Fla. 3 DCA 1980). Jenkins Trucking, Inc. v. Emmons, 107 So.2d 280 (Fla. 3 DCA 1968).

A tenant can file an appeal after vacating the premises as long as it is within the thirty days. If the tenant wins the appeal, it is possible that they will be allowed to move back into the premises, so it is not a good idea for the landlord to enter into a long-term lease with a new tenant if there is a chance the tenant will win on appeal.

If the tenant files a frivolous appeal, the landlord may be able to collect damages. Florida Statutes, Section 57.105 was recently strengthened to allow attorney's fees and sanctions to be awarded for frivolous claims.

Tenant's Bankruptcy

If a tenant files bankruptcy, all legal actions must stop immediately. This provision is automatic from the moment the bankruptcy petition is filed. (United States Code (U.S.C.), Title 11, Section 362.) If you take any action in court, seize the tenant's property, try to impose a landlord's lien, or use the security deposit for unpaid rent, then you can be held in contempt of federal court. It is not necessary that you receive formal notice. Verbal notice is sufficient. If you do not believe the tenant, then you should call the bankruptcy court to confirm the filing.

The stay lasts until the debtor is discharged, the case is dismissed, or until the property is abandoned or voluntarily surrendered.

Relief from Stay. The landlord may ask for the right to continue with the eviction by filing a *Motion for Relief from Stay* and paying the filing fee. Within thirty days of filing the Motion for Relief from Stay, a hearing is held and it may be held by telephone. The motion is governed by Bankruptcy Rule 9014 and the requirements of how the tenant must be served are contained in Rule 7004. However, for such a hearing, the services of an attorney are usually necessary.

Post-Filing Rent. The bankruptcy stay only applies to amounts owed to the landlord at the time of filing the bankruptcy. Therefore, the landlord can sue the tenant for eviction and rent owed for any time period after the filing unless the bankruptcy trustee assumes the lease. The landlord can proceed during the bankruptcy without asking for relief from the automatic stay under three conditions:

➲ the landlord can only sue for rent due after the filing;

➲ the landlord cannot sue until the trustee rejects the lease (if the trustee does not accept the lease within sixty days of the Order for Relief, then Section 365(d)(1) provides that it is deemed rejected); or,

➲ the landlord must sue under the terms of the lease and may not treat the trustee's rejection as a breach.

In Chapter 13 reorganization bankruptcy, the landlord should be paid the rent as it comes due.

Filing after Judgment. If the tenant filed bankruptcy after a judgment of eviction has been entered, there should be no problem lifting the automatic stay since the tenant has no interest in the property. *In re Cowboys, Inc.*, 14 B.R. (S.D. Fla. 1982).

If your tenant files bankruptcy and you decide it is worth hiring a lawyer, you should locate an attorney who is experienced in bankruptcy work. Prior to the meeting with the attorney, you should gather as much information as possible (type of bankruptcy filed, assets, liabilities, case number, etc.).

Landlord's Appeal

If the landlord loses, then he or she has the right to appeal the judgment. Appeals from county court are usually made to the local circuit court, but the county court judge can certify a question to the district court of appeal. (Rule 9.160, Florida Rules of Appellate Procedure.) If the circuit court makes an error in an appellate ruling, it can be appealed to the District Court of Appeals. Appealing a county court judgment to circuit court may take a matter of weeks or months, but appealing a case to the district court may take a year or longer. *Dooley v. Culver*, 392 So.2d 575 (Fla. 4 DCA 1980).

Grounds for appeal. Our legal system allows one chance to bring a case to court. If you did not prepare for your trial, or thought you would not need a witness, you do not have the right to try again. However, in certain limited circumstances you may be able to have your case reviewed.

➲ If the judge made a mistake in interpreting the law that applies to your case, then that is grounds for reversal.

➲ If new evidence is discovered after the trial that could not have been discovered before the trial, then a new trial might be granted, but this is not very common.

➲ If one party lied at trial and that party was believed by the judge or jury, there is usually not much that can be done.

➲ There are certain other grounds for rehearing such as misconduct of an attorney or errors during the trial, but these matters are beyond the scope of this book. (For more detailed information in this area of the law see *Trawick's Florida Practice and Procedure,* available at most law libraries.)

Motion for Rehearing. The first way to appeal a decision is to ask the judge to listen to the case again. If important new evidence has been discovered or an important court case was overlooked by the judge, then this may work, but if the judge was clearly on the side of the tenant, it may be a waste of time. If the case was a jury trial, the motion used is a *Motion for New Trial,* not a *Motion for Rehearing. A* Motion for Rehearing must be filed within five days of entry of judgment. A Motion for New Trial must be filed within five days of the verdict. When the Motion is filed with the court, a copy is sent to the other party (or their attorney) and a hearing is scheduled before the judge, with notice of the hearing also sent to the other side.

03 When a landlord lost a case and was ordered to pay attorney's fees, he asked for a rehearing. After losing the rehearing, the landlord was ordered to pay an additional $750 in attorney's fees for the rehearing. The judgement was reversed for two reasons, first that a rehearing cannot be called frivolous just because it restates issues since it is normal for rehearing to restate issues and second, that attorney's fees should not be awarded for arguing about attorney's fees. *Miami Beach Equity Investors Ltd. Ptn. v. Granoff,* 4 FLW Supp. 755 (11th Cir. 1997)

Notice of Appeal. If the judge made an error in interpreting the law, or ignored the law (it does happen), then you can appeal to a higher court. This is done by filing two copies of a *Notice of Appeal* within thirty days of the rendition of the judgment and paying the filing fee for the appeal. (If the tenant is the one to file the appeal, the landlord can cross-appeal within ten days.)

➲ Within fifty days of the filing of the Notice of Appeal, the clerk of the circuit court should prepare the record.

➲ Within seventy days of the filing of Notice, the parties should file their *appellate brief.*

➲ Within 110 days of the filing of the Notice, the clerk should transmit the record to the circuit court.

➲ More detailed information on how to proceed with an appeal can be found in the *Florida Rules of Appellate Procedure.*

Satisfaction of Judgment

If, after a judgment has been entered against the tenant, the tenant pays the amount due, it is the landlord's responsibility to file a SATISFACTION OF JUDGMENT, (see Form 61.)

Appendix C

Forms

This appendix contains forms which can be used in your landlording activities. They should not be used unless you understand the legal ramifications of them which is explained in the text, or consult a lawyer.

Forms that have the words "The Florida Bar" at the bottom are the "simplified forms" approved by the Florida Supreme Court for use by paralegals and persons who wish to represent themselves.

All other forms were prepared by the author. As you can see, some were designed to look similar to Florida Bar forms to make them more uniform.

The forms in this appendix are available from the publisher on a CD. See the form in the back of the book to order.

Tenant Application

Name_____ Date of Birth _____

Name_____ Date of Birth _____

Soc. Sec. Nos._____

Drivers' License Nos._____

Children & Ages_____

Present Landlord_____ Phone_____

Address _____ How Long?_____

Previous Landlord_____ Phone_____

Address_____

Second Previous Landlord_____ Phone_____

Address_____

Nearest Relative_____ Phone_____

Address_____

Applicant's Employer_____ Phone_____

Address_____

Second Applicant's Employer_____ Phone_____

Address_____

Pets_____

Other persons who will stay at premises for more than one week_____

_____

Bank Name_____ Acct. #_____

Bank Name_____ Acct. #_____

Have you ever been evicted?_____

Have you ever been in litigation with a landlord?_____

Under penalty of perjury, the undersigned hereby certify and attest that the above information is true and authorize landlord to verify the above information. We understand that any false information provided is grounds for termination of the tenacy.

_____   _____

Authorization to Release Personal Information

We, the undersigned prospective tenants of _____
_____ hereby authorize the Landlord/Lessor to access our credit report to determine our creditworthiness for renting the property.

Date: _____, 20 ____   Prospective tenants:

                                         _____

                                         _____

Inspection Report

Date In _____ , 20 _____   Date Out _____ , 20 _____

Unit: _____

AREA	CONDITION			
	Good	Poor	Good	Poor
Yard/garden				
Driveway				
Patio/porch				
Exterior				
Entry light/bell				
Living room/Dining room/Halls				
Floors/carpets				
Walls/ceilings				
Doors/locks				
Fixtures/lights				
Outlets/switches				
Other				
Bedrooms				
Floors/carpets				
Walls/ceilings				
Doors/locks				
Fixtures/lights				
Outlets/switches				
Other				
Bathrooms				
Faucets				
Toilet				
Sink/tub				
Floors				
Walls/ceiling				
Doors/locks				
Fixtures/lights				
Outlets/switches				
Other				
Kitchen				
Refrigerator				
Range				
Oven				
Dishwasher				
Sink/disposal				
Cabinets/counters				
Floors				
Walls/ceiling				
Doors/locks				
Fixtures/lights				
Outlets/switches				
Other				
Misc.				
Closets/pantry				
Garage				
Keys				
Other				

House or Duplex Unit Lease

LANDLORD:_____   TENANT:_____

_____   _____

PROPERTY:_____

IN CONSIDERATION of the mutual covenants and agreements herein contained, Landlord hereby leases to Tenant and Tenant hereby leases from Landlord the above-described property under the following terms:

1. TERM. This lease shall be for a term of _____ beginning _____, 20___ and ending _____, 20 ____.

2. RENT. The rent shall be $_____ per _____ and shall be due on or before the _____ day of each _____. In the event the rent is received more than three (3) days late, a late charge of $_____ shall be due. In the event a check bounces or an eviction notice must be posted, Tenant agrees to pay a $_____ charge.

3. PAYMENT. Payment must be received by Landlord on or before the due date at the following address: _____ or such place as designated by Landlord in writing. Tenant understands that this may require early mailing. In the event a check bounces, Landlord may require cash or certified funds.

4. DEFAULT. In the event Tenant defaults under any terms of this lease, Landlord may recover possession as provided by law and seek monetary damages.

5. SECURITY. Landlord acknowledges receipt of the sum of $_____ as the last month's rent under this lease, plus $_____ as security deposit. In the event Tenant terminates the lease prior to its expiration date, said amounts are non-refundable as a charge for Landlord's trouble in securing a new tenant, but Landlord reserves the right to seek additional damages if they exceed the above amounts.

6. UTILITIES. Tenant agrees to pay all utility charges on the property except: _____
_____.

7. MAINTENANCE. Tenant has examined the property, acknowledges it to be in good repair and in consideration of the reduced rental rate, Tenant agrees to keep the premises in good repair and to do all minor maintenance promptly (under $_____ excluding labor) and provide extermination service.

8. LOCKS. If Tenant adds or changes locks on the premises, Landlord shall be given copies of the keys. Landlord shall at all times have keys for access to the premises in case of emergencies.

9. ASSIGNMENT. This lease may not be assigned by Tenant without the written consent of the Landlord.

10. USE. Tenant shall not use the premises for any illegal purpose or any purpose which will increase the rate of insurance, will comply with all laws and property covenants and restrictions, and shall not cause a nuisance for Landlord or neighbors. Tenant shall not create any environmental hazards on the premises.

11. LAWN. Tenant agrees to maintain the lawn and shrubbery on the premises at Tenant's expense.

12. LIABILITY. Tenant shall be responsible for insurance on his own property and agrees not to hold Landlord liable for any damages to Tenant's property on the premises.

13. ACCESS. Landlord reserves the right to enter the premises for the purposes of inspection and to show to prospective purchasers.

14. PETS & SMOKING. No pets and no smoking shall be allowed on the premises unless the parties have executed a Pet Agreement or a Smoking Agreement.

15. OCCUPANCY. The premises shall not be occupied by more than _____ adults and _____ children.

16. TENANT'S APPLIANCES. Tenant agrees not to use any heaters, fixtures or appliances drawing excessive current without consent of the Landlord.

17. PARKING. Tenant agrees that no parking is allowed on the premises except: _____
_____. No boats, recreation vehicles or disassembled automobiles may be stored on the premises.

8. FURNISHINGS. Any articles provided to Tenant and listed on attached schedule are to be returned in good condition at the termination of this lease.

19. ALTERATIONS AND IMPROVEMENTS. Tenant shall make no alterations to the property without the written consent of the Landlord and any such alterations or improvements shall become the property of the Landlord.

20. ENTIRE AGREEMENT. This lease constitutes the entire agreement between the parties and may not be modified except in writing signed by both parties.

21. HARASSMENT. Tenant shall not do any acts to intentionally harass the Landlord or other tenants.

22. ATTORNEY'S FEES. In the event it becomes necessary to enforce this Agreement through the services of an attorney, Tenant shall be required to pay Landlord's attorney's fees.

23. SEVERABILITY. In the event any section of this Agreement shall be held to be invalid, all remaining provisions shall remain in full force and effect.

24. RECORDING. This lease shall not be recorded in any public records.

25. WAIVER. Any failure by Landlord to exercise any rights under this Agreement shall not constitute a waiver of Landlord's rights.

26. ABANDONMENT. In the event Tenant abandons the property prior to the expiration of the lease, Landlord may relet the premises and hold Tenant liable for any costs, lost rent or damage to the premises. Lessor may dispose of any property abandoned by Tenant.

27. SUBORDINATION. Tenant's interest in the premises shall be subordinate to any encumbrances now or hereafter placed on the premises, to any advances made under such encumbrances, and to any extensions or renewals thereof. Tenant agrees to sign any documents indicating such subordination which may be required by lenders.

28. SURRENDER OF PREMISES. At the expiration of the term of this lease, Tenant shall immediately surrender the premises in as good condition as at the start of this lease.

29. LIENS. The interest of the Landlord shall not be subject to any liens for improvements made by the Tenant as provided in section 713.10, Florida statutes.

30. RADON GAS. Radon is a naturally occurring radioactive gas that, when it has accumulated in a building in sufficient quantities, may present health risks to persons who are exposed to it over time. Levels of radon that exceed federal and state guidelines have been found in buildings in Florida. Additional information regarding radon and radon testing may be obtained from your county public health unit.

31. SMOKE DETECTORS. Tenant shall be responsible for supplying smoke detectors, for keeping them operational and for changing the battery when needed.

32. HOA APPROVAL. If Tenant must be approved by a Homeowner's Association, tenant agrees to use diligence in applying for approval, and this lease is contingent upon receiving approval.

33. ABANDONED PROPERTY. BY SIGNING THIS RENTAL AGREEMENT THE TENANT AGREES THAT UPON SURRENDER OR ABANDONMENT, AS DEFINED BY CHAPTER 83 FLORIDA STATUTES, THE LANDLORD SHALL NOT BE LIABLE OR RESPONSIBLE FOR STORAGE OR DISPOSITION OF THE TENANT'S PERSONAL PROPERTY.

34. MISCELLANEOUS PROVISIONS. _____

_____

_____

_____.

WITNESS the hands and seals of the parties hereto as of this _____ day of _____, 20____.

LANDLORD: TENANT:

_____   _____

_____   _____

Apartment Lease

LANDLORD:_____   TENANT:_____

_____   _____

PROPERTY:_____

IN CONSIDERATION of the mutual covenants and agreements herein contained, Landlord hereby leases to Tenant and Tenant hereby leases from Landlord the above-described property under the following terms:

1. TERM. This lease shall be for a term of _____ beginning _____, 20___ and ending _____, 20___ .

2. RENT. The rent shall be $_____ per _____ and shall be due on or before the _____ day of each _____. In the event the rent is received more than three (3) days late, a late charge of $_____ shall be due. In the event a check bounces or an eviction notice must be posted, Tenant agrees to pay a $_____ charge.

3. PAYMENT. Payment must be received by Landlord on or before the due date at the following address: _____ or such place as designated by Landlord in writing. Tenant understands that this may require early mailing. In the event a check bounces, Landlord may require cash or certified funds.

4. DEFAULT. In the event Tenant defaults under any terms of this lease, Landlord may recover possession as provided by law and seek monetary damages.

5. SECURITY. Landlord acknowledges receipt of the sum of $_____ as the last month's rent under this lease, plus $_____ as security deposit. In the event Tenant terminates the lease prior to its expiration date, said amounts are non-refundable as a charge for Landlord's trouble in securing a new tenant, but Landlord reserves the right to seek additional damages if they exceed the above amounts.

6. UTILITIES. Tenant agrees to pay all utility charges on the property except: _____ _____.

7. MAINTENANCE. Tenant has examined the property, acknowledges it to be in good repair. Tenant shall immediately repay any and all damage to the premises caused by Tenant or Tenant's guests. In the event of maintenance problems not caused by Tenant, they shall be immediately reported to Landlord or Landlord's agent.

8. LOCKS. If Tenant adds or changes locks on the premises, Landlord shall be given copies of the keys. Landlord shall at all times have keys for access to the premises in case of emergencies.

9. ASSIGNMENT. This lease may not be assigned by Tenant without the written consent of the Landlord.

10. Tenant shall not use the premises for any illegal purpose or any purpose which will increase the rate of insurance, will comply with all laws and property covenants and restrictions, and shall not cause a nuisance for Landlord or neighbors. Tenant shall not create any environmental hazards on the premises.

11. CONDOMINIUM. In the event the premises are a condominium unit, Tenant agrees to abide by all rules, regulations and the declaration of condominium. Maintenance and recreation fees are to be paid by _____. This lease is subject to approval by the condominium association and Tenant agrees to pay any fees necessary for such approval.

12. LIABILITY. Tenant shall be responsible for insurance on his own property and agrees not to hold Landlord liable for any damages to Tenant's property on the premises.

13. ACCESS. Landlord reserves the right to enter the premises for the purposes of inspection and to how to prospective purchasers.

14. PETS. No pets shall be allowed on the premises except: _____ and there shall be a $_____ non-refundable pet deposit.

15. OCCUPANCY. The premises shall not be occupied by more than _____ adults and _____ children.

16. TENANT'S APPLIANCES. Tenant agrees not to use any heaters, fixtures or appliances drawing excessive current without consent of the Landlord.

17. PARKING. Tenant agrees that no parking is allowed on the premises except:_____
_____. No boats, recreation vehicles or disassembled automobiles may be stored on the premises.

18. FURNISHINGS. Any articles provided to Tenant and listed on attached schedule are to be returned in good condition at the termination of this lease.

19. ALTERATIONS AND IMPROVEMENTS. Tenant shall make no alterations to the property without the written consent of the Landlord and any such alterations or improvements shall become the property of the Landlord.

20. ENTIRE AGREEMENT. This lease constitutes the entire agreement between the parties and may not be modified except in writing signed by both parties.

21. HARASSMENT. Tenant shall not do any acts to intentionally harass the Landlord or other tenants.

22. ATTORNEY'S FEES. In the event it becomes necessary to enforce this Agreement through the services of an attorney, Tenant shall be required to pay Landlord's attorney's fees.

23. SEVERABILITY. In the event any section of this Agreement shall be held to be invalid, all remaining provisions shall remain in full force and effect.

24. RECORDING. This lease shall not be recorded in any public records.

25. WAIVER. Any failure by Landlord to exercise any rights under this Agreement shall not constitute a waiver of Landlord's rights.

26. ABANDONMENT. In the event Tenant abandons the property prior to the expiration of the lease, Landlord may relet the premises and hold Tenant liable for any costs, lost rent or damage to the premises. Lessor may dispose of any property abandoned by Tenant.

27. SUBORDINATION. Tenants interest in the premises shall be subordinate to any encumbrances now or hereafter placed on the premises, to any advances made under such encumbrances, and to any extensions or renewals thereof. Tenant agrees to sign any documents indicating such subordination which may be required by lenders.

28. SURRENDER OF PREMISES. At the expiration of the term of this lease, Tenant shall immediately surrender the premises in as good condition as at the start of this lease.

29. LIENS. The interest of the Landlord shall not be subject to any liens for improvements made by the Tenant as provided in section 713.10, Florida statutes.

30. RADON GAS. Radon is a naturally occurring radioactive gas that, when it has accumulated in a building in sufficient quantities, may present health risks to persons who are exposed to it over time. Levels of radon that exceed federal and state guidelines have been found in buildings in Florida. Additional information regarding radon and radon testing may be obtained from your county public health unit.

31. SMOKE DETECTORS. Tenant shall be responsible for keeping smoke detectors operational and for changing battery when needed.

32. ABANDONED PROPERTY. BY SIGNING THIS RENTAL AGREEMENT THE TENANT AGREES THAT UPON SURRENDER OR ABANDONMENT, AS DEFINED BY CHAPTER 83 FLORIDA STATUTES, THE LANDLORD SHALL NOT BE LIABLE OR RESPONSIBLE FOR STORAGE OR DISPOSITION OF THE TENANT'S PERSONAL PROPERTY.

33. MISCELLANEOUS PROVISIONS. _____
_____
_____.

WITNESS the hands and seals of the parties hereto as of this _____ day of _____, 20 _____.
LANDLORD: TENANT:

_____   _____

_____   _____   199

House or Duplex Unit Rental Agreement

Form 6

LANDLORD:_____   TENANT:_____

_____   _____

PROPERTY:_____

IN CONSIDERATION of the mutual covenants and agreements herein contained, Landlord hereby rents to Tenant and Tenant hereby rents from Landlord the above-described property under the following terms:

1. TERM. This Rental Agreement shall be for a month-to-month tenancy which may be cancelled by either party upon giving notice to the other party at least 15 days prior to the end of a month

2. RENT. The rent shall be $_____ per month and shall be due on or before the _____ day of each month. In the event the rent is received more than three (3) days late, a late charge of $_____ shall be due. In the event a check bounces or an eviction notice must be posted, Tenant agrees to pay a $_____ charge.

3. PAYMENT. Payment must be received by Landlord on or before the due date at the following address: _____ or such place as designated by Landlord in writing. Tenant understands that this may require early mailing. In the event a check bounces, Landlord may require cash or certified funds.

4. DEFAULT. In the event Tenant defaults under any terms of this agreement, Landlord may recover possession as provided by Law and seek monetary damages.

5. SECURITY. Landlord acknowledges receipt of the sum of $_____ as the last month's rent under this lease, plus $_____ as security deposit against rent or damages. In the event Tenant vacates the premises without giving proper notice, said amounts are non-refundable as a charge for Landlord's trouble in securing a new tenant, but Landlord reserves the right to seek additional payment for any damages to the premises.

6. UTILITIES. Tenant agrees to pay all utility charges on the property except: _____
_____.

7. MAINTENANCE. Tenant has examined the property, acknowledges it to be in good repair and in consideration of the reduced rental rate, Tenant agrees to keep the premises in good repair and to do all minor maintenance promptly (under $_____ excluding labor) and provide extermination service.

8. LOCKS. If Tenant adds or changes locks on the premises, Landlord shall be given copies of the keys. Landlord shall at all times have keys for access to the premises in case of emergencies.

9. ASSIGNMENT. This agreement may not be assigned by Tenant without the written consent of the Landlord.

10. USE. Tenant shall not use the premises for any illegal purpose or any purpose which will increase the rate of insurance, will comply with all laws and property covenants and restrictions, and shall not cause a nuisance for Landlord or neighbors. Tenant shall not create any environmental hazards on the premises.

11. LAWN. Tenant agrees to maintain the lawn and shrubbery on the premises at his expense.

12. LIABILITY. Tenant shall be responsible for insurance on his own property and agrees not to hold Landlord liable for any damages to Tenant's property on the premises.

13. ACCESS. Landlord reserves the right to enter the premises for the purposes of inspection and to show to prospective purchasers.

14. PETS & SMOKING. No pets and no smoking shall be allowed on the premises unless the parties have executed a Pet Agreement or a Smoking Agreement.

15. OCCUPANCY. The premises shall not be occupied by more than _____ adults and _____ children.

16. TENANT'S APPLIANCES. Tenant agrees not to use any heaters, fixtures or appliances drawing excessive current without consent of the Landlord.

200

17. PARKING. Tenant agrees that no parking is allowed on the premises except: _____ _____. No boats, recreation vehicles or disassembled automobiles may be stored on the premises.

18. FURNISHINGS. Any articles provided to tenant and listed on attached schedule are to be returned in good condition at the termination of this agreement.

19. ALTERATIONS AND IMPROVEMENTS. Tenant shall make no alterations to the property without the written consent of the Landlord and any such alterations or improvements shall become the property of the Landlord.

20. ENTIRE AGREEMENT. This rental agreement constitutes the entire agreement between the parties and may not be modified except in writing signed by both parties.

HARASSMENT. Tenant shall not do any acts to intentionally harass the Landlord or other tenants.

22. ATTORNEY'S FEES. In the event it becomes necessary to enforce this agreement through the services of an attorney, Tenant shall be required to pay Landlord's attorney's fees.

23. SEVERABILITY. In the event any section of this agreement shall be held to be invalid, all remaining provisions shall remain in full force and effect.

24. RECORDING. This agreement shall not be recorded in any public records.

25. WAIVER. Any failure by Landlord to exercise any rights under this agreement shall not constitute a waiver of Landlord's rights.

26. ABANDONMENT. In the event Tenant abandons the property prior to the expiration of the lease, Landlord may relet the premises and hold Tenant liable for any costs, lost rent or damage to the premises. Lessor may dispose of any property abandoned by Tenant.

27. SUBORDINATION. Tenants interest in the premises shall be subordinate to any encumbrances now or hereafter placed on the premises, to any advances made under such encumbrances, and to any extensions or renewals thereof. Tenant agrees to sign any documents indicating such subordination which may be required by lenders.

28. SURRENDER OF PREMISES. At the expiration of the term of this agreement, Tenant shall immediately surrender the premises in as good condition as at the start of this agreement.

29. LIENS. The interest of the Landlord shall not be subject to any liens for improvements made by the Tenant as provided in section 713.10, Florida statutes.

30. RADON GAS. Radon is a naturally occurring radioactive gas that, when it has accumulated in a building in sufficient quantities, may present health risks to persons who are exposed to it over time. Levels of radon that exceed federal and state guidelines have been found in buildings in Florida. Additional information regarding radon and radon testing may be from your county public health unit.

31. SMOKE DETECTORS. Tenant shall be responsible for keeping smoke detectors operational and for changing battery when needed.

32. HOA APPROVAL. If Tenant must be approved by a Homeowner's Association, tenant agrees to use diligence in applying for approval, and this lease is contingent upon receiving approval.

33. ABANDONED PROPERTY. BY SIGNING THIS RENTAL AGREEMENT THE TENANT AGREES THAT UPON SURRENDER OR ABANDONMENT, AS DEFINED BY CHAPTER 83 FLORIDA STATUTES, THE LANDLORD SHALL NOT BE LIABLE OR RESPONSIBLE FOR STORAGE OR DISPOSITION OF THE TENANT'S PERSONAL PROPERTY.

4. MISCELLANEOUS PROVISIONS. _____
_____.

WITNESS the hands and seals of the parties hereto as of this _____ day of _____, 20 ____ .

LANDLORD: TENANT:

_____   _____

_____   _____

LANDLORD:_____   TENANT:_____

_____   _____

PROPERTY:_____

IN CONSIDERATION of the mutual covenants and agreements herein contained, Landlord hereby rents to Tenant and Tenant hereby rents from Landlord the above-described property under the following terms:

1. TERM. This Rental Agreement shall be for a month-to-month tenancy which may be cancelled by either party upon giving notice to the other party at least 15 days prior to the end of a month

2. RENT. The rent shall be $_____ per month and shall be due on or before the _____ day of each month. In the event the rent is received more than three (3) days late, a late charge of $_____ shall be due. In the event a check bounces or an eviction notice must be posted, Tenant agrees to pay a $_____ charge.

3. PAYMENT. Payment must be received by Landlord on or before the due date at the following address: _____ or such place as designated by Landlord in writing. Tenant understands that this may require early mailing. In the event a check bounces, Landlord may require cash or certified funds.

4. DEFAULT. In the event Tenant defaults under any terms of this agreement, Landlord may recover possession as provided by law and seek monetary damages.

5. SECURITY. Landlord acknowledges receipt of the sum of $_____ as the last month's rent under this lease, plus $_____ as security deposit against rent or damages. In the event Tenant vacates the premises without giving proper notice, said amounts are non-refundable as a charge for Landlord's trouble in securing a new tenant, but Landlord reserves the right to seek additional payment for any damages to the premises.

6. UTILITIES. Tenant agrees to pay all utility charges on the property except: _____
_____.

7. MAINTENANCE. Tenant has examined the property, acknowledges it to be in good repair and in consideration of the reduced rental rate, Tenant agrees to keep the premises in good repair and to do all minor maintenance promptly (under $_____ excluding labor) and provide extermination service.

8. LOCKS. If Tenant adds or changes locks on the premises, Landlord shall be given copies of the keys. Landlord shall at all times have keys for access to the premises in case of emergencies.

9. ASSIGNMENT. This agreement may not be assigned by Tenant without the written consent of the Landlord.

10. USE. Tenant shall not use the premises for any illegal purpose or any purpose which will increase the rate of insurance, will comply with all laws and property covenants and restrictions, and shall not cause a nuisance for Landlord or neighbors. Tenant shall not create any environmental hazards on the premises.

11. LAWN. Tenant agrees to maintain the lawn and shrubbery on the premises at his expense.

12. LIABILITY. Tenant shall be responsible for insurance on his own property and agrees not to hold Landlord liable for any damages to Tenant's property on the premises.

13. ACCESS. Landlord reserves the right to enter the premises for the purposes of inspection and to show to prospective purchasers.

14. PETS & SMOKING. No pets and no smoking shall be allowed on the premises unless the parties have executed a Pet Agreement or a Smoking Agreement.

15. OCCUPANCY. The premises shall not be occupied by more than _____ adults and _____ children.

16. TENANT'S APPLIANCES. Tenant agrees not to use any heaters, fixtures or appliances drawing excessive current without consent of the Landlord.

17. PARKING. Tenant agrees that no parking is allowed on the premises except: _____

_____. No boats, recreation vehicles or disassembled automobiles may be stored on the premises.

18. FURNISHINGS. Any articles provided to tenant and listed on attached schedule are to be returned in good condition at the termination of this agreement.

19. ALTERATIONS AND IMPROVEMENTS. Tenant shall make no alterations to the property without the written consent of the Landlord and any such alterations or improvements shall become the property of the Landlord.

20. ENTIRE AGREEMENT. This rental agreement constitutes the entire agreement between the parties and may not be modified except in writing signed by both parties.

21. HARASSMENT. Tenant shall not do any acts to intentionally harass the Landlord or other tenants.

22. ATTORNEY'S FEES. In the event it becomes necessary to enforce this agreement through the services of an attorney, Tenant shall be required to pay Landlord's attorney's fees.

23. SEVERABILITY. In the event any section of this agreement shall be held to be invalid, all remaining provisions shall remain in full force and effect.

24. RECORDING. This agreement shall not be recorded in any public records.

25. WAIVER. Any failure by Landlord to exercise any rights under this agreement shall not constitute a waiver of Landlord's rights.

26. SUBORDINATION. Tenants interest in the premises shall be subordinate to any encumbrances now or hereafter placed on the premises, to any advances made under such encumbrances, and to any extensions or renewals thereof. Tenant agrees to sign any documents indicating such subordination which may be required by lenders.

27. SURRENDER OF PREMISES. At the expiration of the term of this agreement, Tenant shall immediately surrender the premises in as good condition as at the start of this agreement.

28. LIENS. The interest of the Landlord shall not be subject to any liens for improvements made by the Tenant as provided in section 713.10, Florida statutes.

29. RADON GAS. Radon is a naturally occurring radioactive gas that, when it has accumulated in a building in sufficient quantities, may present health risks to persons who are exposed to it over time. Levels of radon that exceed federal and state guidelines have been found in buildings in Florida. Additional information regarding radon and radon testing may be from your county public health unit.

30. SMOKE DETECTORS. Tenant shall be responsible for keeping smoke detectors operational and for changing battery when needed.

31. ABANDONED PROPERTY. BY SIGNING THIS RENTAL AGREEMENT THE TENANT AGREES THAT UPON SURRENDER OR ABANDONMENT, AS DEFINED BY CHAPTER 83 FLORIDA STATUTES, THE LANDLORD SHALL NOT BE LIABLE OR RESPONSIBLE FOR STORAGE OR DISPOSITION OF THE TENANT'S PERSONAL PROPERTY.

32. MISCELLANEOUS PROVISIONS. _____

_____.

WITNESS the hands and seals of the parties hereto as of this _____ day of _____, 20 ____.

LANDLORD: TENANT:

_____   _____

_____   _____

Agreement Regarding Abandoned Property
Under Florida Statutes §83.67(5)

This agreement is made between _____ as Landlord and _____ as Tenant of property described as _____.

Pursuant to Florida Statutes section 83.67(3) the undersigned Landlord and Tenant agree that BY SIGNING THIS AGREEMENT THE TENANT AGREES THAT UPON SURRENDER, ABANDONMENT OR RECOVERY OF THE DWELLING UNIT DUE TO THE DEATH OF THE LAST REMAINING TENANT, AS PROVIDED BY CHAPTER 83 FLORIDA STATUTES, THE LANDLORD SHALL NOT BE LIABLE OR RESPONSIBLE FOR STORAGE OR DISPOSITION OF THE TENANT'S PERSONAL PROPERTY.

Date: _____, 20____   Landlord:

_____

_____

Tenant:

_____

_____

EARLY TERMINATION FEE/LIQUIDATED DAMAGES ADDENDUM

[ ] I agree, as provided in the rental agreement, to pay $_____ (an amount that does not exceed 2 months' rent) as liquidated damages or an early termination fee if I elect to terminate the rental agreement and the landlord waives the right to seek additional rent beyond the month in which the landlord retakes possession.

[   ] I do not agree to liquidated damages or an early termination fee, and I acknowledge that the landlord may seek damages as provided by law.

_____   _____
Landlord's Signature   Date

_____   _____
Landlord's Signature   Date

_____   _____
Landlord's Signature   Date

_____   _____
Tenant's Signature   Date

_____   _____
Tenant's Signature   Date

Pet Application

Tenants:

_____

Property to be rented: _____

List of all pets to be living at premises:

Name	Type	Breed	Age	Approx. weight
_____	_____	_____	_____	_____
_____	_____	_____	_____	_____
_____	_____	_____	_____	_____
_____	_____	_____	_____	_____
_____	_____	_____	_____	_____

Veterinarian name, address and phone:

_____

References (former landlords or neighbors) name, address and phone:

_____

_____

_____

We certify this information is true.

Date: _____, 20 _____

Tenant:

_____

_____

Pet Agreement

THIS AGREEMENT is made pursuant to that certain Lease dated _____ between _____ as Landlord and _____as Tenant for property at _____ .

In consideration of $_____ as non-refundable cleaning payment and $_____ as additional security deposit paid by Tenant to Landlord, Tenant is allowed to keep the following pet(s): _____ on the premises _____ under the following conditions:

1. In the event the pet produces a litter, Tenant may keep them at the premises no longer than one month past weaning.

2. Tenant shall not engage in any commercial pet-raising activities.

3. No pets other than those listed above shall be kept on the premises without the further written permission of the Landlord.

4. Tenant agrees at all times to keep the pet from becoming a nuisance to neighbors and/or other tenants. This includes controlling the barking of the pet, if necessary and cleaning any animal waste on and about the premises.

5. In the event the pet causes destruction of the property, becomes a nuisance, or Tenant otherwise violates this agreement, Landlord may terminate the Lease according to Florida law.

Date: _____ , 20 ____

Landlord: Tenant:

_____   _____

_____   _____

Co-signer Guaranty of Lease

Name and address:

_____

_____

_____

Home phone: _____

Cell phone: _____

Email: _____

Social security number(s):_____

I/we hereby agree to co-sign for _____

for his/her leasing of the premises at _____

_____.

As inducement for landlord to rent the unit to the above-referenced person, I/we agree to pay for all unpaid rents, utilities and damages owed by the above-referenced person for the above-referenced property.

Date: _____, 20 ____   Co-signer/guarantor(s)

_____

_____

Smoking Agreement

THIS AGREEMENT is made pursuant to that certain Lease dated _____ between _____ as Landlord and _____ as Tenant for property at _____.

In consideration of $_____ as non-refundable cleaning payment and $_____ as additional security deposit paid by Tenant to Landlord, Tenant is allowed to smoke tobacco products on or about the premises.

In the event that damage from burns or smoke exceeds the above payments, Tenant agrees to be liable for any additional amounts paid for cleaning or repairs.

Date: _____, 20 ____

Landlord: Tenant:

_____   _____

_____   _____

Disclosure of Information on Lead-Based Paint and/or Lead-Based Paint Hazards

Lead Warning Statement

Housing built before 1978 may contain lead-based paint. Lead from paint, paint chips, and dust can pose health hazards if not managed properly. Lead exposure is especially harmful to young children and pregnant women. Before renting pre-1978 housing, lessors must disclose the presence of known lead-based paint and/or lead-based paint hazards in the dwelling. Lessees must also receive a federally approved pamphlet on lead poisoning prevention.

Lessor's Disclosure

(a) Presence of lead-based paint and/or lead-based paint hazards (check (i) or (ii) below):

　(i) _____ Known lead-based paint and/or lead-based paint hazards are present in the housing (explain).

　_____

　_____

　(ii) _____ Lessor has no knowledge of lead-based paint and/or lead-based paint hazards in the housing.

(b) Records and reports available to the lessor (check (i) or (ii) below):

　(i) _____ Lessor has provided the lessee with all available records and reports pertaining to lead-based paint and/or lead-based paint hazards in the housing (list documents below).

　_____

　_____

　(ii) _____ Lessor has no reports or records pertaining to lead-based paint and/or lead-based paint hazards in the housing.

Lessee's Acknowledgment (initial)

(c) _____ Lessee has received copies of all information listed above.

(d) _____ Lessee has received the pamphlet *Protect Your Family from Lead in Your Home.*

Agent's Acknowledgment (initial)

(e) _____ Agent has informed the lessor of the lessor's obligations under 42 U.S.C. 4852(d) and is aware of his/her responsibility to ensure compliance.

Certification of Accuracy

The following parties have reviewed the information above and certify, to the best of their knowledge, that the information they have provided is true and accurate.

Lessor	Date	Lessor	Date
Lessee	Date	Lessee	Date
Agent	Date	Agent	Date

This sample form may be used by firms to document compliance with the requirements of the Federal Lead-Based Paint Renovation, Repair, and Painting Program after April 2010.

Occupant Confirmation

Pamphlet Receipt

___ I have received a copy of the lead hazard information pamphlet informing me of the potential risk of the lead hazard exposure from renovation activity to be performed in my dwelling unit. I received this pamphlet before the work began.

Owner-occupant Opt-out Acknowledgment

___ (A) I confirm that I own and live in this property, that no child under the age of 6 resides here, that no pregnant woman resides here, and that this property is not a child-occupied facility.

Note: A child resides in the primary residence of his or her custodial parents, legal guardians, foster parents, or informal caretaker if the child lives and sleeps most of the time at the caretaker's residence.

Note: A child-occupied facility is a pre-1978 building visited regularly by the same child, under 6 years of age, on at least two different days within any week, for at least 3 hours each day, provided that the visits total at least 60 hours annually.

If Box A is checked, check either Box B or Box C, but not both.

___ (B) I request that the renovation firm use the lead-safe work practices required by EPA's Lead-Based Paint Renovation, Repair, and Painting Rule; or

___ (C) I understand that the firm performing the renovation will not be required to use the lead-safe work practices required by EPA's Lead-Based Paint Renovation, Repair, and Painting Rule.

_____

Printed Name of Owner-occupant

_____   _____

Signature of Owner-occupant   Signature Date

Renovator's Self Certification Option (for tenant-occupied dwellings only)

Instructions to Renovator: If the lead hazard information pamphlet was delivered but a tenant signature was not obtainable, you may check the appropriate box below.

___ **Declined** – I certify that I have made a good faith effort to deliver the lead hazard information pamphlet to the rental dwelling unit listed below at the date and time indicated and that the occupant declined to sign the confirmation of receipt. I further certify that I have left a copy of the pamphlet at the unit with the occupant.

___ **Unavailable for signature** – I certify that I have made a good faith effort to deliver the lead hazard information pamphlet to the rental dwelling unit listed below and that the occupant was unavailable to sign the confirmation of receipt. I further certify that I have left a copy of the pamphlet at the unit by sliding it under the door or by (fill in how pamphlet was left)._____

_____   _____

Printed Name of Person Certifying Delivery   Attempted Delivery Date

_____

Signature of Person Certifying Lead Pamphlet Delivery

_____

_____

Unit Address

Note Regarding Mailing Option — As an alternative to delivery in person, you may mail the lead hazard information pamphlet to the owner and/or tenant. Pamphlet must be mailed at least 7 days before renovation. Mailing must be documented by a certificate of mailing from the post office.

Renovation Notice

(For use in notifying tenants of renovations in common areas of multi-family housing)

The following renovation activities will take place in the following locations:

_____

Activity (e.g., sanding, window replacement)

_____

Location (e.g., lobby, recreation center)

The expected starting date is _____ and the expected ending date is

_____. Because this is an older building built before 1978, some

of the paint disturbed during the renovation may contain lead. You may obtain a copy of

the pamphlet, *Protect Your Family From Lead In Your Home*, by telephoning me at

_____. Please leave a message and be sure to include your name, phone

number and address. I will either mail you a pamphlet or slide one under your door.

_____   _____
Date   Printed name of renovator

                                          _____
                                          Signature of renovator

Radon Gas Notice

To: _____

Property: _____

Florida law requires us to provide you with this notice:

Radon is a naturally occurring radioactive gas that, when it has accumulated in a building in sufficient quantities, may present health risks to persons who are exposed to it over time. Levels of radon that exceed federal and state guidelines have been found in buildings in Florida. Additional information regarding radon and radon testing may be obtained from your county public health unit.

Notice of Holding Security Deposit

To:_____

From:_____

Date: _____, 20_____

Pursuant to Florida statutes §83.49(2) this notice is to advise you that your security deposit is being held as follows:

1. The account is at the following depository: _____
_____

2. The funds are:
    ___ in a separate account solely holding security deposits
    ___ in an account commingled with landlord's funds

3. The account is:
    ___ interest-bearing
    ___ not interest-bearing

4. Florida statutes provide as follows:

§83.49(3)(a) Upon the vacating of the premises for termination of the lease, if the landlord does not intend to impose a claim on the security deposit, the landlord shall have 15 days to return the security deposit together with interest if otherwise required, or the landlord shall have 30 days to give the tenant written notice by certified mail to the tenant's last known mailing address of his or her intention to impose a claim on the deposit and the reason for imposing the claim. The notice shall contain a statement in substantially the following form:

This is a notice of my intention to impose a claim for damages in the amount of _____ upon your security deposit, due to _____. It is sent to you as required by s. 83.49(3), Florida Statutes. You are hereby notified that you must object in writing to this deduction from your security deposit within 15 days from the time you receive this notice or I will be authorized to deduct my claim from your security deposit. Your objection must be sent to (landlord's address) .

If the landlord fails to give the required notice within the 30-day period, he or she forfeits the right to impose a claim upon the security deposit.
(b) Unless the tenant objects to the imposition of the landlord's claim or the amount thereof within 15 days after receipt of the landlord's notice of intention to impose a claim, the landlord may then deduct the amount of his or her claim and shall remit the balance of the deposit to the tenant within 30 days after the date of the notice of intention to impose a claim for damages.
(c) If either party institutes an action in a court of competent jurisdiction to adjudicate the party's right to the security deposit, the prevailing party is entitled to receive his or her court costs plus a reasonable fee for his or her attorney. The court shall advance the cause on the calendar.
(d) Compliance with this section by an individual or business entity authorized to conduct business in this state, including Florida-licensed real estate brokers and salespersons, shall constitute compliance with all other relevant Florida Statutes pertaining to security deposits held pursuant to a rental agreement or other landlord-tenant relationship. Enforcement personnel shall look solely to this section to determine compliance. This section prevails over any conflicting provisions in chapter 475 and in other sections of the Florida Statutes, and shall operate to permit licensed real estate brokers to disburse security deposits and deposit money without having to comply with the notice and settlement procedures contained in s. 475.25(1)(d).

Amendment to Lease/Rental Agreement

    The undersigned parties to that certain agreement dated _____, 20____ on the premises known as _____, hereby agree to amend said agreement as follows:

All other terms and conditions remain in full force and effect.

WITNESS the hands and seals of the parties hereto this ____ day of _____, 20____.

Landlord: Tenant:

_____   _____

_____   _____

Consent to Assignment or Subletting

Current Tenant:

_____

New Tenant:

_____

Rental Premises:

_____

_____

The undersigned landlord hereby consents to the

☐ Assignment

☐ Subletting

of the above-referenced premises. The current tenant ☐ WILL / ☐ WILL NOT be held liable for all obligations under the lease agreement

Date: _____, 20____   Current tenant:

_____

_____

Landlord:

_____

Access Request

Date: _____, 20____

To: _____
    Tenant

It will be necessary to enter your dwelling unit for the purpose of _____

_____.

If possible we would like access on _____ at ____ o'clock ___.m.

In the event this is not convenient, please call to arrange another time.

Sincerely,

_____

Landlord

Address:

_____

_____

Phone:_____

Statement for Repairs

Date: _____, 20____

To: _____
       Tenant

It has been necessary to repair damage to the premises which you occupy which was caused by you or your guests. The costs for repairs were as follows:

This amount is your responsibility under the terms of the lease and Florida law and should be forwarded to us at the address below.

Sincerely,

_____
Landlord

Address:

_____
_____

Phone:_____

Notice of Change of Terms

Date: _____ , 20____

To: _____
      Tenant

    You are hereby notified that effective _____ , 20_____ the terms of your rental agreement will be changed as follows:

    If you elect to terminate your tenancy prior to that date kindly provide 15 days notice as provided by law.

                  Sincerely,

                  _____
                  Landlord

                  Address:
                  _____
                  _____

                  Phone:_____

Letter - Vacating Tenant

Date:

To:

Dear _____

    This letter is to remind you that your tenancy will expire on _____, 20____. Please be advised that we do not intend to renew or extend it.

    The keys should be delivered to us at the address below on or before the end of the lease along with your forwarding address. We will inspect the premises for damages, deduct any amounts necessary for repairs and refund any remaining balance as required by law.

               Sincerely,

               _____

               Address:

               Phone:

Annual Letter - Continuation of Tenancy

Date:

To:

Dear _____

      This letter is to remind you that your lease will expire on _____, 20_____. Please advise us within _____ days as to whether you intend to renew your lease. If so, we will prepare a new lease for your signature(s).

      If you do not intend to renew your lease, the keys should be delivered to us at the address below on or before the end of the lease along with your forwarding address. We will inspect the premises for damages, deduct any amounts necessary for repairs and refund any remaining balance as required by law.

      If we have not heard from you as specified above we will assume that you will be vacating the premises and will arrange for a new tenant to move in at the end of your term.

                                          Sincerely,

                                          _____

                                          Address:

                                          Phone:

Property Management Agreement

THIS AGREEMENT is made on _____, 20_____ between _____
_____ as Owner and _____
_____ as Manager, of the Property, known as _____
_____

WHEREAS Owner wishes to hire Manager to take over the day to day management of the Property and Manager wishes to take over such duties,

THEREFORE, in consideration of the mutual agreements contained herein, the parties agree as follows:

1. Authority. Manager is hereby appointed exclusive agent with power and authority to lease and manage the Property.

2. Term. This agreement shall be for a term of _____ months, beginning _____, 20____ and ending, _____, 20____.

3. Duties. Manager shall rent, manage and control the property using its best efforts to find and keep tenants. Manager shall negotiate all leases on terms agreed by Owner. Manager shall contract for all necessary repairs to the property. Manager shall collect all rents and remit to Owner after payment of _____. Payments shall be made to Owner of net amounts, less $_____ kept on deposit for expenses, at least once every _____ days.

4. Leases. Manager shall execute all leases and rental agreements:

____ in Manager's name as landlord.

____ in Owner's name. Manager is hereby appointed as attorney-in-fact to execute such agreements.

Manager shall have authority to serve any legal notices on tenants and to take any legal action as is permitted by law to enforce leases, evict tenants, or collect money owed.

5. Compensation. The manager shall be paid as follows: _____
_____.

6. Sale of Property. In the event of a bona fide sale of the property, Owner may terminate this contract upon giving thirty days notice.

_____   _____
Owner   Manager

Notice of Termination of Agent

Date:

To:

You are hereby advised that _____ is no longer our agent effective _____. On and after this date he or she is no longer authorized to collect rent, accept notices or to make any representations or agreements regarding the property.

Rent should thereafter be paid to us directly unless you are instructed otherwise by in writing.

If you have any questions you may contact us at the address or phone number below.

Sincerely,

_____

Address:

Phone:

Notice of Appointment of Agent

Date: _____, 20____

To: _____
      Tenant

    You are hereby advised that effective _____, 20____, our agent for collection of rent and other matters regarding the property will be:

      Name: _____

      Phone: _____

However, no terms of the written lease may be modified or waived without our written signatures.

If you have any questions you may contact us at the address or phone number below.

               Sincerely,

               _____
               Landlord

               Address:

               _____
               _____

               Phone:_____

To: _____
        Tenant's Name

        _____
        Address

        _____
        City, State, Zip Code

Date: _____

This is a notice of my intention to impose a claim for damages in the amount of $_____ [insert amount of damages] upon your security deposit due to _____ _____ [insert damage done to premises or other reason for claiming security deposit].

This notice is sent to you as required by §83.49(3), Florida Statutes. You are hereby notified that you must object in writing to this deduction from your security deposit within 15 days from the time you receive this notice or I will be authorized to deduct my claim from your security deposit. Your objection must be sent to _____ [insert Landlord's address].

                        _____
                        Landlord's Name_____
                        Address _____

                        _____
                        Phone Number _____

Approved for use under rule 10-2.1(a) of
the Rules Regulating the Florida Bar

The Florida Bar 2010

This form was completed
with the assistance of:
Name:
        Address:
Telephone Number:

Receipt and Release

The undersigned tenant of the property located at _____
_____ acknowledges receipt of the sum of _____
Dollars ($_____) by ☐ cash ☐ check ☐ money order

Said payment is made
        ☐ as a return of tenant's security deposit
        ☐ as a as full settlement of all claims related to said property and tenant's occupancy thereof.

In consideration for said payment promptly made to tenant, tenant hereby releases landlord from all claims tenant has or may have against landlord in any capacity whatsoever known or unknown.

Date: _____, 20_____

                    Tenants:

                    Sign _____
                    Print _____

                    Sign _____
                    Print _____

NOTICE FROM LANDLORD TO TENANT --TERMINATION
FOR FAILURE TO PAY RENT

To: _____
      Tenant's Name

      _____
      Address

      _____
      City, State, Zip Code

From: _____

Date: _____

    You are hereby notified that you are indebted to me in the sum of $_____ [insert amount owed by Tenant] for the rent and use of the premises located at _____ _____, Florida [insert address of premises, including county], now occupied by you and that I demand payment of the rent or possession of the premises within three days (excluding Saturday, Sunday, and legal holidays) from the date of delivery of this notice, to-wit: on or before the _____ day of _____, 20_____ [insert the date which is three days from the delivery of this notice, excluding the date of delivery, Saturday, Sunday, and legal holidays].

                              _____
                              Signature

                              _____
                              Name of Landlord/Property manager
                              [Circle one]

                              _____
                              Address [street address where Tenant can deliver rent]

                              _____
                              City, State, Zip Code

                              _____
                              Phone Number

Hand Delivered On

Posted On

Approved for use under rule 10-2.1(a) of
the Rules Regulating the Florida Bar

The Florida Bar 2010

This form was completed
with the assistance of:
Name:
Address:
Telephone Number:

NOTICE FROM LANDLORD TO TENANT NOTICE OF
NONCOMPLIANCE OTHER THAN FAILURE TO PAY RENT

To: _____

Tenant's Name

_____

Address

_____

City, State, Zip Code

From: _____

Date: _____

You are hereby notified that you are not complying with your rental agreement in that _____. [insert noncompliance, default or violation]. Demand is hereby made that you remedy the noncompliance , default or violation within seven days of receipt of this notice or your rental agreement shall be deemed terminated and you shall vacate the premises upon such termination. If this same conduct or conduct of a similar nature is repeated within twelve months, your tenancy is subject to termination without you being given an opportunity to cure the noncompliance, default or violation.

_____

Landlord's Name_____

Address _____

Phone Number _____

Approved for use under rule 10-2.1(a) of
the Rules Regulating the Florida Bar

The Florida Bar

This form was completed
with the assistance of:
Name:
Address:
Telephone Number:

NOTICE OF TERMINATION

(Tenant's Name and Address)

Dear _____ :
　　　　　　(Tenant's Name)

Pursuant to Florida Statutes §83.56(2)(a):

　　　You are hereby notified that your lease is terminated immediately. You shall have seven (7) days from delivery of this letter to vacate the premises. This action is taken because:

_____
Landlord's Name_____
Address _____
Phone Number _____

Hand Delivered On

Posted On

This form was completed
with the assistance of:
Name:
Address:
Telephone Number:

NOTICE OF NON-RENEWAL

(Tenant's Name and Address)

Dear _____:
           (Tenant's Name)

      You are notified that your tenancy will not be renewed at the end of the present term. You will be expected to vacate the premises on or before _____, 20 ____. In the event that you do not vacate the premises by said date, legal action may be taken in which you may be held liable for double rent, court costs and attorney fees.

                                               _____

                                             Landlord's Name_____

                                             Address _____

                                             Phone Number _____

This form was completed
with the assistance of:
Name:
Address:
Telephone Number:

FORM 1.997. CIVIL COVER SHEET

The civil cover sheet and the information contained herein neither replace nor supplement the filing and service of pleadings or other papers as required by law. This form is required for the use of the Clerk of Court for the purpose of reporting judicial workload data pursuant to Florida Statute 25.075. (See instructions on the reverse of the form.)

I. CASE STYLE

(Name of Court) _____

Plaintiff _____

Case #: _____

_____

vs.

Defendant _____

_____

II. TYPE OF CASE

(Place an x in one box only. If the case fits more than one type of case, select the most definitive.)

Domestic Relations	Torts	Other Civil
☐ Simplified dissolution	☐ Professional malpractice	☐ Contracts
☐ Dissolution	☐ Products liability	☐ Condominium
☐ Support C IV-D	☐ Auto negligence	☐ Real property/Mortgage foreclosure
☐ Support C Non IV-D	☐ Other negligence	☐ Eminent domain
☐ UIFSA C IV-D		☐ Challenge to proposed constitutional amendment
☐ UIFSA C Non IV-D		☐ Other Civil
☐ Domestic Violence		**Tenant Eviction**
☐ Other domestic relations		

III. IS JURY TRIAL DEMANDED IN COMPLAINT?

☐ Yes

☐ No

Date _____

_____
SIGNATURE OF ATTORNEY/PARTY FOR PARTY INITIATING ACTION

IN THE COUNTY COURT, IN AND FOR
_____COUNTY, FLORIDA
[insert County in which rental property is located]

CASE NO.: _____

                                    [Insert case number assigned
                                    by Clerk of the Court]

_____,

[Insert name of Landlord]
                         Plaintiff,

vs.   COMPLAINT FOR EVICTION AND
                                    DAMAGES

_____,

[Insert name of Tenant]
                         Defendant.

_____/

Plaintiff,_____ [insert name of Landlord], sues Defendant,
_____, [insert name of Tenant] and alleges:

COUNT I
Tenant Eviction

1.   This is an action to evict the tenant from real property in _____ [insert
county in which the property is located] County, Florida.

2.   Plaintiff owns the following described real property in the County: _____
_____ [insert legal or street description of
the property including, if applicable, unit number].

3.   Defendant has possession of the real property under a (oral/written) agreement to pay rent
of $_____ [insert rental amount] payable _____ [insert
terms of rental payments, i.e., weekly, monthly, etc.]. A copy of the written agreement, if any, is attached
as Exhibit "A."

4.   Defendant failed to pay the rent due_____, 20_____ [insert date of
payment Tenant has failed to make].

5.   Plaintiff served Defendant with a notice on _____, 20 _____ [insert date
of notice], to pay the rent or deliver possession but Defendant refuses to do either. A copy of the notice is
attached as Exhibit "B."

WHEREFORE, Plaintiff demands judgment for possession of the property against Defendant.

COUNT II
Damages

6. This is an action for damages that do not exceed $15,000.

7. Plaintiff restates those allegations contained in paragraphs 1 through 5 above.

8. Defendant owes Plaintiff $_____ that is due with interest [insert past due rent amount] since _____, 20 _____ [insert date of last rental payment Tenant failed to make].

WHEREFORE, Plaintiff demands judgment for damages against Defendant.

Landlord's Name_____

Address, Unit Number _____

Phone Number:_____

Approved for use under rule 10-2.1(a) of
the Rules Regulating the Florida Bar

The Florida Bar 2010

This form was completed
with the assistance of:
Name:
Address:
Telephone Number:

IN THE COUNTY COURT, IN AND FOR
_____COUNTY, FLORIDA
[insert County in which rental property is located]

CASE NO.: _____

[Insert case number assigned
by Clerk of the Court]

_____,
(Insert name of Landlord)
                    Plaintiff,

vs.   COMPLAINT FOR EVICTION

_____,
(Insert name of Tenant)
                    Defendant.
_____/

Plaintiff,_____ [insert name of Landlord], sues Defendant,
_____, [insert name of Tenant] and alleges:

1.   This is an action to evict the tenant from real property in _____ [insert county in which the property is located] County, Florida.

2.   Plaintiff owns the following described real property in the County: _____
_____ [insert legal or street description of the property including, if applicable, unit number].

3.   Defendant has possession of the real property under a (oral/written) agreement to pay rent of $_____ [insert rental amount] payable _____ [insert terms of rental payments, i.e., weekly, monthly, etc.]. A copy of the written agreement, if any, is attached as Exhibit "A."

4.   Defendant failed to pay the rent due_____, 20_____ [insert date of payment Tenant has failed to make].

5.   Plaintiff served Defendant with a notice on _____, 20 _____ [insert date of notice], to pay the rent or deliver possession but Defendant refuses to do either. A copy of the notice is attached as Exhibit "B."

WHEREFORE, Plaintiff demands judgment for possession of the property against Defendant.

_____
Signature

_____
Name of Landlord/Property manager
(Circle one)

_____
Address

_____
City, State, Zip Code

_____
Phone Number

Approved for use under rule 10-2.1(a) of
the Rules Regulating the Florida Bar

The Florida Bar 2010

This form was completed
with the assistance of:
Name:
Address:
Telephone Number:

IN THE COUNTY COURT, IN AND FOR
_____ COUNTY, FLORIDA
[insert County in which rental property is located]

_____,   CASE NO.: _____

[Insert name of Landlord]   [Insert case number assigned
                   Plaintiff,   by Clerk of the Court]

vs.

_____,

[Insert name of Tenant]   COMPLAINT FOR EVICTION
               Defendant.

_____/

     Plaintiff,_____ [insert name of Landlord], sues Defendant,
_____, [insert name of Tenant] and alleges:

    1.   This is an action to evict the tenant from real property in _____ [insert
county in which the property is located] County, Florida.

    2.   Plaintiff owns the following described real property in the County: _____
_____ [insert legal or street description of
the property including, if applicable, unit number].

    3.   Defendant has possession of the real property under a (oral/written) agreement to pay
rent
of $_____ [insert rental amount] payable _____ [insert
terms of rental payments, i.e., weekly, monthly, etc.]. A copy of the written agreement, if any, is attached
as Exhibit "A."

    4. Plaintiff served Defendant with a notice on _____, 20 _____ [insert date
of notice], giving written notice to the Defendant that the Defendant was in violation of its rental agreement. A copy of the notice, setting forth the violations of the rental agreement, is attached hereto as
Exhibit "B."

    5. Defendant has failed to correct or discontinue the conduct set forth in the above-mentioned
notice.

    WHEREFORE, Plaintiff demands judgment for possession of the property against Defendant.

Landlord's Name _____
Address _____

_____
Phone Number_____

Approved for use under rule 10-2.1(a) of   This form was completed
the Rules Regulating the Florida Bar   with the assistance of:
                                           Name:
The Florida Bar 2010   Address:
                                           Telephone Number:

IN THE COUNTY COURT, IN AND FOR
_____COUNTY, FLORIDA
[insert County in which rental property is located]

_____,   CASE NO.: _____

[Insert name of Landlord]

                Plaintiff,   [Insert case number assigned
by Clerk of the Court]

vs.

_____,

[Insert name of Tenant]   COMPLAINT FOR EVICTION
              Defendant.   HOLDOVER TENANT

_____/

Plaintiff,_____ [insert name of Landlord], sues Defendant,
_____, [insert name of Tenant] and alleges:

COUNT I
Tenant Eviction

    1.   This is an action to evict the tenant from real property in _____ [insert county in which the property is located] County, Florida.

    2.   Plaintiff owns the following described real property in the County: _____ _____ [insert legal or street description of the property including, if applicable, unit number].

    3.   Defendant has possession of the real property under a (oral/written) agreement to pay rent of $_____ [insert rental amount] payable _____ [insert terms of rental payments, i.e., weekly, monthly, etc.]. A copy of the written agreement, if any, is attached as Exhibit "A."

    4. Defendant failed to vacate the premises at the end of said agreement.

WHEREFORE, Plaintiff demands judgment for possession of the property against Defendant.

COUNT II
Damages - Double Rent

5. This is an action for double rent.

6. Defendant(s) owe Plaintiff the sum of $_____ for each day Defendant(s) remain(s) in the premises since the termination of the tenancy.

WHEREFORE, Plaintiff demands judgment for possession of the property and rent owed against Defendant(s).

_____
Landlord's Name _____
Address _____

_____
Phone Number_____

STATE OR FLORIDA   )
)
COUNTY OF _____   )

The undersigned, being the Plaintiff in the foregoing complaint, being first duly sworn, deposes and says:

    1. That the allegations in the attached Complaint for Eviction are true.

    2. That the Defendants are not in the military service of the United States.

                                  _____
                                  Plaintiff

    Sworn to and subscribed before me by _____ who is personally known to me or produced _____ as identification on this _____ day of _____, 20_____

                                  _____
                                  Notary Public
                                  My commission expires:

(Attach a copy of this form to your Complaint)

IN THE COUNTY COURT, IN AND FOR
_____ COUNTY, FLORIDA
[insert County in which rental property is located]

_____ ,   CASE NO.: _____

[Insert name of Landlord]   [Insert case number assigned
                Plaintiff,   by Clerk of the Court]

vs.

_____ ,

[Insert name of Tenant]   EVICTION SUMMONS - RESIDENTIAL
             Defendant.

_____ /

TO: _____ [insert name,
address and phone number of Tenant].

PLEASE READ CAREFULLY

You are being sued by _____ [insert
Landlord's name] to require you to move out of the place where you are living for the reasons given in
the attached complaint.

You are entitled to a trial to decide whether you can be required to move, but you MUST do ALL
of the things listed below. You must do them within 5 days (not including Saturday, Sunday, or any legal
holiday after the date these papers were given to you or to a person who lives with you or were posted at
your home.

THE THINGS YOU MUST DO TO CHALLENGE THE EVICTION ARE AS FOLLOWS:

    1.   Write down the reason(s) why you think you should not be forced to move. The written
reason(s) must be given to the Court Clerk at _____ [insert address of courthouse].

2. Mail or take a copy of your written reason(s) to: _____
[insert Landlord's name and address].

3. Give the court clerk the rent that is due. You MUST pay the clerk the rent each time it becomes due until the lawsuit is over. Whether you win or lose the lawsuit, the Judge may pay this rent to
the landlord. [By statute, public housing tenants or tenants receiving rent subsidies shall be required to
deposit only that portion of the full rent for which the tenant is irresponsible pursuant to federal, state
or local program in which they are participating.]

    4.   If you and the landlord do not agree on the amount of rent owed, you must file a written
request (motion) which asks the Judge to decide how much money you must give to the Court Clerk.
The written request must be filed with your written answer to the Eviction Complaint. A copy of your
motion must also be mailed or hand delivered to the plaintiff(s) attorney, or if the Plaintiff(s) has no
attorney, to the Plaintiff.

IF YOU DO NOT DO ALL OF THESE THINGS WITHIN 5 DAYS (NOT INCLUDING SATURDAYS, SUNDAYS , AND LEGAL HOLIDAYS FOR YOUR COURTHOUSE), YOU MAY BE EVICTED WITHOUT A HEARING OR FURTHER NOTICE

THE STATE OF FLORIDA:
TO EACH SHERIFF OF THE STATE:

You are commanded to serve this summons and a copy of the complaint in this lawsuit on the above-named defendant.

DATED on THE _____ DAY OF _____, 20____

Clerk of the Court

By:_____
Deputy Clerk

Clerk's Address: _____

_____
Telephone number _____

Approved for use under rule 10-2.1(a) of
the Rules Regulating the Florida Bar

The Florida Bar 2010

This form was completed
with the assistance of:
Name:
Address:
Telephone Number:

IN THE COUNTY COURT, IN AND FOR
_____COUNTY, FLORIDA
[insert County in which rental property is located]

_____,   CASE NO.: _____

[Insert name of Landlord]   [Insert case number assigned
                    Plaintiff,   by Clerk of the Court]

vs.

_____,

[Insert name of Tenant]   SUMMONS
                    Defendant.   ACTION FOR BACK RENT AND DAMAGES
_____/

      Each Defendant is further required to serve written defenses to the demand or back rent and all other damages to the premises contained in the Complaint upon the above-named _____ _____ [insert Landlord's name] at the above-named address within 20 days after service of this Summons upon the Defendant, exclusive of the day of Service, and to file the original of said written defenses with the Clerk of said court either before service on _____ [insert Landlord's name] or thereafter. If you fail to do so, a default will be entered against Defendant for the relief demanded in that portion of the Complaint.

      WITNESS my hand and seal of the Court this _____ day of _____,20____ .

(COURT SEAL)   Clerk of Court

                                      By:_____
                                               Deputy Clerk

Approved for use under rule 10-2.1(a) of
the Rules Regulating the Florida Bar

The Florida Bar 2010

This form was completed
with the assistance of:
Name:
Address:
Telephone Number:

IN THE COUNTY COURT, IN AND FOR
_____COUNTY, FLORIDA
[insert County in which rental property is located]

CASE NO.: _____

[Insert case number assigned
by Clerk of the Court]

_____,

[Insert name of Landlord]

Plaintiff,

vs.

_____,

[Insert name of Tenant]

Defendant.

_____/

MOTION FOR CLERK'S DEFAULT—
RESIDENTIAL EVICTION

Plaintiff moves for entry of a default against _____ [name],
for failure to respond as required by law Plaintiff's Complaint for residential eviction.

_____

Name _____

Address _____

_____

Telephone Number_____

DEFAULT—RESIDENTIAL EVICTION

A default is entered in this action against the Defendant for eviction for failure to respond as
required by law.

DATE:_____

CLERK OF THE COURT

By:_____

Deputy Clerk

cc: _____

[Insert name of Landlord]

_____

[Insert name and address of Tenant]

Approved for use under rule 10-2.1(a) of
the Rules Regulating the Florida Bar

The Florida Bar 2010

This form was completed
with the assistance of:
Name:
        Address:
Telephone Number:

IN THE COUNTY COURT, IN AND FOR

_____COUNTY, FLORIDA

[insert County in which rental property is located]

CASE NO.: _____

[Insert case number assigned
by Clerk of the Court]

_____,

[Insert name of Landlord]

Plaintiff,

vs.

_____,

[Insert name of Tenant]

Defendant.

_____/

MOTION FOR CLERK'S DEFAULT—
DAMAGES (RESIDENTIAL EVICTION)

Plaintiff moves for entry of a default against _____ [name], for failure to respond as required by law Plaintiff's Complaint for damages.

_____

Name _____

Address _____

_____

Telephone Number _____

DEFAULT—DAMAGES

A default is entered in this action against the Defendant for eviction for failure to respond as required by law.

DATE: _____

CLERK OF THE COURT

By: _____

cc: _____

[Insert name of Landlord]

_____

[Insert name and address of Tenant]

This form was completed
with the assistance of:
Name:
Address:
Telephone Number:

IN THE COUNTY COURT, IN AND FOR
_____COUNTY, FLORIDA
[insert County in which rental property is located]

_____,   CASE NO.: _____

[Insert name of Landlord]   [Insert case number assigned
                                                                by Clerk of the Court]

            Plaintiff,

vs.

_____,   MOTION FOR DEFAULT FINAL
(Insert name of Tenant)   JUDGMENT—RESIDENTIAL EVICTION

            Defendant.
_____/

        Plaintiff asks the court to enter a Default Final judgment against _____
[name],
Defendant, for damages and says:

    1.   Plaintiff filed a Complaint alleging grounds for residential eviction of Defendant.

    2.   A default was entered by the Clerk of this Court on _____ [date].

        WHEREFORE, Plaintiff asks this Court to enter a Final judgment For Residential Eviction
against Defendant.

_____

                                                        Name _____
                                                        Address _____

                                                        _____
                                                        Telephone Number_____

cc: _____
        (Insert name and address of Tenant)

Approved for use under rule 10-2.1(a) of   This form was completed
the Rules Regulating the Florida Bar   with the assistance of:
                                                  Name:
The Florida Bar   Address:
                                                  Telephone Number:

IN THE COUNTY COURT, IN AND FOR

_____COUNTY, FLORIDA

[insert County in which rental property is located]

_____,   CASE NO.: _____

[Insert name of Landlord]   [Insert case number assigned
                          Plaintiff,   by Clerk of the Court]

vs.   MOTION FOR DEFAULT FINAL

_____,   JUDGMENT—DAMAGES

(Insert name of Tenant)   (RESIDENTIAL EVICTION)

                          Defendant.

_____/

        Plaintiff asks the court to enter a Default Final judgment against _____
[name],
Defendant, for damages and says:

        1.   Plaintiff filed a Complaint alleging grounds for residential eviction of Defendant.

        2.   A default was entered by the Clerk of this Court on _____ [date.

        3.   In support of this Motion, Plaintiff submits the attached Affidavit of Damages.

        WHEREFORE, Plaintiff asks this Court to enter a Final judgment against Defendant.

        I CERTIFY that I ___ mailed, ___ faxed and mailed, or ___ hand delivered a copy of this motion
and attached affidavit to the Defendant at _____
_____[insert address at which tenant was served and fax number if sent by fax].

                                  _____
                                  Name _____
                                  Address _____

                                  _____
                                  Telephone Number _____

Approved for use under rule 10-2.1(a) of   This form was completed
the Rules Regulating the Florida Bar   with the assistance of:
                                                    Name:
The Florida Bar   Address:
                                                    Telephone Number:

IN THE COUNTY COURT, IN AND FOR
_____COUNTY, FLORIDA
[insert County in which rental property is located]

_____,   CASE NO.: _____

[Insert name of Landlord]   (Insert case number assigned

          Plaintiff,   by Clerk of the Court)

vs.

_____,

[Insert name of Tenant]   AFFIDAVIT OF DAMAGES

          Defendant.

_____,

STATE OF FLORIDA   )
COUNTY OF   )

BEFORE ME, the undersigned authority, personally appeared_____ [name] who being first duly sworn, states as follows:

1.   I am ____ the Plaintiff or ___ the Plaintiff's agent (check appropriate response) in this case and am authorized to make this affidavit.

2.   This affidavit is based on my own personal knowledge.

3.   Defendant has possession of the property which is the subject of this eviction under an agreement to pay rent of $_____ [rental amount] per _____ _____ [week, month, or other payment period].

4.   Defendant has not paid the rent due since _____.
                               [date of payment tenant has failed to make]

5.   Defendant owes Plaintiff $ _____ [past due rent amount] as alleged in the complaint plus interest.

6.   Defendant owes Plaintiff $_____ [amount of other damages] as alleged in the complaint plus interest

_____

Name_____

Acknowledged before me on _____ [date], by
_____ [name], who _____ is personally known to me/ _____ produced
_____ [document] as identification, and who took an oath.

I CERTIFY that I ____ mailed, ____ faxed and mailed, or ____ hand delivered a copy of this motion and attached affidavit to the Defendant at _____
_____.[insert address at which tenant was served and fax number if sent by fax]

IN THE COUNTY COURT, IN AND FOR

_____COUNTY, FLORIDA
[insert County in which rental property is located]

_____,   CASE NO.: _____

[Insert name of Landlord]   [Insert case number assigned
                Plaintiff,   by Clerk of the Court]

vs.

[Insert name of Tenant]   **NONMILITARY AFFIDAVIT**
           Defendant.

     On this day personally appeared before me, the undersigned authority, _____
_____, who after being duly sworn, says:

     Defendant, _____, is unknown by Affiant not to be in the
military service or any governmental agency or branch subject to   the provisions of the Soldiers' and
Sailors' Civil Relief Act.

DATED: _____   _____
                                                Signature of Affiant
                                              Name_____
                                              Address_____

                                              _____
                                              Telephone No._____

Sworn and subscribed before me on _____ [date], by _____
_____ [name], who ____ is personally known to me/ ____ produced _____
[document] as identification, and who took an oath.

                                              _____
                                              NOTARY PUBLIC-STATE OF FLORIDA
                                              Name: _____
                                              Commission No.: _____
                                              My Commission Expires: _____

I CERTIFY that I have ____ mailed, ____ faxed and mailed, or ____ hand delivered a copy of this
motion and attached affidavit to the Defendant at _____
[insert address at which Tenant was served and fax number if sent by fax] to: Attorney for opposing

Name _____
Address _____
Fax No. _____

Approved for use under rule 10-2.1(a) of   This form was completed
the Rules Regulating the Florida Bar   with the assistance of:
                                          Name:
The Florida Bar   Address:
                                          Telephone Number:

IN THE COUNTY COURT, IN AND FOR
_____COUNTY, FLORIDA
[insert County in which rental property is located]

_____,   CASE NO.: _____

[Insert name of Landlord]   [Insert case number assigned
                  Plaintiff,   by Clerk of the Court]

vs.

_____,

[Insert name of Tenant]
                  Defendant.

_____/

FINAL JUDGMENT—EVICTION

THIS ACTION came before the Court upon Plaintiff's Complaint for Eviction. On the evidence presented, it is

ADJUDGED that Plaintiff, _____[insert Landlord's name], recover from Defendant, _____[insert Tenant's name], possession of the real property described as follows:

_____

[insert legal or street description of rental premises including, if applicable, unit number]

and $ _____ as court costs, FOR WHICH LET WRITS OF POSSESSION AND EXECUTION NOW ISSUE.

ORDERED in _____[insert city in which court is located], _____ [insert county in which court is located] COUNTY, FLORIDA on _____, 20_____.

                            _____
                            County Judge

cc: _____

       [Insert name of Landlord]

     _____

       [Insert name of Tenant]

Approved for use under rule 10-2.1(a) of
the Rules Regulating the Florida Bar

The Florida Bar

This form was completed
with the assistance of:
Name:
Address:
Telephone Number:

IN THE COUNTY COURT, IN AND FOR
_____COUNTY, FLORIDA
[insert County in which rental property is located]

_____,   CASE NO.: _____

[Insert name of Landlord]

               Plaintiff,   [Insert case number assigned
                                         by Clerk of the Court]

vs.

_____,

[Insert name of Tenant]

               Defendant.

_____/

FINAL JUDGMENT—DAMAGES

THIS ACTION came before the Court upon Plaintiff's Complaint for unpaid rent. On the evidence presented, it is ADJUDGED that Plaintiff, _____ [insert Landlord's name], whose principal address is _____ [insert Landlord's address] recover from Defendant, _____ [insert Tenant's name], whose principal address is _____ [insert Tenant's address] the sum of $_____ with costs in the sum of $ _____, making a total of $ _____, that shall bear interest at the legal rate pursuant to section 55.03, Florida Statutes FOR WHICH LET EXECUTION NOW ISSUE.

ORDERED in _____[insert city in which court is located], _____ [insert county in which court is located] COUNTY, FLORIDA on _____, 20_____.

_____
County Judge

cc: _____

[Insert name of Landlord]

_____

[Insert name of Tenant]

This form was completed
with the assistance of:
Name:
Address:
Telephone Number:

IN THE COUNTY COURT, IN AND FOR
_____ COUNTY, FLORIDA
[insert County in which rental property is located]

_____ ,   CASE NO.: _____

[Insert name of Landlord]   [Insert case number assigned
                  Plaintiff,   by Clerk of the Court]

vs.

_____ ,

[Insert name of Tenant]
                  Defendant.   NOTICE OF HEARING

_____ /

To: _____

           _____

           _____

      PLEASE TAKE NOTICE that on the _____ day of _____, _____, at _____ o'clock ___.M. or as soon thereafter as can be heard, the undersigned will bring on to be heard Plaintiff's Motion to Strike and Motion for Default before the Honorable _____ one of the judges of the above Court in his/her Chambers in Room _____ in the Courthouse at _____, in _____ County, Florida.

Time set aside: _____.

PLEASE GOVERN YOURSELF ACCORDINGLY.

DATED this _____ day of _____, _____.

      I HEREBY CERTIFY that a copy hereof is being furnished by regular U.S. Mail on this date to the above-mentioned addressee.

                            _____
                            Plaintiff

                            _____
                            Address

                            _____
                            Phone

IN THE COUNTY COURT, IN AND FOR
_____COUNTY, FLORIDA
[insert County in which rental property is located]

_____,   CASE NO.: _____

[Insert name of Landlord]

               Plaintiff,

vs.

_____,   [Insert case number assigned
by Clerk of the Court]

MOTION TO STRIKE

[Insert name of Tenant]

               Defendant.

_____/

COMES NOW the Plaintiff and moves this Court to Strike the Answer of Defendant, and in support of his Motion states as follows:

The Defenses contained in Defendant's Answer fail to state a defense, legal or equitable, to Plaintiff's complaint to Remove Tenant, more particularly:

1.   This is an action for possession of real property as authorized and governed by Chapter 83 of the Florida Statutes.
2.   The Defendant's Defenses do not allege that the Defendant paid or tendered payment of the amount of rent when due or within three (3) days after delivery of written demand for rent or possession by the Plaintiff as provided by Florida Statutes 83.56(3).
3.   The Defendant's Defenses do not allege that the Plaintiff accepted, or agreed to accept, payment of rent at any time after expiration of the three (3) day period con templated by Florida Statutes 83.56(3).
4.   The Plaintiff has terminated the rental agreement in accordance with Florida Statutes 83.56(3) and is entitled to possession of the premises as provided by Florida Statutes 83.56.
5.   Defendants have not deposited the rent alleged to be due into the registry of the court.

I HEREBY CERTIFY that a copy of the foregoing has been sent by U.S. MAIL to _____(Defendant), at _____, Florida, this ____ day of _____, 20_____.

_____

Plaintiff

_____

Address

IN THE COUNTY COURT, IN AND FOR
_____COUNTY, FLORIDA

[insert County in which rental property is located]

_____,   CASE NO.: _____

[Insert name of Landlord]   [Insert case number assigned
                    Plaintiff,   by Clerk of the Court]

vs.

_____,

[Insert name of Tenant]   **MOTION FOR DEFAULT**
                    Defendant.

_____/

    Plaintiff moves for entry of a default against _____ [name],
for damages for failing to respond as required by law plaintiff's complaint.

Name _____

Address _____

_____

Telephone Number _____

DEFAULT

    A default is entered in this action against the Defendant for eviction for failure to respond as required by law.

    DATE:_____

_____

County Judge

cc: _____

[Insert name of Landlord]

_____

[Insert name of Tenant]

This form was completed
with the assistance of:
Name:
Address:
Telephone Number:

253

IN THE COUNTY COURT, IN AND FOR
_____COUNTY, FLORIDA
[insert County in which rental property is located]

_____,   CASE NO.: _____

[Insert name of Landlord]   [Insert case number assigned

Plaintiff,   by Clerk of the Court]

vs.

_____,

[Insert name of Tenant]

Defendant.   STIPULATION

_____/

The parties to this action hereby stipulate as follows:

1. The defendant acknowledges the sum of $_____ to be due and owing to the plaintiffs.

2. In partial payment of the above debt, the defendant(s) agree(s) to immediately pay to the plaintiff(s) the amount of $_____, and the balance of the above debt will be paid as follows:

$_____ due on _____ $_____ due on _____
$_____ due on _____ $_____ due on _____

In addition to the above-stated amounts, the defendant, as a further condition hereof, agrees to pay to the plaintiffs the sum of $_____ on the ___ day of each month, in cash, representing periodic installments payable under the rental agreement between the parties for rent of the subject residential premises.

3. If all of the foregoing sums are paid as set out above, in full, in cash, and when due, this action shall be dismissed with prejudice, and each party does hereby release the other by a general release as if set out here in full.

4. If any of the above sums are not paid as set out above, the plaintiffs shall be entitled to a Writ of Possession to be executed forthwith upon the filing of an Affidavit of Non-Payment. Defendant hereby waives a hearing on plaintiffs' application for an order of tenant removal in such case.

If defendant should default in any of the above payments, and defendant abandons possession of the dwelling or is lawfully evicted by reason of such default, it is agreed that plaintiffs shall be entitled to a money judgment for any of such payments as are in default at the time of defendant's abandonment or eviction. Defendant waives notice and hearing on plaintiffs' application for such money judgment.

Dated: _____, 20____.

_____   _____
Plaintiff   Defendant

_____   _____
Plaintiff   Defendant

IN THE COUNTY COURT, IN AND FOR
_____COUNTY, FLORIDA
[insert County in which rental property is located]

_____,   CASE NO.: _____
[Insert name of Landlord]
                        Plaintiff,   [Insert case number assigned
                                            by Clerk of the Court]
vs.

_____,   MOTION TO SET CAUSE FOR TRIAL
[Insert name of Tenant]
                        Defendant.
_____/

        The Plaintiff _____ state that this action is at issue and
ready to be set for trial and request the date for trial be set by the Court.
        The estimated time for trial is 30 minutes.
        I HEREBY CERTIFY that a copy of the foregoing has been sent by regular U.S. Mail to
_____.

                                    _____
                                    Plaintiff

                                    Address: _____
                                    _____
                                    Phone: _____

                        ORDER

        THIS CAUSE coming on to be heard upon Motion to Set Cause for Trial, it is
        ORDERED that this cause, being the issue, be and it is hereby set for trial before the Honorable
_____ in the Courthouse in _____, Florida on the _____
day of _____, 20____ at _____ o'clock ____.M in Room _____.
        DONE AND ORDERED in Chambers in _____, _____
County, Florida, this ____ day of _____, 20____.

                                    _____
                                    COUNTY JUDGE
cc:
        _____
        [Insert name of Landlord]

        _____
        [Insert name of Tenant]

255

IN THE COUNTY COURT, IN AND FOR
_____COUNTY, FLORIDA

CASE NO.: _____

[Insert case number assigned
by Clerk of the Court]

_____,

(Insert name of Landlord)

                Plaintiff,

vs.

_____,   PLAINTIFF'S NOTICE FOR TRIAL

(Insert name of Tenant)

            Defendant.

_____/

     PLEASE TAKE NOTICE that the above captioned action is at issue and is set for trial before the honorable _____, Judge of the County Court, on _____, the _____ day of _____, 20____, at _____ o'clock ____.m., in room _____ of the _____ County Courthouse at _____.

_____

Plaintiff

Address: _____

_____

Phone: _____

     I hereby certify that a copy of this Notice has been furnished to the defendant by hand delivery this _____ day of _____, 20_____.

_____

Plaintiff

IN THE COUNTY COURT, IN AND FOR
_____COUNTY, FLORIDA

CASE NO.: _____

[Insert case number assigned
by Clerk of the Court]

_____,
(Insert name of Landlord)

      Plaintiff,

vs.   WRIT OF POSSESSION

_____,
(Insert name of Tenant)

      Defendant.

_____/

STATE OF FLORIDA
TO THE SHERIFF OF _____ COUNTY, FLORIDA:
   (insert county in which rental property is located)

  YOU ARE COMMANDED to remove all persons from the following described property in
_____,County, Florida: _____
(insert county in which rental property is located)   (insert legal or street

_____
   description of rental premises including, if applicable, unit number)
and to put_____ in possession of it.
   (insert Landlord's name)

  DATED on _____ day of _____ , 20_____.

        Clerk, County Court

(SEAL)

       By:_____
        Deputy Clerk

Approved for use under rule 10-2.1(a) of   This form was completed
the Rules Regulating the Florida Bar   with the assistance of:
               Name:
The Florida Bar   Address:
               Telephone Number:

IN THE COUNTY COURT, IN AND FOR
_____COUNTY, FLORIDA

CASE NO.: _____

[Insert case number assigned
by Clerk of the Court]

_____,

[Insert name of Landlord]

Plaintiff,

vs.

_____,

[Insert name of Tenant]

Defendant.

_____/

MOTION TO DISBURSE FUNDS
FROM THE COURT REGISTRY

The Plaintiff requests that the Court order the clerk to disburse the rent payments paid into the court registry in this cause and in support would show:

1. This is an action for possession of real property based upon nonpayment of rent.

2. Plaintiff's expenses for debt service, taxes, insurance, utilities and maintenance on the property are continuing to accrue on a daily basis and Plaintiff's sole source of income to meet those expenses is the rent from the premises. Unless plaintiff receives the rent payments now being posted into the registry of the court, plaintiff will have to borrow funds from other sources to meet his obligations.

3. Plaintiff requests that he be allowed to apply ex parte for an order of disbursement on the first business day following deposit of continuing rent in this action.

I hereby certify that a copy of the foregoing has been furnished to defendant by _____ mail _____ hand delivery this _____ day of _____, 20____.

_____
Plaintiff

Address: _____

_____

Phone: _____

IN THE COUNTY COURT, IN AND FOR   Form 59
_____COUNTY, FLORIDA

CASE NO.: _____

[Insert case number assigned
by Clerk of the Court]

_____,
[Insert name of Landlord]
                              Plaintiff,

vs.

_____,   ORDER DISBURSING FUNDS FROM
[Insert name of Tenant]   THE COURT REGISTRY
                              Defendant.
_____/

THIS CAUSE coming on to be heard upon Motion to Release Funds from the Court Registry, it is

ORDERED that the funds being held by the clerk in this cause be released to Plaintiff forthwith.

DONE AND ORDERED in Chambers in _____, _____
County, Florida, this _____ day of _____, 20_____

                                        _____
                                        County Judge

cc: _____
        [Insert name of Landlord]

        _____
        [Insert name of Tenant]

259

FORM 1.998. FINAL DISPOSITION FORM

This form shall be filed by the prevailing party for the use of the Clerk of Court for the purpose of reporting judicial workload data pursuant to Florida Statutes section 25.075. (See instructions on the reverse of the form.)

I.   CASE STYLE

                    (Name of Court)_____

Plaintiff _____   Case #:_____

               _____   Judge: _____

vs.

Defendant _____

                 _____

II.   MEANS OF FINAL DISPOSITION (Place an "x" in one box for major category and one subcategory, if applicable, only)

☐ Dismissed Before Hearing
    ☐ Dismissed Pursuant to Settlement – Before Hearing
    ☐ Dismissed Pursuant to Mediated Settlement – Before Hearing
    ☐ Other - Before Hearing
☐ Dismissed After Hearing
    ☐ Dismissed Pursuant to Settlement – After Hearing
    ☐ Dismissed Pursuant to Mediated Settlement – After Hearing
    ☐ Other After Hearing – After Hearing
☐ Disposed by Default
☐ Disposed by Judge
☐ Disposed by Non-jury Trial
☐ Disposed by Jury Trial
☐ Other

DATE _____   _____

                                     SIGNATURE OF ATTORNEY FOR PREVAILING PARTY

IN THE COUNTY COURT, IN AND FOR
_____ COUNTY, FLORIDA
[insert County in which rental property is located]

CASE NO.: _____

[Insert case number assigned
by Clerk of the Court]

_____ ,

[Insert name of Landlord]

                    Plaintiff,

vs.   SATISFACTION OF JUDGMENT

_____ ,

[Insert name of Tenant]

                    Defendant.

_____ /

    This document is signed by _____ , [insert: "individually" or "as agent of Plaintiff"] _____ on _____ , 20_____ .

    Plaintiff, _____ [insert: "individually" or "as agent of Plaintiff"] to acknowledge full payment of the judgment signed by the Judge on _____ , 20_____ . Plaintiff agrees that Defendant(s) do(es) not owe the Plaintiff any more monies for the judgment.

_____   _____
(Witness)   (Plaintiff)

_____
(Witness)

Acknowledged before me on _____ [date], by _____
[name], who _____ is personally known to me/ _____ produced _____ [document] as identification.

_____
NOTARY PUBLIC-STATE OF FLORIDA
Name: _____
Commission No.: _____
My Commission Expires: _____

Approved for use under rule 10-2.1(a) of
the Rules Regulating the Florida Bar

The Florida Bar

This form was completed
with the assistance of:
Name:
Address:
Telephone Number:

To:_____

_____

_____

Re: Your Check No._____
Criminal remedies:
Pursuant to Florida Statutes, section 832.07:
You are hereby notified that a check numbered_____ in the face amount of $_____, issued by you on _____, 20_____ drawn upon _____(bank) and payable to _____ has been dishonored. Pursuant to Florida law, you have 7 days from receipt of this notice to tender payment in cash of the full amount of the check plus a service charge of $25, if the face value does exceeds $50 but does not exceed $300, $40, if the face value exceeds $300, or 5 percent of the face amount of the check, whichever is greater, the total being $_____ and _____ cents. Unless this amount is paid in full within the time specified above, the holder of such check may turn over the dishonored check and all other available information relating to this incident to the state attorney for criminal prosecution. You may be additionally liable in a civil action for triple the amount of the check, but in no case less than $50, together with the amount of the check, a service charge, court costs, reasonable attorney fees and incurred bank fees, as provided in section 68.065.

Civil remedies:
Pursuant to Florida Statutes, section 68.065:

You are hereby notified that a check numbered_____ in the face amount of $_____, issued by you on _____, 20____ drawn upon _____(bank) and payable to _____ has been dishonored. Pursuant to Florida law, you have 30 days from receipt of this notice to tender payment in cash of the full amount of the check plus a service charge of $25, if the face value does exceeds $50 but does not exceed $300, $40, if the face value exceeds $300, or 5 percent of the face amount of the check, whichever is greater, the total being $_____ and _____ cents. Unless this amount is paid in full within the 30-day period, the holder of the check or instrument may file a civil action against you for three times the amount of the check, but in no case less than $50, in addition to the payment of the check plus any court costs, reasonable attorney fees, and any bank fees incurred by the payee taking this action.

Payment should be made to: _____

_____

_____

Sent by Certified Mail, return receipt requested.

Notice of Right to Reclaim Abandoned Property
(Property of former tenant valued under $500)

TO:_____

_____

_____

When you vacated the premises at _____ Apt. ____, the following personal property remained:

You may claim this property _____
_____. Unless you pay the reasonable costs of storage and advertising, if any, for all the above-described property and take possession of the property which you claim no later than _____, 20____* this property may be disposed of pursuant to s. 715.109.

Because the property is believed to be worth less than $500, it may be kept, sold, or destroyed without further notice if you fail to reclaim it within the time indicated above.

Dated:_____, 20_____

_____
Landlord_____
Telephone:_____
Address:_____

_____

*Insert date not fewer than 10 days after notice is personally delivered or, if mailed, not fewer than 15 days after notice is deposited in the mail.

Notice of Right to Reclaim Abandoned Property
(Property of person other than tenant valued under $500)

TO:_____

_____

_____

When _____ vacated the premises at
_____ Apt. _____, the following personal property remained:

If you own any of this property, you may claim this property at:_____
_____.

Unless you pay the reasonable costs of storage and advertising, if any, for all the above-described property and take possession of the property which you are entitled no later than _____, 20_____* this property may be disposed of pursuant to s. 715.109. Because the property is believed to be worth less than $500, it may be kept, sold, or destroyed without further notice if you fail to reclaim it within the time indicated above.

Dated:_____, 20_____   _____
                                        Landlord_____
                                        Telephone:_____
                                        Address:_____

                                        _____

*Insert date not fewer than 10 days after notice is personally delivered or, if mailed, not fewer than 15 days after notice is deposited in the mail.

Notice of Right to Reclaim Abandoned Property
(Property of former tenant valued over $500)

TO:_____

_____

_____

When you vacated the premises at _____

_____ Apt. _____, the following personal property remained:

You may claim this property at:_____

_____.

Unless you pay the reasonable costs of storage and advertising, if any, for all the above-described property and take possession of the property which you claim no later than _____,
20_____* this property may be disposed of pursuant to s. 715.109.
If you fail to reclaim the property, it will be sold at a public sale after notice of the sale has been given by publication. You have the right to bid on the property at this sale. After the property is sold and the costs of storage, advertising and sale are deducted, the remaining money will be paid over to the county. You may claim the remaining money at any time within one year after the county receives the money.

Dated:_____, 20_____

_____

Landlord_____

Telephone:_____

Address:_____

_____

*Insert date not fewer than 10 days after notice is personally delivered or, if mailed, not fewer than 15 days after notice is deposited in the mail.

Notice of Right to Reclaim Abandoned Property
(Property of person other than tenant valued over $500)

TO:_____

_____

_____

When _____ vacated the premises
at _____ Apt. _____ , the
following personal property remained:

If you own any of this property, you may claim this property at_____

_____.

Unless you pay the reasonable costs of storage and advertising, if any, for all the above-described property and take possession of the property which you are entitled no later than _____, 20_____ * this property may be disposed of pursuant to s. 715.109.
If you fail to reclaim the property, it will be sold at a public sale after notice of the sale has been given by publication. You have the right to bid on the property at this sale. After the property is sold and the costs of storage, advertising and sale are deducted, the remaining money will be paid over to the county. You may claim the remaining money at any time within one year after the county receives the money.

Dated:_____, 20_____

_____
Landlord_____
Telephone:_____
Address:_____

_____

*Insert date not fewer than 10 days after notice is personally delivered or, if mailed, not fewer than 15 days after notice is deposited in the mail.

Index

Law Books by Attorney Mark Warda

Florida Titles

☐ Florida **Landlords'** Rights and Strategies (NEW! 2012) 34.95 ☐ with CD 49.95
☐ Florida **Landlords'** Rights and Strategies CD only 19..95
☐ **Land Trusts** in Florida (9th ed.) with CD 34.95
☐ How to Form an **LLC** in Florida (4th ed.) 29.95
☐ How to **Start a Business** in Florida (8th ed.) 34.99
☐ How to Make a Florida **Will** (7th ed.) 18.95

National Titles

☐ **Personal Property Trusts** (1st national ed.) 34.95 ☐ *Book with CD* 49.95
☐ Complete Guide to **Asset Protection** Strategies (2nd Ed. 2012) 34.95
☐ **Land Trusts** for Privacy & Profit (3rd national ed.) 39.95 ☐ *Book with CD* 54.95
☐ **Land Trusts** for Privacy & Profit Forms only on CD 19.95
☐ Secrets of **Lease Option** Profits (2nd ed. by Jack Shea & Mark Warda) 34.95
☐ Secrets of **Lease Option** Profits Forms only on CD 19.95 ☐ *Book with CD* 49.95
☐ How to Register Your Own **Copyright** (5th ed.) 24.95
☐ Complete Book of Real Estate **Contracts** with CD 18.95
☐ Complete Book of Real Estate **Leases** with CD 18.95
☐ Form Your Own **Corporation** (5th ed.) with CD 29.95
☐ Complete **Limited Liability Company** Kit with CD 24.95
☐ Complete **Nonprofit Corporation** Kit with CD 34.95
☐ **Incorporate** in **Nevada** from Any State 24.95
☐ Make Your Own Simple **Will** (4th ed.) with CD 26.95
☐ The Complete Book of **Personal Legal Forms** with CD 28.95
☐ **Homeowner's** Rights 19.95
☐ **Neighbor vs. Neighbor** (2nd) 16.95

You can order by mail (Galt Press, P. O. Box 186, Lake Wales, FL 33859), by fax (863-678-0155), by phone (863-678-0011) or by email (mark@warda.net). If ordering by email, put half of your credit card number in each of 2 separate emails and include the expiration date with one of them. All orders must be prepaid. We accept Discover, MasterCard and Visa. New credit card processing rules require us to have your credit card billing zip code.

Credit Card No. _____ Exp. _____ Phone _____
Zip code on credit card billing address _____ Last 3 digits on back of card _____
Name _____   Books total $_____
Address _____   Florida sales tax*   _____
City, State _____Zip _____ Shipping**   _____

Signature for credit card _____   Total order $_____
*Sales tax only if shipped to Florida

**Shipping: Add $3.62 for book rate or $5.65 for priority mail to order (not per book). CD shipping $2.56